Lords of the Ring

Lords of the Ring

Marsh, Warren and the Business of Boxing

HARRY LANSDOWN & ALEX SPILLIUS

HEINEMANN : LONDON

William Heinemann Ltd
Michelin House, 81 Fulham Road, London SW3 6RB
LONDON   MELBOURNE   AUCKLAND

First published 1991
Copyright © Harry Lansdown and Alex Spillius 1991

A CIP catalogue record for this book
is held by the British Library
ISBN 0 434 73876 X

Picture Credits

1a All Sport 1b All Sport/Russell Cheyne 1c All Sport/Ben Radford 1d All Sport/Trevor Jones 3 All Sport/Dan Smith 4 Jerry Munson 5 All Sport/Michael King 6 All Sport/Bob Martin 7 Roy Chaplin 8 Rex Features 9 London News Service 10 Ambrose Mendy/John McDonald 11 All Sport/Bob Martin 12 London News Service 13 All Sport 14 John McDonald 15 Rex Features 16 All Sport/Russell Cheyne

Phototypeset by Deltatype Ltd, Ellesmere Port, Cheshire
Printed in Great Britain by
Clays Ltd, St. Ives Plc

Contents

Acknowledgements   vi
Preface   vii
1. Down the Old Kent Road   1
2. Another East End Fighter   5
3. Lord of the Unlicensed Ring   20
4. The Business of Boxing   45
5. The Establishment   63
6. The Making of a Fighter   84
7. Warren Busts the Cartel   98
8. A Promoter's Dream, Almost   128
9. Things Fall Apart   139
10. The Shooting   161
11. Trial and Error   187
12. The Buy-Up   219
13. The Punch-Up   233
14. Any Way Back?   261

Acknowledgements

The authors would like to thank the seventy or so people who kindly agreed to be interviewed for this book: the promoters, managers, boxers, trainers, agents, officials, journalists, staff, friends and relations of some of the main characters. We are particularly grateful to Terry Marsh for speaking so candidly, and to Nick Pitt of the *Sunday Times* and Jon Robinson for their assistance. Numerous attempts were made to speak to Frank Warren, but we were told by his lawyer he would be unlikely to do something like this unless there was some remuneration, which there wasn't.

'Hello, is that Alex Spillius?'

'Yes.'

'It's Frank Warren.'

'Hello.'

'Before I decide to see you, what I am interested to know is how much you're getting paid for the book, how much do you intend to market it for, and how much do you want to pay me for the interview?'

We had been trying to interview Frank Warren for a year, he finally telephoned us in June 1991.

'I don't really want to say how much we are getting paid.'

'You want to know where my money comes from, where does your money come from? You're going to make money out of what you see as me being an interesting character . . . I'm in the business of making money myself . . . What relationship have you got with Mendy?'

'We talked to him, and listened to what he said and weighed it up . . . he's not a friend, if that's what you mean.'

'No, not at all, I'm just very intrigued . . . I've never had people go and knock on members of my family's doors before and I take exception to it. My uncle has nothing to do with my business, he's my uncle and that's the end of it.'

'If you're trying to get an idea of what someone's like . . .'

'I'm sure you'd only hear good things from him.'

'Well I'm quite happy to hear good things.'

'What I'd like you to do is fax through a copy of that letter you sent to me – we've moved our office.'

'As for money for an interview, I don't really know what you think about that.'

'I'm thinking your publisher and yourself are going to make money out of a book . . . and it seems to me the thrust of it seems to be about Marsh and myself . . . and as that's the way you're going . . . If you can get that fax to me I'll give it some thought and get back to you in the next couple of days.'

Mr Warren never called back.

CHAPTER ONE

Down the Old Kent Road

'I could tell you a few things. I've been married four times, all lovely girls – except the last one. I'm a poor Sinatra.' Everyone in boxing has a story, though some are bigger than others. Ted looks after the day to day running of the Henry Cooper gym in the Old Kent Road, SE1, the cheapest property on the London Monopoly board.

The gym lies a few hundred yards south of the more famous boxing haunt, the Thomas A Beckett. It is sited above a pub, once called the Wellington, but renamed by the landlord after the former British heavyweight champion 'Our 'Enery', whose story is that he once knocked over Muhammad Ali. It is surrounded by a series of run-down cafes, mini-markets and under-patronised shops. Opposite there is a garage, where a second-hand pink limousine with tinted windows is parked outside. Who could this belong to? Perhaps Don King, the flamboyant American promoter, has come to town to check on some British opponent. In fact it belongs to a man known as George, a pimp from Peckham.

Next to the gym is a patch of wasteland, a building development hit by recession; weeds gather, and a group of kids play football between piles of rubble. Inside the gym is an oasis of healthy activity. Naked men come out of the shower, sweat replaced by steam, and slowly towel themselves down. A skinny, black would-be welterweight in a Lonsdale shirt and pink and black cycling shorts spars in front of a full-length mirror. An older heavyweight, his pink flesh bulging through his T-shirt, hits a punchbag. Another pounds away on a running machine.

Black and white photographs line the walls – of Ali, Frazier and Cooper, all in their prime. And there is a ring. Two men circle round one another, sparring, perpetually on their toes, trying to score imaginary points like amateurs rather than knock each other out. Only they are not amateurs. One is a title contender; the other, a pale, wiry figure, with short, curly hair, is a former world champion. He is also a man acquitted on a charge of attempting to murder his former manager. He is now trying to box again, to return to past glory. Now there's a story. Terry Marsh.

A couple of old-timers walk in, and stand knowingly by the ropes.

'He still looks the business don't he?'

'Yeh, and you should have seen him helping out the kids down here the other day. Marvellous. They love him.'

Back in the changing room, Harry Stevens – 'Aitchie' – is holding court: a 59-year-old south Londoner, ex-fighter and former window cleaner, part-time singer and MC. Tales of injustice in the boxing game spin off his tongue.

'D'you know how much John H. Stracey got paid for winning the world welterweight title? I do, 'cos he's a good friend of mine, and he was on about it just the other day. Can you guess 'ow much? Can you guess it? You could put it in the palm of your hand, and let's face it, you couldn't fit that many £50 notes in the palm of your hand now could you?'

A silence passes for agreement on this.

'He got £3,500. For *winning* the world title off Jose Napoles, in 1975. Bloody diabolical. His manager said they'd had to buy the fight and pay Napoles a fortune to defend it.'

The conversation drifts from fight purses to wages. 'How's your boy doing Aitchie?'

'He's all right, he's got the window-cleaning business now, clears about £800 a week – ain't bad is it? He's got Heathrow, and parts of Regent Street. 'Course, it was my business, and I take £200 week off him every week, which 'e don't like, 'e don't like it at all. But that's tough. I gotta have my whack. I've told him, next time we 'ave a row, that'll be it, I'll sell it.'

When the glove is on the other hand, the guv'nor taking his whack is not so bad after all.

Terry Marsh left the gym and went to Hackney to see an old friend and boxing acquaintance, Jon 'Tiny' Robinson, about plans to fight again in America. For five years, Robinson worked as Frank Warren's general manager. A former character actor and model, he still reports on boxing for the *Hackney Gazette*, though he is now vice-president of one of the main world boxing organisations, the International Boxing Federation. His cosy office is above his family business – a modest flower shop at the Bethnal Green end of Hackney Road. He once moved in to a more up-market headquarters in the West End, but no one dropped in to see him. It was too out of the way. The East End is much more convenient.

Jon is known as 'Tiny' because he weighs 30 stone. Once he was officially Britain's heaviest man. 'There was a guy called George McAree who claimed to weigh more than me. So we went down for a weigh-in at the Theatre Royal in Stratford. The press was there. He was six stone more but I stuck some weights in my trousers and beat him, 37 stone to 36 stone.'

Funny, up-front, he is one of the senior brothers of the fraternity, a man whom everyone in boxing knows. He was with Frank Warren when he moved in to the bigtime and began signing promising young fighters. One of his new men was Terry Marsh.

Warren and Marsh were close, their careers rose in tandem. Marsh became a champion, and Warren one of the top managers and promoters. Then they fell out in mysterious circumstances. Warren diversified into new leisure and entertainment businesses, and started building London's first large-scale venue for 60 years. His own kingdom in Docklands. His prestige grew. Then one day at the end of 1989, as he stepped out of his Bentley arriving for a promotion in East London, he was shot. Miraculously, he survived.

To begin with the police seemed to be making no headway. Then on 16 January 1990, they arrested Terry Marsh and within 24 hours charged him with attempted murder. There was incredulity inside and outside boxing. Marsh was still a public favourite, the boxer who even as a champion had kept his job as a fireman. The story seemed to be a parody of perceived images of boxing and London's East End. It revived a nostalgia for a lost age of villainy, a feeling which, however mistaken, was felt to be more acceptable because the victim had survived. And it revolved around a sport that fascinates millions, which creates bigger heroes and more losers than any other game. Like all the best stories, it is about fate, timing and luck. There is a good guy and a bad guy, though the casting of the roles remains an open question.

CHAPTER TWO

Another East End Fighter

Perhaps because boxing is just a controlled form of fighting and the most primitive form of sport, there is no precise date for its beginning. Unlike rugby for instance, begun in 1823 when a school boy called William Ellis picked up the ball in a soccer match and began running. Some historians have traced boxing back to ancient Greece, and around 900 BC, when a ruler named Thesus watched two fighters hammering one another with their fists. The Romans developed it, but only to the extent that they merged it into their gladiatorial contests – until these were banned under the emperors Constantine and Theodoric.

It seems that for hundreds of years fighting disappeared as a recognised sport until the early eighteenth century, when the ancestor of modern day boxing began to emerge – English bare knuckle prize-fighting. The prize ring was an area around which spectators, usually at a village fair, would gather and form a loose circle with rope and watch an unsupervised fight governed only by vague concepts of fair play. Betting was an important part of the spectacle. 'The Noble Art', as prize-fighting was called, began as part of working peoples' entertainment and then grew in popularity with the aristocracy.

James Figg, the first champion of England in 1719, fought in front of George I and is regarded as one of the fathers of boxing. Figg opened an amphitheatre in London's Tottenham Court Road, and dedicated it to teaching 'the manly art of foul play, back-sword, cudgelling and scientific boxing'. One of his successors, Jack Broughton, introduced rules to stop wrestling and kicking.

In 1838 the London Prize Ring Rules sought to make all fights uniform. However, the sport had declined in popularity since the Regency period and the days of the first great East End Jewish fighter, Daniel Mendoza; new rules were not enough to revive it. As is still to some extent the case today, boxing's popularity rested less on specific rules than on who was fighting and whether their personality caught on with the public.

Boxing needed a new hero and along came Tom Sayers, one of the great bare knuckle fighters of the mid-nineteenth century. Sayers' most famous fight was against the American heavy-weight champion John C. Heenan in 1860, in a field in Farnborough watched by a crowd of around 1200 people. They had travelled there on dawn trains that left London in secret, for this was a period when the sport was an underground practice. Yet one spectator claimed he 'rubbed shoulders with pugilists and poets, statesmen and publicans, dandies, men of letters, and even divines.' The big fights were something to go to and somewhere to be seen at, as they are today.

Sawyers and Heenan fought for 37 rounds lasting two hours and 20 minutes: the battle was only ended by the arrival of the police. Heenan was reported to be in a critical condition for 48 hours, while Sayers turned up the next day to have his photograph taken and prove how little he had been hurt. He died a few years later of consumption in 1865. His funeral procession, which began in Camden Town and went up to Highgate Cemetery, was the largest working-class funeral in London that century, with an estimated 100,000 people lining the three miles to pay their respects to England's champion. It was not an occasion for a rally of any sort, and there was no particular organisation behind it. And yet as the *Illustrated Sporting News* remarked: 'Great warriors and great statesmen, carried to their marble tombs in all the pride and pomp of death have failed to attract such crowds.'

The heroism of boxers is not simply a media-induced pheno-menon, stemming from hype or money, but a fascination that comes from something deep within many people, and which goes far back in time. The emotions provoked by boxing derive from more basic human instincts such as aggression and survival. Tom Sayers was a peoples' hero much the way in which Henry Cooper is a century later. Amid the Victorian spirit of progress, Sayers' popularity was an affront to established middle-class ideology, and its notion of evolution to a more humanitarian society, bound up with values of moderation and religious piety.

And yet boxing itself was moving with the humanitarian times. In 1867, the same year that 'respectable' working-class men were enfranchised, the Marquis of Queensberry introduced his Queensberry Rules, which are the foundation for the rules of modern boxing. These rules introduced gloves (called 'pillows' by their detractors) brought in mainly to stop fighters' hands from breaking, and not to protect their faces. The rules also provided for a contestant being disqualified for delivering a foul blow, unintentionally or otherwise, and introduced a third man, the referee, who is allowed to stop the fight at his own discretion. Boxing was no longer akin to a street fight. However, it took the rules around 25 years to catch on, and replace the bare knuckle tradition.

The last bare knuckle fight for the world heavyweight title took place in America in 1882, and was won by John L. Sullivan, who held the title for 10 years. By the time Bob Fitzsimmons from Cornwall had felled 'Gentleman' Jim Corbett in Nevada in 1897 to win the heavyweight title for Britain, gloves, and a greater degree of finesse and skill, were firmly established.

Today boxers unwittingly stand out against a number of prejudices and while the sport has a solid minority following, it is condemned by a far larger number of people who believe it should be banned. And yet even amongst boxing's detractors, a fascination with boxers remains. If they become involved in anything outside the ring, as they periodically do, their alleged activities create an interest unrivalled by other sportsmen. It is as if people believe that if a boxer is there anything might be possible.

In Britain boxing gained legal status, and in 1929, the British

Board of Control was founded, emerging out of the National Sporting Club which had previously decided all championships. By the start of the 1930s, the Jewish community could boast the largest number of world champions of any defined ethnic group. They had four: Benny Bass, Al Singer, Maxie Rosenbloom, from the US, and from London, Jack 'Kid' Berg, alias 'the Whitechapel Whirlwind'.

The sport's popularity among Jews in the Bronx, New York, was reflected on the other side of the Atlantic in the East End of London. Today the Jewish involvement in boxing has declined, although the East End is where a great many influential boxing people hail from, including the top promoters and managers, and it has a number of successful amateur clubs. It is boxing country.

To outsiders, the East End still presents a formidable image of closed-off poverty – tough, isolated and streetwise. However, the area resists easy definition, and there are many differing interpretations of its boundaries. It is certainly east of Aldgate, taking in Hoxton, Bethnal Green, Wapping, Stepney, Bow, Poplar, Whitechapel and Limehouse. The Cockney's traditional rule is that the area has always been within the sound of Bow Bells. In fact today it spreads much further, taking in places such as Stratford and East Ham. But in any case the East End represents more than just a geographical description: it also stands for an alternative culture.

The celebrated landmarks of its history – the Ripper murders in 1888 which took place off Brick Lane, the anarchist 'Sidney Street Siege' in 1911, the battle of Cable Street, and of course, the reign of the Kray twins in the 1960s – evoke fear, distaste but also admiration. For as well as the violence, there is a reputation for a zest for life among its people, which is not a romantic myth.

What is indisputable is that the East End, with its great docklands, has provided a natural and significant breeding ground for boxers. Immigrants tend to settle near the ports at which they have arrived, and in the late Victorian era East London experienced the largest arrival of newcomers up until the Commonwealth influx of the 1950s. Between 1870 and 1914 around 120,000 Eastern Europeans arrived, mainly

Russian and Polish Jews, and the character of the East End was re-defined. It became increasingly stratified, with tightly defined communities of people, who had lost their old roots and were re-establishing a new framework for their lives. But they joined an indigenous population of cockney Londoners and also the Irish – the settlers from an earlier wave of immigration. In this racially splintered area, the rough edge of grinding poverty prevailed. It is not hard to understand why boys and men used to fight in the streets.

Boxing with gloves, as opposed to bare fist fighting, became an accepted way to settle an argument, often with a third man acting as a referee, albeit a rather informal one. The lure of the ring was similar to that of the musical halls, and there were a number of local venues such as Wonderland, the Judaean, the Poplar Hippodrome, and the most famous of all, Premierland in Back Church Lane, Whitechapel. Like the stage, the ring offered a chance of local fame, and the opportunity for the talented to get away. Not every ambitious lad with a desire to break out of the ghetto could win a scholarship to a grammar school.

The story of former East End hero, the late Jack 'Kid' Berg alias 'the Whitechapel Whirlwind' who died in 1991, illustrates how boys came to fight.

'I was outside the Premierland one day, and a Frenchman asked me to mind his car. He paid me half a crown. So I was sitting in it, and this other lad came along and started bouncing up and down on the bonnet. I got out and told him to get off. We ended up having a fight. I hit him so hard that a bloke came out of the Premierland and told me I didn't need to fight on the street for nothing when I could do it in there and get paid. I agreed. He paid me 17 shillings for my first ever professional fight. That's how I started.'

Jack 'Kid' Berg went on to become the light-welterweight champion of the world. Along with another, Ted 'Kid' Lewis, he was a hero to a local Jewish population in particular, proving that Jews did not have to take everything lying down, but could hit back – and hard. Boxing flourished in the East End for practical as well as cultural reasons. It was something people could either watch or take part in, without a lot of money or elaborate facilities. It was not as easy to find and preserve a decent cricket pitch, or neatly mown tennis courts, as it was to have a ring in a hall or warehouse. Betting on fighters spiced up even the most minor bout. In an area where toughness counted for everything, boxing had to be the sport.

It was in this fighting tradition that Terry Marsh was born in Stepney on 7 February 1958, one of four sons of Jim and Maisie Marsh. The family lived in Hardinge Street, which runs off Cable Street, in a typical two-up, two-down East End house with an outside lavatory. Jimmy Marsh worked on the docks at West India and St Catherine's. Maisie, a tough, strong-willed woman, ran the household. There was not a lot of spare money to go round, and the already considerable demands on a woman of raising a family were exacerbated by the stress of caring for a mentally retarded child, James, known as Jimmy, who is Terry's elder brother. 'Almost everyone looks back at things with nostalgia,' says Terry, 'but at the time it was tough. My brothers and I were all very sensitive to Jimmy being handicapped. I believed he was my *raison d'être*. We used to get in a lot of fights, as other kids made fun of him. We found ourselves in battles where often the odds were stacked against us.'

But Terry was also different from the rest of his family. He did well at school, and instead of going to a local comprehensive he was offered a place at Westminster City Grammar School, in Palace Street, SW1. It was a big step for a boy from a close-knit, East End family, but he was unlikely to get picked on at his new school, for at the age of 10 he had already started boxing at St George's Amateur Boxing Club in Cable Street.

Cable Street, which still has some of its original Georgian houses standing alongside concrete flats, runs parallel between Commercial Road and the old London Docks at Wapping. Its name derives from the ships' cables that used to be made there; it is redolent of the East End fighting tradition. In 1936 it was the site of a great battle. Sir Oswald Moseley's Black Shirts attempted to march through the East End, a provocative gesture to its substantial Jewish population. A confrontation took place in spite of a police presence – or some say because of it – and developed in to a bloody battle. The Black Shirts were beaten back by the local population, some of whom were Communists, and some of whom were simply there for the fight. The crowd cried out 'They shall not pass', imitating the Spanish Communist slogan, of '*No pasaran*'.

St George's ABC was founded in 1962 in Berners Street. It began as the Berner Boys Club. It moved to the crypt at St George's Church and then after a series of short stays in shared gyms and halls the club settled at St George's Town Hall, Cable Street, where it remained until 1990. Marsh is not its only famous son. John H. Stracey, the former world welterweight champion was a member of St George's, as was former Commonwealth middleweight champion, Rod Douglas. The club is still thriving and has recently moved to just behind Cable Street, to an old library, not far from a pub called the Artful Dodger.

The East End may have changed, but the type of training and the sweaty, workmanlike atmosphere at St George's gym is as intimidating and yet also as friendly as when it first started. This is not an establishment where earnest professionals in lurid tracksuits work off flab. There are no exercise machines, only free weights, half a dozen punch bags, and of course, a ring. The place is spartan, with just a few faded posters of long ago fights on the bare, white walls, and a picture of the East End's most recent hero, Nigel Benn. There is a Lonsdale clock which has an alarm going off at three-minute intervals to give the fighters, mainly teenage boys, a 60-second rest. The only concession to modernity is the endless cycle of soul, hip-hop and house music booming out of a tape machine, while some of the fighters skip. And there is a scroll written out on the wall:

'Boxing is a science, the study of a lifetime, in which you
may exhaust yourself but never your subject. It is a
contest, a duel, calling for skill and self control. It is a test
of temper, a trial of honour, a revealer of character. It

affords the chance to play the man and act the
gentleman. It provides not only physical health, but a
natural force. It includes companionship with friends and
opportunities to excel in your chosen sport. So go to it,
you would be champions and may you enjoy every
moment of your chosen sport. But remember, we cannot
all be champions.'

Darren Mohammed, an expectant, 18-year-old bantamweight, and typical of many generations of young boxers to have
trained at St George's, is waiting to spar, dancing and circling
round a punchbag to the Alexander O'Neal song, All True Man.
He wears a vest and tracksuit bottoms with velvet black
Lonsdale boxing shorts pulled up over them. He is just five foot
four inches tall. But he is a very confident five foot four. His
mother is white and comes from Brixton, and his father was
born in Zanzibar, East Africa. Darren was born and brought up
in Cable Street. His dark glinting eyes search you out, assessing
what weight you might be.

He is quick and willing to give anyone his life story. 'I was
boxing years ago, but I took it up again seriously when I finished
as a labourer. I took a few courses but I couldn't get another job.
Now I don't work at all. I do what I have to do down here and
people help me, like me family and that, for money.

'I've been in trouble with the law and my brothers don't really
get on with me, but I'm still sweet with my mum and dad.'

Crime is no longer part of his life. 'I've come out of all that.
Boxing teaches you the right way – you just don't have time for
no trouble, know what I mean? Anyway it was just theft and
fighting. Fighting a lot – on street corners, firms and all that.
Silliness it is. Against the Pakis mainly. But that's when you're
young. I blame it on the area, but I suppose it's the same in every
area.

'I've had an adult life; I've had to look after myself since I was
16. I've got my own flat and that. I've been in prison, detention
centre, and in remand in Brixton, but just for a week, 'cos they
had nowhere else to send me. But you're not doing yourself any

favours carrying on like that. I'm over it now. I hope to go professional and be a star. I want to do it for my trainer. He's a wicked geezer. He does everything for you. He tells you the right way, puts you on the straight and narrow.'

Darren lost the previous night, but it had not affected his confidence too much. 'I just wasn't fit enough. I used to smoke a lot, you know. And it's still inside me. But I only lost by a point and the referee said I was the better boxer. I'll fight him again and beat him.'

St George's had always been one of the strongest clubs in London, so it was not helpful for Terry Marsh's fighting prospects when his family decided to leave Stepney for Basildon in Essex. He was just 13. Jimmy Marsh was offered a job in Tilbury, working for the Port of London Authority. Like all new towns Basildon is a target for jokes. But for many families like the Marshes it meant a better house, with a bathroom, and for the first time relatively spacious, unpolluted green surroundings. They lived in Pitsea, to the east side of town. Temporarily, Terry left St George's and joined the Bluehouse Amateur Boxing Club. However, it was just a small converted barn rigged up with a ring and two bags. He only stayed a year, before he and his younger brother John returned to St George's.

Moving to Basildon had also meant a change of school. Terry now went to Chalvedon Comprehensive. This was not a school that was able to push him in the way that ambitious Westminster City had done, and at 16 made the suggestion he go and get himself a trade. Had he stayed at Westminster City School the whole pattern of his life might have been very different. He might have become an officer in the Forces and never been tempted into professional boxing. As things stood, Terry Marsh may have moved away from the East End, but boxing was still his main means of gaining recognition.

Boxing manager Burt McCarthy, who knew the family well, recalls, 'I used to watch Terry's progress as an amateur because he was Jimmy Marsh's boy. He made the best of himself all right.

But then East End kids take all their advantages because they have to, don't they?'

Terry Marsh seems to have done. In 1973 and 1974 he won two junior ABA titles and a National Schools title. Two years later he represented Young England.

Bert Lilley, a former docker and amateur boxer, born in West Ham, is the secretary at St George's, as well as a Labour councillor. He is a typically gruff, East End patriot. 'Terry was a joker; a very jovial lad. We all thought the world of him. The boy used to train very hard. He was dedicated; and then when he fought he'd jab and get out the way – a real ring craftsman who knew how to get in to a lead and then sit on it. We knew he was special.'

However, Terry Marsh had got off to an inauspicious start, losing his first ever fight to an opponent called Tommy Mooney, the only boxer who can ever really claim to have got the better of Marsh. In all, the two boys fought 11 times, with Mooney winning eight of the contests. Marsh was not particularly big for his age, and his renowned ring craftsmanship was forced upon him because he was not strong enough to stand in the ring and trade punches. He had no particular ambition to become a professional boxer. He did not love the sport for its own sake, but relished beating the odds against more physically developed opponents. And he was tough. 'When I was 15, I had a skinhead, Dr Martins, and a Crombie. I was a dedicated follower of fashion.'

At the age of 17 he had to switch to senior boxing. Equally skinny, inexperienced, crude opponents were replaced by tough campaigners, some of whom had boxed at the Olympics. Yet Marsh made the transition easily. In 1977, he won the London lightweight title and finished a semi-finalist for the British title. He lost to a fighter called George Gilbody, on a split decision, no mean feat as Gilbody had once fought Thomas 'The Hit Man' Hearns.

By then Marsh had left Chalvedon Comprehensive with four 'CSE' grade ones, which considering his exams had coincided with an ABA final was an achievement.

The president at St George's was a local bookmaker called Tommy Newton, and for his first job Marsh worked in one of Newton's betting shops as a settler, the person who calculates the return on a winning bet. 'I used to take bets as well,' said Terry, 'but I made it clear to the punters that they didn't have to pay tax.'

He may have been pulled out of his grammar school, but Terry Marsh, intelligent, quick-witted and determined, was never someone who was going to remain in a back street bookies. He decided to join the Forces, which had been a long-term ambition of his, ever since becoming a member of the cadet force at Westminster City. However, he was not content with becoming an ordinary soldier. In 1978 he signed up for the Royal Navy as a marine commando.

Like all recruits, he had to endure a routine of little sleep and endless petty duties, mixed in with other more arduous ones. Kit inspection, runs, exercises, map reading, field craft, route marching (for which the Marines are famous) and the notorious 'beastings' – demanding, impromptu training exercises to sort out who is really cut out to be a marine. It is not merely a case of being accepted; recruits have to earn the right to stay on, and there is a high fall-out rate. Marsh dealt with everything that was thrown at him.

He also continued to win boxing titles, including the 1978 lightweight ABA championship, and he made his full England début. The mental toughness that characterised his greatest professional boxing performances was initially tested and reinforced by his time as a marine. He finished first in his group in the basic commando training course. The signs that he had enormous mental motivation, remarkable athleticism and stamina were clear to see. And yet to look at he was just a rather pale, wiry, 10-stone man, and not the classic embodiment of what a boxing action man should look like. He was actually stronger than he appeared, with a competitive, pig-headed character to match.

During the 1978 Commonwealth Games in Edinburgh, Marsh was receiving some friendly teasing from other members of the boxing team. They were all at the pool, when it was discovered Marsh could not dive. But rather than accept their taunts he went up to the top board of an Olympic standard pool and dived off – backwards. He then got out of the water and did it again. Terry can be a bit wild when he is out with the lads. Courage has never been a problem for him, though his courage may have been for other people.

Two years later the first moment of controversy hit Marsh's boxing career. Although he was amateur welterweight champion he was not automatically selected for the Moscow Olympics. In May he was told to box-off for a place with a fighter called Joey Frost whom he had already beaten the month before by a unanimous points decision. Marsh was furious at being treated in such a manner, and refused to fight, thereby vacating his place. He argued that as reigning champion he should automatically qualify, telling *Boxing News*: 'I'm bitterly disillusioned with the way the ABA have treated me and as far as I am concerned they are finished.'

His mother Maisie joined in the row, giving good, solid East End family support. She wrote a letter to *Boxing News* saying that Terry had beaten Frost fair and square. She went on to suggest there was an ABA conspiracy against her boy, who was about to serve in Northern Ireland. For its part the ABA did not feel that Marsh had yet proved himself, and strenuously denied that they were prejudiced against him because he was a soldier.

Marsh gained premature release from the Marines in 1981. He wanted to gain more qualifications, for, as he once said, 'I would have loved to have been an officer in the Marines, but I just didn't have the "O" levels.' The highest rank he could have risen to was sergeant. 'I didn't see much point hanging around only to say "Sir" to an 18-year-old officer with "A" levels.' Instead he enrolled at Basildon College of Further Education and decided to turn professional 'to nick a few bob while I was studying.'

The progression to professional boxer may seem straight-forward but Terry Marsh was no ordinary fighter. At his college in Basildon he passed eight 'O' levels and embarked on a two year 'A' level course in mathematics, physics and chemistry. Affable and articulate, Marsh could probably already claim to be the most professionally qualified fighter in Britain. He had signalled his intelligence long before, when in 1969, aged 11, he became London Schools Chess Champion. There are parallels between chess and boxing. American writer George Plimpton wrote that 'no sport [other than boxing] exists in which one's attention is so directly focused on the opposition for such a long time – except perhaps chess, so that matters of psychological pressure are certainly in effect.'

In her essay *On Boxing* Joyce Carol Oates writes that 'as the chess grand master channels his powerful aggressive impulses on to the game board, which is the world writ small, so the "born" boxer channels his strength into the ring against the opponent. And in the ring, if he is a good boxer, and not a mere journeyman, he will cultivate yet another split personality, to thwart his opponent's game plan *vis-à-vis* him. Boxers, like chess players, must be able to think on their feet, must be able to improvise in mid-fight, so to speak.'

During a bout Marsh could switch from an orthodox stance to southpaw (leading with his right hand), and he was always expert at unbalancing his opponents making them unable to punch with their full weight. He could certainly improvise. Indeed, he had little alternative because of the relative lightness of his punches. He could not just stand in the middle of the ring and bang away.

Marsh has always stressed that he aimed to nullify an opponent's strength. In his world title fight against Joe Louis Manley, he raised his fist at the end of every round and winked at the crowd to demoralise his enemy and the American's corner-men.

In 1982 Marsh sustained a hand injury and had to stop fighting for a while. By this time he was hanging around with a pretty, dark-haired girl he had first met while he was in the Marines at a disco in Stoke-on-Trent where she worked as a shop assistant. He had showed off to her to the sounds of Human League and Spandau Ballet and the combination of a disco-dancing soldier who boxed on the side was irresistable to 19-year-old Jacqui Beffel from Newcastle. In March 1982, they were married at Brentwood registry office. 'I had a physics lecture in the morning, and I had to go to the gym in the afternoon,' recalls Marsh, 'so we squeezed the wedding in somewhere in between.'

Meanwhile the Falklands War had made it more difficult to become an officer in the Marines. 'The Falklands factor helped Maggie Thatcher, but it never helped me,' says Marsh. 'The Marines were suddenly oversubscribed and you now needed "A" levels as well to be an officer.'

Married, and with no regular income, Terry abandoned his plans to become an officer and gave up his 'A' level course. 'I'm satisfied in my own mind that it was something that was once obtainable to me, and that I showed I was capable of belonging to that club of people I had to call "sir".'

He joined the Essex Fire Brigade and thrived in the all male atmosphere of practical jokes, friendly banter, and perpetual challenges. He was not taking his fighting seriously enough to want to fight full-time. Or perhaps boxing, and the incredible reserves of physical and mental stamina that it requires, were not enough of a challenge for him? He had to have more. The responsibilities and dangers of being a fireman attracted Marsh.

Marsh had won 50 of his 54 senior bouts as an amateur, and had reached a stage in his career when he needed a manager. Frank Maloney, then a trainer who during a long career has worked with Duff, Warren and Ambrose Mendy, remembers going to sign Marsh in September 1981. Five foot three and a half inches tall, with close-cut hair, Maloney would be a casting director's dream for a gangster film. He makes Bob Hoskins look lanky and his East London credentials are impeccable. 'I grew up on the terraces of Millwall, and I am still going and still suffering.' At the time Maloney was working with a young, ambitious manager called Frank Warren, who had only recently become involved in boxing.

'We met outside some barracks in Dorset. There was Warren, a promoter called Kieran Murphy, and myself. I was the trainer.

The three of us had a company called Pirate Promotions. We looked like the Mafia, in our suits and Crombie coats, three likely lads. We went to a cafe in Poole. We talked for a long time, and Terry treated it all as a bit of a joke. We put a proposition to him of £1,000 for his first six fights which at that time was quite good money. Most of it was all agreed there and then. It was very informal.'

'I remember being impressed by Frank's youthfulness,' says Marsh. 'I thought all boxing managers were aged about 50, and I didn't realise you didn't have to be middle-aged to be a businessman.'

A deal was signed. The Marsh-Warren relationship had begun.

CHAPTER THREE

Lord of the Unlicensed Ring

Frank Warren once successfully sued a national newspaper for saying he had risen from 'the gutter'. He hadn't. He had risen from the Priory Green Estate in the Angel, Islington, north London, an eight-storey council block. Born on 28 February 1952, Frank John Warren was the first child of Frank and Iris Warren. Three more children were to follow: Christine, Robert and Mark. Priory Green, sited off the Pentonville Road on the way down to King's Cross, houses about a thousand people in three large blocks of flats. It has always been reasonably well kept. There are no towers and mid-air walkways, no broken lifts and very little graffiti. Simply designed, with a white stone outer shell, dark brown brick facade, blue doors and red railings, it is uniform without being dismal. Washing hangs out to dry. Young mothers laden with kids and shopping struggle along the path through the landscaped green space in between the blocks. There are few cars. It is an almost wholly white working-class part of the borough with other similar estates stretching up to the centre of Islington. Inside, the flats are in fair condition, but with low ceilings easily conducting noise from above and below, it is the sort of place where the neighbours could make life hell, or become your best friends. Priory Green is not somewhere so grim as to deter any hopes of an improved material life.

The hopes of the Warren family were fairly high for the eldest son when he passed the 11-plus and won a place at Highbury Grove Grammar School in 1963. Frank was not an exceptional child but he was bright, and it was a decent school, the pick of the bunch locally, better than Philip Magnus or Holloway, which were rough places. Highbury Grove at least presented a chance of a few 'O' Levels, maybe even of further education. The headmaster at the time was Rhodes Boyson, now a Tory MP instantly recognisable by his Dickensian whiskers, who later held several ministerial posts in Margaret Thatcher's government. Friends of the family remember the young Warren as a polite, level-headed boy, at least to his family and elders, but he had a tearaway streak and was expelled for fighting at the age of 15, on the verge of taking his only 'O' Level, Art. His biggest regret is not making more of school, but Highbury Grove at least planted an interest in literature and art which have bloomed in Warren's adult life. Everyday school routine did not captivate him.

The main drag in Islington, Upper Street, is now famous for its bars, brasseries and theatres patronised by young professionals, and *City Limits* readers. Yuppification of parts of the borough in the 1970s and 1980s followed a slower period of gentrification which saw areas such as Barnsbury and Canonbury turned into pockets of considerable affluence. But the indigenous, white working-class world that Frank Warren grew up in prevails. Islington as a whole has never been as deprived as neighbouring places like Hackney or Haringey, and families, often large, have their roots firmly fixed here for years, feeling proud of their manor, with its clearly defined boundaries: City Road to the south and west, Newington Green to the north, and Southgate Road to the east. Working class Islington was an environment of familiarity: familiar faces, familiar places, familiar patterns of life. Everyone knew each other; friends looked after each other, enemies sorted each other out or kept their distance. But it was and is still a hard part of town, with a number of 'problem' estates and rising crime and violence. In 1975 a man was shot dead; a letter to the local paper said it had been a revenge killing committed by a hired hitman. Gang fights were common.

A short walk up the hill from Priory Green leads to Chapel Street market at the Angel, the hub of the manor. Now just confined to one street, it used to spread over four or five. It was the place to hang out and live the street life. Grubby but friendly it is a typical inner city market. Stalls outside middle-range shops sell fruit and veg, knickers and boxer shorts, nylons and tights. Stallholders yell about yet another bargain, mothers and shoppers stop and chat, teenagers shuffle around disgruntledly, open pub doors offer snatches of babbled conversation and laughter clouded by smoke and the aroma of alcohol.

This was where young Frank Warren spent much of his spare time, in a street culture of wheeling and dealing, working as it comes, a common aversion to official forms and the Establishment. It was 'them' and 'us', though not in an aggressively bitter sense of a starved ghetto.

Frank Warren was an ordinary teenager, doing the things the other kids did. Mickey Droy, the former Chelsea footballer, spent four or five years in his teens knocking around with Warren. Droy came from the opposite end of Islington, the Highbury end, but like Warren came from an established local family. His father, Horace Droy, ran a few bookmaker's shops, his uncle worked at Smithfield meat market. There was a gang of ten or so, including Kevin Jenden, an architect now with a practice in Islington, who helped pop promoter Harvey Goldsmith organise Band Aid; and names like Alfie Sculley, John Giovanni and Ray Farrell which belong to faces that Warren hasn't seen for years.

'Frank was just one of the lads. You couldn't print what we used to get up to,' says Droy, smiling mischievously. 'There wasn't a terrific lot to do. We used to go to pubs, arcades, discos, it wasn't anything terribly clever. We used to get into a few scraps, Frank was always one to muck in, everyone did. But we weren't real tearaways.

'It all happened in the pubs. We used to go to pubs where we knew we would get a drink as for a time we were under age. Often there used to be after-hours drinking. If you didn't have any money you went out with the people who did.'

Crime was there for those who wanted to indulge, says Droy – stealing cars, working for racketeers, handling stolen goods – but neither he nor Warren ever got involved in any of that nonsense. The bravado of the gang was enough.

'In those days there were lots of gangs, some had names, we never did. There was a bit of rivalry. I mean if there was trouble you always had mates to help you. If you went out of the area, it was always best to go with your mates, say if you went drinking in Bethnal Green or to a club in Dalston, like the Downbeat. It was a sign of the times that there was always gangs of some description. We didn't go looking for trouble, unless someone had done something to a friend.' In which case having Mickey around wouldn't have been a bad idea – six foot four inches and as broad as a bus – no one picked a lot of trouble with him.

Warren has described his youth as tough. 'I was in a gang like just about everybody else my age. We used to hang around the markets and it could get a little rough but never too bad. I was never in to scooters, I always preferred cars.'

Before he or any of his mates drove, times were often spent dancing at a club called Tiles off the Tottenham Court Road, and Saturday nights at the Royal in Tottenham. Just after the peak of the mod era, it was the time of the 'suedehead' – medium-length, smooth, moppish hair brushed forward. Dressing up meant mohair suits, a Ben Sherman button-shirt and a pair of brogues, or if you were showing off, a pair of Italian Salatio loafers. Dressing down meant Levis, a shirt and V-neck sweater. At the clubs they stared at girls dancing round their handbags, unable to pluck up the courage to chat up any of them, as the soul sounds of Stax, Atlantic and Motown and a little bit of Bluebeat blasted out. 'We were all trying to be macho but just stood there like a bunch of idiots,' remembers Droy.

Every other Saturday was spent on the terraces at Highbury watching Arsenal and in particular a slightly older ex-Highbury Grove boy they all knew, Charlie George. One of the original Fancy Dans and bad lads, George was role model for thousands of kids. Long after a career in which ill-discipline let down his enormous talent, Charlie-boy is back in the manor now, running a garage in the arches behind King's Cross station. Warren has always known Charlie, and they both used to like a flutter. As he reached his late teens, Warren got in the habit of going down the dogs at Haringey and losing a bit, winning a bit, but usually losing a bit.

For Arsenal 1970–71 was the glory year of the League and Cup double, with George scoring the FA Cup winner at Wembley. By then he was wearing his hair long and messy, with sideburns creeping down towards his jaw. Islington lads were wearing tulip-collar shirts, big heels, baggy brush-denim jeans and tank tops. Everyone was a lad now, listening to another north Londoner – Rod Stewart and his band the Faces. Being dedicated followers of fashion and hanging out was a laugh, but none of the crowd was really doing much.

'We were friends but I always thought Frank was a bit more serious. He would like a laugh, but the others were scatterbrains, some of them would do anything. I had no inkling of what he would do,' says Droy. 'Really he had no direction any more than the rest of us. In those days it was hard to get a decent job, when we left school we used to go round in threes and fours looking for work – there just seemed to be loads of kids leaving school looking for a job at the same time.'

Droy's uncle found him work at Smithfield, where Warren was also later employed, before football lifted him out of the drudgery of continually shifting, unfulfilling employment. Droy signed as a professional for Chelsea at the age of 19 in 1970 and quickly lost touch with most of his old friends, Warren included. He became one of the greatest characters of the game in his era – the bearded defensive giant who could head a ball as far as most could kick it. He stayed at Chelsea for 14 years – 'there were lots of offers from big clubs, believe me, but my wife didn't want to go up north and it was so easy driving to Chelsea'. Eventually he moved to Crystal Palace, then Brentford and retired in 1986: 'I was playing in the third division at the end, and I've never played that rubbish, I thought it was time to pack it in.' Work now is running an electrical goods wholesalers off Harrow Road in West London; his home is still in Islington.

Bereft of academic qualifications, Warren at least had the advantage of a strong family to help him. The Warrens were well known in Islington, along with other solid, well-established families like the Adamses and Rileys, partly because there were four brothers, Jimmy, who now works nights in the black cab radio room, Frank senior, Bob, and George, who died a couple of years ago. A brood of males brings confidence, identity and protection in a largely disenfranchised world where quick wits and wheeling and dealing have to carry you through. All four Warren brothers tried their hand at boxing, the established escape route to wealth and fame, but like 99 per cent of other aspirants never approached the first staging post. They all fought as amateurs, but none were good enough to turn professional. It was back to the street life and less glamorous trades.

The Warren family is particularly proud and private. 'They always kept themselves to themselves and were a close-knit family,' says Mary Powell, an Islington shopkeeper and friend of the Warrens for 30 years. 'They have always had to fend for themselves and they have had to be very careful, and they don't talk about their business.'

Droy, despite being a close friend of Warren, never visited his home and never talked about his family, though everyone knew Frank's Uncle Bob was a bit of a character. He knew a few faces, he used to drink with Henry Cooper and Jim Wicks in the West End, he was friends with Stanley Baker the actor. Bob had lived a bit.

Little riles Warren more than the link made between his career and his uncle's imprisonment for his involvement in wounding a gangster in the 1950s. He believes the incident has been used as a brush of criminality to tar him, as if because he has an uncle with underworld links in the past he must be suspect himself. Time and time again Warren has emphasised he was just a small boy when the incident happened – 'I was three years of age at the time so I had nothing to do with it.'

The incident belongs to London's gangland folklore, to an age when men with smart titfers, camel-hair coats and Coronas ran Soho, when, later, the Kray twins Ronnie and Reggie held sway over the East End and much of the West End in an orgy of organised violence, when arguments were often settled by the slash of a blade on face.

Jack 'Spot' Comer was a self-confessed leading underworld figure in the 1950s, a gangster with a capital G. A big, bombastic man who smoked large cigars continuously, he was the son of Polish Jewish immigrants, born in 1912 in Whitechapel, part of an East End steeped in crime and violence. After working as a street bookmaker and a brief spell of thieving during which he was caught and bound over twice, Spot concentrated on running crooked fairground games and unorthodox forms of bookmaking at big race meetings.

Bookmaking and betting were a lowlife Alma Mater, an education in how money worked and how to make it quickly. Few were, or are, smart enough or tough enough to learn all the lessons. Spot was. Gradually, through his Upton Park Mob, he took control of the bookies' pitches at several racecourses, and expanded his operations into a Soho empire based on nightclubs, gambling houses, and protection rackets. By the early fifties he felt confident enough to write an autobiography called *King of the Underworld*. Another gangster, Billy Hill, also claimed the title; the two had been allies in sewing up the West End, though in 1955 they fell out spectacularly.

Spot had developed a rivalry with a much smaller operator called Albert Dimes, aka 'Italian Albert', a north Londoner with West End ambitions of his own, who was most probably working for Hill at the time of the incident. After a fight with a stiletto knife in a greengrocer's shop in Frith Street, in the heart of Soho, in August 1955, both Spot and Dimes were charged with wounding the other. Spot convinced the jury he had acted in self-defence and was acquitted; the case against Dimes was not proceeded with. This tale of dark and deathly deeds more than sated the public's and media's thirst for a criminal world both repulsive and compelling. It was the trial of the year partly because of Spot's blatant celebration: he was accompanied from the Old Bailey by two minders, 'Sonny the Yank' and 'Moisha Blue Boy'. He invited reporters to his luxury apartment in Marylebone as he drank champagne with friends and his 'beautiful, raven-haired Irish wife' Rita, as the papers described her.

The bitterness between Spot and Dimes festered. Bob Warren, as his nephew has said, was a friend of Dimes. So was Francis Fraser, or 'Mad Frankie' Fraser as he was called, a sobriquet perhaps not surprisingly attached after Fraser was twice certified insane.

Late in April 1956 a gang rival to Spot's heard he was planning to take over some of their patches. The gang was informed that Spot had gathered about 30 Irishmen in a Paddington pub to scheme the invasion. Without checking the story, it was decided to stop Spot. One evening as he was walking home to Hyde Park Mansions with Rita and a friend, Spot was set upon by two or more men, who kicked him to the floor and smacked him repeatedly with cudgels and coshes in a vicious attack lasting three to four minutes. Spot was left bleeding heavily on the steps of the mansion block, as his assailants escaped.

Bob Warren and Fraser appeared at the Old Bailey shortly afterwards charged with attacking Spot with intent to cause bodily harm. Warren, then 28, gave his profession as a scaffolder; Fraser, 32, said he was a turf accountant. Fraser at least, who took the leading role in the attack, was identified by Rita Comer, who was threatened repeatedly before the trial. In court Spot, bearing the marks of 90 stitches – or as he said, 'so many stitches the doctors run out of thread they had to go to the tailors' – appeared to stick to a law of the underworld followed down the years: never turn in anyone, no matter what harm they have caused. In court he said he couldn't see who any of the men were, 'No it was all too quick you see.' As Burt McCarthy, a boxing manager and friend of Frank Warren says: 'If you come from that kind of background, you don't just grass on someone to the police – whatever they have done to you.' Bob Warren and Fraser each got seven years.

Spot, at the age of 42, wound down his operations from then on. He bought a furniture shop in the Gloucester Road. He lives off the North End Road in Hammersmith.

Albert Dimes died in 1972 from cancer. At his funeral a brunette unknown to the family laid a wreath from the Kray twins at his graveside, bearing the simple message, 'To a fine gentleman – Ron and Reg Kray'. Charlie and Eddie Richardson, the other famous pair of gangland brothers, also in prison at the time, sent a wreath, as did Mad Frankie from his cell in Hull prison, where he was serving 20 years for his part in another crime.

The whole story is part of an era that has an irresistible appeal of sleazy glamour for many; a nostalgia for a bygone age of roguery. The reality was grim.

Frank Warren has never seen any mileage in remembering that era, or being associated with it via his uncle. Bob Warren was no Frankie Fraser, there is no record of him having any connection with the Krays, but he isn't exactly an accountant from Mill Hill. The sort of reputation that follows a crime of the type he committed doesn't die quickly; in the manor, it commands respect. And Bob Warren has lived his life as a builder and a bookmaker – chiefly at point-to-points. Like his three brothers, he has stayed in the manor he was born in. Today, in his early 60s, he lives in a council flat in Hoxton, just east of Islington, an area with none of the architectural pleasantries of its wealthier neighbour – a landscape of empty streets, cheerless estates and patches of wasteland.

Tall, broad-shouldered, tough-looking, with thick, swept back, badly-dyed hair, and a crackling voice that commands attention, it is easy to see how Bob Warren was invaluable to Frank when he was young. Bob saw there was some hope for Frankie, he encouraged him to get on, to be lucky and stay sharp. His uncle, more than his father, offered sound counsel: who could be trusted, who should be steered clear of, what was a good or bad business scheme. In his early twenties, when Warren's ambition began to surface, he needed his uncle's wisdom, accumulated over many years on the streets.

Jon Robinson, who worked for Warren for years, says: 'Bob gave Frank confidence. He was in the era of Jack Spot and so on and he stopped anyone muscling in on Frank.'

Acquaintances of the family all speak highly of Bob Warren. 'He is a very nice, genuine honest type of guy and you've got to speak well of them because there aren't too many about,' says Burt McCarthy. 'I've heard remarks Mickey Duff has made about Frank's uncle, but as a person, Mickey couldn't clean his shoes. There's many other people who are up to all kinds of villainy who never get caught, and they look down on the people who do.'

The agent Ambrose Mendy, now the best of enemies with Warren, but once a colleague, first met him in 1974. 'He had an uncle who was a great guy, Mr Street Credibility. Bob had a Robin Hood image, he'd talk to anyone, just a really good guy. He helped draw people to Frank. I don't think his father was in the same league in those terms.'

Warren in turn stands by Bob. 'I am proud he is my relation. In actual fact he is the one person, if I have had any success, it's down to,' he once said. 'He is the one who said whatever you do, keep away from this or that type of people, don't get involved in this and conduct your life properly. He was always emphasising this to me, and I took notice of that from a young age. What happened to him happened 35 years ago – there is a thing in this country called spent conviction.'

Mary Powell's husband, Jack, a former fighter and founder of the London Ex-Boxers Association charity, has known the family for longer than he can remember: 'Bob helped Frank by being there. That's how I would look at that kind of thing – people would think twice about taking liberties with Frank.'

Mary Powell recalls the young Warren as always being very polite, but never as standing out from the gaggle of local kids. Now, transformed into a national figure, he still shows the same regard for her as in his youth. 'Frank has never forgotten me at a birthday or Christmas. As soon as he heard about Jack's stroke, he said "Mary, if you have to go anywhere I'll have a car round". If you ever need anything, you can count on him. I could never run him down.' And as the years have gone on, he has remained firmly in the family's bosom, inevitably seeing less of his relatives day to day, but always turning up for family dos and get togethers.

From the age of 12, Warren helped his father run his bookie's pitch at the races. He learnt the useful art of keeping a book and managing money, and the thrill of a quick, profitable deal. Much later Warren said his favourite word was 'agreed'. It was a young age to be around a trade which isn't recognised by the Royal Society of Arts. He was surrounded by people who knew there was cash to be made outside the conventional means of a nine-to-five job, that for working-class lads there were alternatives to counting out other people's money behind the window at Lloyds or putting the finishing touches to a Ford Escort on the production line. Frank Warren senior and his brother could at times make decent money from gambling. Warren remained out of the mainstream for years to come.

The life of a bookie can be mundane – seeing the same people at the same racecourses week after week – and is very rarely a stepping stone to greater things, but on big race days it is an exciting world, dominated by money and an urge to jazz life up a little. Racecourses in full swing are a carnival of style and spending, which impressed the young Frank. Bookies have to think on their feet, pitting their wits each day against the punters, working out odds that will draw the money in but which won't expose the bookie to too much risk. It is a world where charm and personality multiply chances of success – something Warren picked up from Uncle Bob.

Gambling can educate a clever man quickly, or ruin an over-indulgent one fast. Though Warren bet for years, once he matured, he more or less gave it up, knowing it was smarter to be laying the bets than making them. In the world where Warren was raised, there are always a handful of smart kids, who take the glimmer of a chance to make something of themselves, and there are those who can't struggle free of the mediocrity that awaits them, even if they should wish to. Warren acquired the primitive capitalist instinct that sustained his father and uncle, the obstinacy to achieve economic self-determination that an early life without luxury can breed. But he made more of it than they ever had, or imagined that young Frank ever would. Having blown his education and any prospects of a professional career, there was no option. 'You start to scuffle around and you work hard and you get lucky and suddenly you are making money. I never planned to be a millionaire. I just got on with it and then things seemed to happen. I think I got it from working at the races with my Dad,' Warren told the journalist Lynn Barber, in one of her revealing profiles.

'Ever since I was a kid I've always gone to good tailors to get suits made, and I always drove a decent car . . . If you've got money, it makes life easier, doesn't it?'

After leaving Highbury Grove, Warren took a series of jobs. What he really wanted to do was be a cameraman – it had been hoped he would find work as a trainee in the film company of Stanley Baker, but it didn't work out and he started off as an office boy, then as a solicitor's clerk at the quaintly Dickensian-named, J Tickle & Co. It was quickly clear Frank wasn't suited to a legal career, but it was a useful insight into the law, which Warren was later to exploit to enormous advantage. Before long he became a salesman in Smithfield meat market. The hours were tough, but the money was good – £250 a week in the early seventies. Warren liked the busy atmosphere. He moved into a smart rented flat and satisfied his burgeoning passion for sports cars by buying an E-type Jaguar. Once he realised the bummarees, or porters, made more money, he switched jobs. There were opportunities for private deals. He offered to deliver meat to a restaurateur from Cambridge who wasn't happy with travelling down to London. As Warren sold to the man, he determined the price, buying the meat elsewhere for less, delivering it, and pocketing the difference.

Frank had everything a young man could wish for: a job, a flat and a car. He was a smart working class lad doing well for himself, and true to the traditions of his class and family, he married young. In 1972 he tied the knot with Barbara, a local girl from Chapel Market. A couple of years later they had a son Jamie. Frank began managing a pub called the Three Brewers in Essex Road, Islington. Life seemed to be going well.

Then in late 1975, he was accused of attempting to rape an 18-year-old girl one evening at his pub. Frank John Warren, 23, of Elmore Street, which is round the corner from the pub, and where his former wife still lives with their son Jamie, appeared at Highbury Magistrates court on Tuesday 2 December. An incident was alleged to have taken place on Sunday 30 November. He was released on bail of £100 plus a surety of the same amount. On a second appearance a month later Warren was committed to Crown Court and again bailed. Four months later in April 1976, his case was heard at the Old Bailey. In his testimony Warren told the court that the girl's story of an alleged sex assault had been made up and that she was lying. On 12 April, after a three day trial in front of Judge Peter Mason, a jury acquitted him. They also returned not guilty verdicts on two other counts of alleged indecent assault and assault causing actual bodily harm.

Around this time Frank left Islington for a while. Perhaps it was because of the inevitable local gossip surrounding the trial, or may be he just felt he needed a break. He went to Spain for about a year, where he stayed with relatives and lazed around for a time. But typically, he spotted a business opportunity, namely, vending machines.

They were all the rage out there, but only just entering the market back home. 'From there I got the idea and I just came back and got stuck into it.' Warren is good at getting stuck into things; he begins a project impulsively, then sticks to it tenaciously. Warren leased these new drinks machines, as well as cigarette machines and pool tables to pubs or offices and collected the rent. It worked.

His reputation grew in the Islington manor as a bit of a sharp operator. One of the young Warrens was doing all right for himself, he had his own little business, Dawell Pool Limited, run with a partner, John Dale, from an office in Amwell Street, Islington, he had already run a pub. Now he was providing pool tables for pubs in north and east London as a new craze took off. Pubs like the *Spanish Patriot* in Islington, *Rose of Denmark* and the *Dragon Arms* staged darts and pool matches, often with topless girls to get the punters in. Frank sometimes turned up when his pool tables were part of the evening's entertainment, which was often in aid of local charities. It was all part of a scene which was very popular for two or three years, then faded.

By his own admission Warren was a bit of a 'Jack the Lad'. The marriage did not last too much longer. 'The only thing wrong with it was me. I just wasn't ready to settle down. It was a classic case of marrying too early.' By now he knew he didn't want to stay in Islington all his life. He knew he wasn't going to be a Cavalier-owning, unaspiring C2, standing on the North Bank at Highbury for years to come. At some point, he didn't know how exactly, he would have all the trappings of success: a Rolls, a top tax bracket and a season ticket in the upper tier. Already he had more money than his peers, but even then he still hadn't really got going. Warren didn't have a mission. Still one of the lads, still gambling on the dogs, he always had a deal in mind and something clever to say.

One day in 1977 Warren bumped into his cousin Lenny McLean. McLean, then 26, worked as a bouncer at north London nightclubs and lived in Hoxton. Big, broad, with cropped hair, Lenny soon earned the nickname, 'Lean, Mean', though the latter was far more appropriate than the former. He is now to be found working the door of the Hippodrome nightclub in the West End. A couple of days before this chance meeting, Warren had seen McLean fight at an unlicensed boxing show in a pub backroom. He lost badly.

Despite his father and uncles' boxing careers and a good friend who boxed when they were younger, Frank was never taken with the game, and had never fancied doing it himself. But he knew enough to see McLean could have won the fight if he had done some training outside the pub.

Ambrose Mendy says he went with him to the fight at Sinatra's in Croydon. 'He was managing a pub next to one of the children's clothes shops I had and one day he asked me to go to the boxing with him. It was incredible, there were about 800 screaming their heads off. A free-for-all fight, everything goes. The potential was clear.'

A couple of days later Warren ran into McLean, who was trying to get a return match. Warren persuaded him of the virtues of training and took him to see someone who trained fighters. McLean won the return at the Finsbury Park Rainbow in the first round. Frank has since claimed he won £25,000 in a bet.

The other fighter's manager approached Warren and McLean about a third encounter. All of a sudden young Frank was calling the shots. He recalls saying, 'Well, hang about. Why should you put it on and get all the money? So we had this big argument and I said "He can fight anyone, he doesn't need you." So then I had to get him [McLean] a fight. The first one was unbelievable, a complete farce. What went wrong? You name it.'

Just as Warren had learnt that it was smarter to be a bookmaker than a punter, he now realised it could pay to be in control of boxing rather than just be a hanger-on.

The unlicensed boxing scene was big in those days. They were unpleasant, seedy events, staged in pub back rooms or small halls in Essex and north and east London. Tough guys, almost invariably overweight, slugged it out after hours, roared on by boozed-up male audiences thirsty for a good scrap, a winning bet and a bit of blood or more. The boxers mostly wore gloves, sometimes not. Medical supervision was non-existent. Betting, often for large amounts, was part of the ritual, as were sidestakes, whereby each fighter would have backers who would bet on their man, with the winning fighter picking up a cut. These sidestakes went as high as £5,000, £10,000 and even £20,000 when Warren's shows got going.

Frank Warren has never had a taste for violence – he even finds it hard to defend the level of violence in the sport which made him successful – and the conditions of the shows he was seeing shocked him. Instead of walking away in disgust, he reacted with typical initiative and tenacity, realising he could clean up the whole business and make himself a tidy sum.

Warren had had the spark of inspiration but he couldn't do it alone. His uncle Jimmy recalls, 'I don't know how Frank got the idea, but he did, and we all helped him put it together.' The Warren family production team was augmented by old friends of Bob, the McCarthy brothers, Burt and Leslie. Burt had managed boxers for years, and if things had gone differently, he could have been a big name in the sport. As it was, he became a millionaire businessman, and at this stage was concentrating on a new electronics business. Brought up in the East End, McCarthy has, like Frank Warren, exceeded expectations. Despite his sophistication and smart clothes, McCarthy bears many hallmarks of his upbringing: a sharp turn of phrase, keen eyes, and natural suspicion. Short, stocky, with slightly ruddy cheeks and wiry hair, he is friendly and a lively talker, like so many boxing people.

Over a lengthy meal in an Italian restaurant, McCarthy nostalgically recalled Warren's early days. He was impressed by young Frank, whom Bob Warren introduced him to a little while before the McLean fight. Burt remembers Warren was full of ideas, without being particularly flash or confident. 'Frank always had a presence but he's not the sort of boy who throws himself about.'

Burt's brother Leslie has had connections with Charles and Eddie Richardson, the south London gangland brothers sent down for over 25 years in 1967. He was convicted for trying to nobble the jury in Charlie's trial in 1967. It was the so-called 'torture trial', in which the headlines were grabbed by the brothers' treatment of supposedly disloyal or incompetent members of their gang in their Park Lane offices – pliers on teeth and fingernails, electrode therapy and other niceties. Along with another man, Albert Stayton, Leslie McCarthy, then 33, was found guilty at the Old Bailey of 'conspiring to pervert the course of public justice by attempting to influence and induce jurors concerned in the trial of Charles Richardson and others in favour of one or more of the accused'.

A Mr Kenneth Horsecraft, brother of a Francis Horsecraft, a juror in the trial, was introduced to McCarthy and Stayton in a pub. One of them said to him: 'Have you a brother on the "torture trial" jury?' Horsecraft answered he had, then the man said: 'Any chance of doing any business?'

Horsecraft replied: 'No, you've got the wrong brother. No, no chance.' Nothing more was said or done by the two men. McCarthy and Stayton were both jailed for 18 months.

Leslie McCarthy has worked for Frank for 12 years. Early on his knowledge of the unlicensed scene – the venues, the fighters, and so one – was invaluable; he was part of the team, with others soon joining the fold, including Jon Robinson and Mary Powell, who used to help with the tickets. Frank was in charge, but the older people around him were invaluable, and enjoyed working with one of their own who was trying to achieve the sort of thing they had only dreamt of.

Frank, still only in his mid-twenties, was not an imposing physical figure. Medium build, five foot eleven inches tall, with mousy brown hair and a slightly podgy face, he was always smartly turned out, in the best suits he could afford, and had a certain charisma, an impish smile and an infectious, slightly anxious enthusiasm for what he was doing. His easy-going manner won people over. He wasn't threatening; shy at first meetings, with a quiet voice, he had tics, still evident today, like scratching his cheek with his little finger if a little unsure of himself, and dropping his head and peering up while listening to someone. He had what they call a quiet authority.

Frank's knowledge of boxing may have been patchy, but as well as being a quick learner, he could spot a winner and a crowd pleaser, a talent that served him well later.

The early shows were chaotic. The fighters were too old and too fat, the fights were undignified, brutal scraps. The audience often decided to have a go themselves, flinging fists and chairs about with riotous abandon. One fighter would hold another's head under his arm and belt him. The referee didn't have much authority. It was one up from bare fists in the back room of a pub in Essex. It was farcical, fun if you could take it, but not what most people would call boxing. There were plenty of characters at ringside, flat noses and cigars all round, with their Bentleys, BMWs and Mercs parked outside.

The chair-throwing didn't last too long. Warren realised the shows had to smarten up a bit. But at this stage it hadn't occurred to him to go legitimate and apply for a British Boxing Board of Control licence. Burt McCarthy, with plenty of experience of professional boxing, had made it clear it was a self-serving, protective body keen to preserve the status quo, which had administered British boxing since 1929. But the Board was self-appointed. It wasn't a government department, its rules weren't laws. He had no respect for the Board, seeing it as a stuffy, traditional closed shop. Why couldn't there be another self-appointed boxing organisation? Between them, Warren, his uncle and the McCarthys came up with an alternative: the National Boxing Council (NBC), which began on 20 May 1979. Unlicensed only meant unlicensed by the Board – there was nothing illegal about Warren's early shows or the NBC, as the Greater London Council and other local authorities gave their permission and the police knew what was happening. So on with the show. It was an idea of brilliant simplicity and an incredibly bold move for a 27- year-old who two years previously was concerned with pool tables not winning punches. A disregard for authority and tradition, or anything that stood in his way, was rewarding him. 'We made a few mistakes to begin with,' Warren told a journalist at the time, 'but we were very green then. Some of our fighters were over- age, and some weren't too fit, but you've got to start somewhere. These days we are a legitimate organisation giving boxers a genuine alternative – and that can only be good for the boxers themselves.'

The NBC's shows grew in to bigger venues: the Rainbow in Finsbury Park, which had once been a major venue for rock concerts, and the Royal in Tottenham, packed in 1,500–2,000 on NBC nights.

The NBC appointed a medical supervisor, Dr John Thurston, a consultant at St Mary's Hospital, Roehampton, and medical officer of Rosslyn Park Rugby Club. To the horror of the British Boxing Board of Control, he would advise fighters that in view of their health and physical condition fighting might not be such a good idea, but would never prevent them going in the ring. The NBC bouts began to resemble licensed shows more and more. The referees, all ex-fighters, wore the familiar white shirt and black bow tie; there were ringside judges, though fights almost invariably went to a knockout or stoppage; proper tickets, posters and programmes were printed. Warren introduced innovations in staging which he continued later on: blaring pop music as fighters, followed by a spotlight, made their way to the ring; bunny-girls paraded with cards showing the number of the next round; the MCs like little Aitchie Stevens announced the bouts with flamboyance and a music hall-style flourish. All this is standard practice today, but Warren was the first to realise punters wanted plenty of embellishments to the boxing itself. They also wanted to see a decent fight, a good scrap, not the turgid, one-sided affairs often presented by established promoters too scared to give their own fighters a decent match.

Despite being technically legal, the NBC evenings acquired a speakeasy status. Some wild touches were thrown in – one night the corner men were in white dress suits and the boxers swilled their mouths out with champagne instead of water. Warren expanded, staging evenings of dinner, cabaret and boxing in Mayfair, charging £17 a head for a meal which included 'Coupe Hawaiian' and 'Dindonneau Rôti aux Chipolata'. Warren pushed himself more in the limelight, promoting the shows under the banner of Warren Sports Promotions. Every seat was always taken. Famous ex-boxers like Terry Downes began to be seen at ringside, and the odd celebrity, like Derek Jameson, the Radio 2 presenter, at that time editorial director of the *Daily Express* and *Daily Star*.

Soon the newspapers began to pick up on Warren's shows. He vigorously defended himself against accusations of organising bloodbaths, and even went to the lengths of commissioning a half-hour long publicity documentary video called 'Box On'. Made by Lindsay Clennell, it presents the NBC as the boxing fans' friend, with Warren cast as the emancipator.

Jameson, dressed in black tie at an NBC evening, appears making a raucous, spluttering defence of Warren.

'If the working class are going to beat each other up, then they should do it for their own people, from their own roots. Why should it be in the National Sporting Club or the Hilton? Shouldn't it belong to the people as it used to when I was a kid? And I think as the editor of a newspaper in Fleet Street I want to know why so many obstacles are put in the way of this young guy Frank Warren, who's trying to make boxing a decent sport again. I don't like what's happening to him.'

The fights show flabby, balding, slow middle-aged men – pugilistic puddings – throwing wild, indiscriminate punches, unable to defend themselves adequately, as their wobbly bellies flap around. At the end of a round, one fighter reels uncontrollably from side to side of the ring, his legs gone, his eyes blank. He is taken back to his corner but, after a minute, is up for the next round. Another boxer admits he hasn't fought for ten years; his job was selling greeting cards.

But Warren was learning the art of public relations, of talking up average commodities into would-be fight heroes. 'Take Colombo (Steve Richards),' he tells the interviewer, 'he fought his way out of Hungary during the revolution and he's been fighting ever since. He's very determined and he always trains hard.' Cliff Field, probably the best of the regular fighters, is shown smashing a car up at work in the wrecker's yard, to an original background tune. The handle of his sledgehammer flies off and he grins in embarrassment.

The stable boxers made a reasonable living for a time out of the shows, earning as much as £500 a fight. But for others it was just a way of taking a belated place in the spotlight and working off some aggression. As one said, 'Look, there's millions of people fighting. This way you get paid for it, and you can't get nicked for it.'

Lenny McLean praised Warren for cleaning up unlicensed boxing. 'There was nutting, kicking, all kinds of stuff until Frankie came along. He's made it sensible, the first one that nuts, that's it, disqualified.'

These days, Warren makes light of this period, shrugging it off as something of an irrelevance. It wasn't. It was where Warren cut his teeth in the basic arts of promotion he was soon to master on a much bigger stage. It took considerable nerve for someone in his mid-twenties to stage those shows. He had to take risks, but after all, Frank was a gambler.

Jon Robinson, before long general manager in Warren's office, says at the time Warren looked like a 'saucy choirboy'. His boyish, pale face was occasionally lit by a canny smile; he wasn't arrogant, but he had something. People listened to Frank.

Except he wasn't Frank in those days, but 'Frankie'. And his accent was almost unrecognisable from what it is today, being then a typical breathless Cockney 'h'-less and 't'-less tone which over the years Warren has improved into one he regards as more acceptable.

Warren has always perceived a snobbery from the public, and certainly the press, towards his roots, when fascination is the more common attitude. Though not openly ashamed of his background, he did once say nothing gave him more satisfaction than driving through Islington without stopping. Whereas many successful people cherish their humbler origins, such sentiment has no place in Warren's repertoire of emotions. Though there is still a lot of affection for him in the area. Alby Hollister, a former boxer, famous for a time for being the first man to go the distance with the great Randolph Turpin, has run the Alma in Chapel Street for 20 years, a tiny pub the size of a living room, with boxing prints and blow-ups of his fight reports on the walls. 'All his family and Frank are very nice people. The family has always been very good to me. Frank used to come in here for a drink, but not any more of course. Everyone round here is very proud of 'im, we like to see one of our own getting on.'

'I didn't see myself living in a council flat for the rest of my life,' Warren once said. And his extraordinary ambition, once in full gear, took him away from Islington, at least physically. Boxing people never leave the manor completely. Warren tries to distance himself from the world he grew up in, and the people who influenced him, but as much as anyone else, Warren is a product of his environment. Frank Warren may have become a millionaire, met Frank Sinatra and danced with Princess Michael of Kent, but, his family, certain friends and associates and a *modus operandi* picked up over the years in Islington, are still very much part of him. He has craved social acceptance and respectability, and never felt it has been awarded as unreservedly as he deserved.

By 1979, Warren, streetwise, determined and anti-authoritarian, was coming of age. As he once admitted, he grew up a bit late, but when he did he grew up fast. He had found something to absorb him. He was motivated by the thrill of making money, which the NBC shows did, and the buzz of pulling off a deal. He had taken his gambling spirit into action with spectacular effect. Things were being 'agreed'.

And Warren possessed in abundance an attribute essential to success of any kind: the ability to work hard. In 1979 he set up an office in an empty shop in Packington Street, Islington, one of the pleasant terraced streets off Upper Street at the Angel end, and built a team of people around him.

'We ran it seven days a week,' recalls Jon Robinson, who was there from day one. 'The average promoter doesn't realise you need an office open all the time. Frank could be a shy boy in public at first, but very strong in private when he worked. He knew what he wanted. He worked hard and he had a terrific habit of writing everything down. He always had a legal brain on him. But he is ruthless. I couldn't get on with him after five years. He'll speak to you one day and not the next.'

In a sport beset by managerial incompetence, Warren realised that simple virtues of diligence and sound organisation would count for a great deal. But from the early days, he had to be in control and had trouble relying on anyone else.

And he always thought big. In August 1980 Warren issued a rather ropey-looking press release on paper headed 'Warren Sports Promotions'. It plugged 'The Race of the Century, Coe v Ovett'. Warren, who signed himself as managing director, pledged to stage 'the most exciting track event of all time, the clash between the giants . . .', promising to raise at least £2 million for the Cancer Research Campaign (CRC) if the race went ahead. It didn't, and negotiations with the two runners, then at the peak of their careers, at the time of the Moscow Olympics, didn't go too far. It never came to anything, but got the attention of the press, not least because it raised what was becoming a major question about Warren: where did his money come from?

Warren admitted that an industrialist was prepared to

underwrite £2 million for the CRC. A journalist went to see the head of the charity, a Mr Sadler. He said Warren had a backer for this race, who was a very wealthy household name, whose reputation was beyond reproach, and whose wife had died of cancer. The reporter some time later put it to Warren that the industrialist was his major backer, full stop. 'He was taken aback, and said it wasn't like that, he said he had done everything himself, but there was someone in the background when the big one – say a major promotion – came along, who would step in to co-operate.' Warren didn't fancy continuing the conversation.

The identity of the industrialist has never been revealed. Jarvis Astaire, *inter alia* a millionaire promoter, businessman and agent, fits every criterion – his first wife had died of the disease in 1974. Though the idea of the man who was soon to become one of Warren's greatest rivals working with him in this way might sound fantastical, at that stage in Warren's career Astaire can not have seen him as an adversary of such potential potency.

Jon Robinson insists there is no mystery about Warren's finances. 'Warren got his money from the bank. He opened an account for each promotion and sold tickets to pay into the account. Frank isn't shady and he didn't have bundles to start with.'

The costs involved in the unlicensed shows were not huge, and each promotion made a profit. Warren may have had a few quid on one side from his vending business, plus that winning bet on the McLean fight, which Warren has said was £25,000.

Frank and money got on very well. It is likely he also borrowed to finance promotions, particularly from a network of publicans who were keen followers of the unlicensed shows. Burt McCarthy is also widely believed to have lent Warren considerable amounts over the years. In other words, Warren bobbed and weaved for money as his career as a promoter went ever upwards.

By 1980 the British Boxing Board of Control were scared of Warren, and the establishment promoters – Mickey Duff, Mike

Barrett, Jarvis Astaire – were growing wary of him. Between them they had major boxing promotions in the capital sewn up; in fact there were very few major shows outside London. The popularity of Warren's shows couldn't be denied, backing up his claim that the NBC represented a widespread disaffection with the monopoly held by the establishment.

For excitement, NBC shows were second to none, at least for those who could bear to watch such hideous spectacles. In 1980 the English boxer Alan Minter's loss to the American Marvin Hagler for the middleweight world title at Wembley Arena ended in a racist-inspired riot, with Hagler unable to leave the ring as drinks cans were hurled in. The accusation often made by the boxing establishment that Warren kept a disorderly boxing house was beginning to sound less convincing.

The Board were already beginning to feel threatened by the NBC, when Warren pulled off a masterstroke. The NBC applied for membership of the World Boxing Association, one of the two bodies then governing the sport. It was unlikely the application would succeed, but if it did, the NBC would have been considerably legitimised, and the Board would have faced having to share its power, a scenario unthinkable after 50 years of unbroken rule.

Ray Clarke, now 70, was general secretary of the Board at the time. In the board room in the Vauxhall Bridge Road offices of the organisation he used to run, Clarke remembered: 'Warren had run those [unlicensed] shows more or less sticking two fingers up at the Board of Control, saying he didn't need the Board, and set up his organisation which later fell by the wayside. We were worried at the image of the unlicensed fights, splashed across the front pages of the tabloids, who were usually calling for this to stop. It was bad for the image of boxing.

'He wasn't actually invited to make an application, but word got out to him, you know, "why don't you go legitimate, you won't get anywhere running this sort of rubbish".'

On 10 December 1980, Frank Warren was awarded a British Boxing Board of Control promoter's licence by the Board's Southern Area Council. He was glad to take it. By now the NBC was running away with itself. Lots of different people had somehow got involved whom he had no time for.

'There was a certain amount of opposition to giving him a licence,' says Clarke, 'but generally speaking it was felt if we had him under our control it would be an end to the unlicensed shows because he was the brains behind them. He was a charmer Frank. I had been a bit worried because of one of his uncles, but I never mentioned that to him. We considered what he was now, that he genuinely wanted to join the Board and become legitimate, and had no police record. We always ask a promoter if he has been in trouble with the police and what he does for a living. He said he'd worked in a lawyer's office, that he was in property. It was a bit vague.' By co-opting Warren, the Board hoped it would tame him. They couldn't have been more wrong.

Two years before the idea of becoming a licensed promoter would have been ridiculous. Now, with Leslie and Burt and Bob and everyone else urging him to go for it, it became the most logical move. The NBC had run its course, and now it was worth having a crack at the real thing, despite all the obstacles. On 1 December, a few days before his licence was officially sanctioned, Warren put on his first show under Board jurisdiction. It was at the Bloomsbury Hotel, and featured two American fighters, Otis Gordon and Jerry 'The Bull' Martin, a world title contender, something unheard of for a promoter's début. It wasn't a great evening, Warren lost £17,000. But his extraordinary transformation from coffee-machine vendor to millionaire boxing promoter was on its way. He was now about to take on the boxing establishment, the biggest challenge of his career.

CHAPTER FOUR

The Business of Boxing

An American boxing manager once said of Don King, the most powerful promoter in the world: 'Don King is a liar and a thief, the greediest bastard I've ever known. This guy wants all the money and all the fighters. He talks about fairness and equality, but he wants everything for himself, and doesn't want to give anything to anybody ... If I was a fighter and needed a promoter, who would I take? Don King. The man is the best. Don King delivers.'

Boxing promotion is all about delivering. It is both the simplest and the most complicated task. On the face of it, all a promoter has to do is hire a venue, put a few fighters together, sell the tickets and persuade a television company to broadcast the show. In fact once upon a time that was virtually all a promoter had to do, without even having to worry about television, in the days when tens of thousands went to see boxing every week at local halls up and down the country. These days, starting with an empty hall and ending with a successful and profitable night's boxing is a precarious task.

A promoter is an employer – of his own team of organisers, publicity officers and ticket handlers, of the night's boxers and their teams; he deals with the media, the national or world boxing authorities who oversee the fight, and the balance sheets at the end of the day.

Success depends on four things: the promoter's charisma, the reliability of his staff, his ability to add up, and having boxers people want to pay to see.

A lot of money also helps. 'Give me half a million pounds and I can make YOU,' says Jon Robinson, pointing an emphatic finger, 'the number two promoter in Britain in five weeks. You need money up front, then the other bits fall in to line.'

If boxing is part-sport and part-theatre, then the promoter is producer and director rolled into one; the main boxers are the leading actors, with a full support cast of less well known performers; the boxers' managers are the actors' agents; the matchmakers are the casting directors; the cornermen are the wardrobe and make-up artists, and the referee, timekeeper, judges and inspectors are the technical crew. Only boxing is unrehearsed entertainment, where anything can happen.

Above all, the promoter has to find the boxers. Nowadays promoters are often managers as well, and have their own boys – 'house' fighters – matched against chosen opposition. There the matchmaker comes in. Matchmakers are walking boxing encyclopaedias, on call 24 hours a day should their mind need to be searched to find a new opponent. They have to be trusted by promoters to find opponents who will give house fighters something to think about, without ever seriously threatening to beat them. In that sense matchmakers are considerable power-brokers, though at times the job seems more akin to pawn-broking – buying in cheap goods which are then recycled.

Ernie Fossey, Frank Warren's matchmaker, has no illusions about the job. 'You have to have the patience of Job. You have to know the limitations of the boys – try and convince the other guy he's got half a chance. There's many managers, despite what you hear, who are not interested in talking about the money. They want to see if their boy has a chance. Then you can start getting them keen with a bit of money.

'Anyone can make a title fight – the Board of Control can do that. It's making the undercard, that's where the headaches come in. I have to look through the fighters' records and then get hold of the manager. If he says having looked at my kid's record that he doesn't fancy it, then I'll say "but who has he beaten?" Persuasion is part of it. But you know nine times out of ten the kid has got half a chance.'

The manager is entitled to a 25 per cent cut of the boxer's fee, though sometimes he will take nothing at all. In the fifties and sixties, promoters were promoters and managers were managers, but latterly the distinction became blurred. Either one man does both, or a group combine to form one promotional and managerial unit. Negotiations for boxing matches are often of labyrinthine complexity, even to the parties involved, or journalists or outsiders taking an interest. Sub-plots about negotiations can assume greater importance than the main event itself, and the more important the fight, the trickier the dealing process becomes. Nothing beats the shenanigans preceding a world heavyweight championship fight.

There are three ways a promoter makes money: from ticket sales, sale of television rights, and sundries such as sponsorship, programmes and spin-off merchandise. A full house will only cover costs; television is where the big money is, which explains why promoters without it resent so strongly those with it, and the rest is icing on the financial cake. The overall size of a promoter's outgoings vary on the scale of the promotion, but always includes the fees of the boxers, cornermen, security men, production of tickets and programmes, hiring the venue, hiring a ring, lights and music facilities and so on. A small hall show at somewhere like the York Hall in Bethnal Green or the Lewisham Theatre could cost from £7,500 to £25,000 to stage. Costs for a major event at a large auditorium would be about £200,000 or more, excluding fighters' fees.

Boxing is like no other sport. Other sports have fixture lists, teams, regular festivals of contest – the World Cup, the Superbowl, the Grand National. Boxing is a contest between two men which has to be arranged by others, so personalities dictate the sport, rather than officialdom. And arrangements involve so many imponderable elements that bartering, haggling and wheeling and dealing are the essence of the game. And part of its attraction. In boxing, every deal is different. It has to be that way, as every individual involved wants to make as much money as he possibly can. Matters of principle rarely govern disputes. In boxing, arguments come down to money. Fighting for money is the root of all boxing.

Every boxing show in Britain must in theory be approved by the British Boxing Board of Control, the national regulatory authority for the sport. It has a board of stewards and eight regional councils, all of which are self-appointed. Bereft of any statutory powers, the Board has endeavoured with some success to control professional boxing, (amateur boxing is controlled by the Amateur Boxing Association), by its own policies and rules. Today the stewards are made up of judges, lawyers, doctors, policemen (including Nipper Read, the man who put the Kray twins away), magistrates and MPs. The current president Sir David Hopkin, is the Metropolitan chief stipendiary magistrate. It is a collection of white middle-class professionals with as far as anyone knows, spotless reputations, though what qualifies them to sit in judgement on boxing matters is questionable. Separated by social class and education, most of boxing's brethren stick two fingers up at the Board in the same way they would to a Jehovah's Witness knocking at the door early on a Sunday morning.

'They are not boxing people, what do they know about boxing?' is a familiar complaint about the Board. 'One rule for us, and one for them' is another, though boxing characters are not renowned for seeing the other man's point of view. Administration is a thankless task.

The promoter and manager Mike Barrett speaks for a number in boxing when he says: 'The Board are all very well, but they are rather toothless. Generally speaking they don't know what time of day it is.'

The general secretary responsible for the day-to-day running of the Board is John Morris. A friendly, efficient, avuncular 56-year-old, with the air of a grammar school headmaster, he was formerly a sports journalist and press officer for the Board, before taking up his current post in 1986. 'Boxing is a sport that must have one central control for each country. Once you get people setting up on their own and diversifying, then you'll get trouble,' he said at the Board's offices.

'Boxing is a peculiar sport, in that its individual promoters put on individual shows, and they basically all want the same fighters and the same fights and there aren't enough to go round. Everything is piecemeal in boxing, nothing is planned more than two or three months ahead, which makes it a hard sport to legislate for. I would like to see a lot less of the stupidities and bitternesses and enmities they [promoters] create. There's a them and us attitude, when they are essentially business rivals. Whether or not they like each other is irrelevant.'

The Board awards licences to promoters, managers, agents, boxers, timekeepers, matchmakers. It approves and supervises every professional match that takes place in Britain. It deals with disciplinary matters. And perhaps most importantly when boxing *per se* has so many enemies, it sets very strict medical guidelines to be followed inside and outside the ring. In other words, it has quite a job on its hands. Over the years it has been criticised for being biased, inefficient and riddled with vested interests. Yet its authority remains intact.

The Board's role has been complicated by the growing number of weight divisions for fighters, and therefore the number of championships. To the original eight divisions – fly, bantam, feather, light, welter, middle, light-heavy and heavy, a few were added just before and after the war, such as light-middle or light-welter, but then came a proliferation into a byzantine hierarchy of weights. There are now seventeen. This increase has been good for boxers, as more weights mean more titles to aim for, with fighters able to move up and down between weights more easily, and the competition more thinly spread. Whereas in the old days there were roughly 14 pounds between divisions, now they are separated by five or six.

The number of world titles has also multiplied as the number of worldwide boxing commissions handing out championships has grown. Before the commissions, the big American promoters called the shots over who fought whom for what title. Then in 1963 the World Boxing Council was formed with a constitution declaring itself as a 'non-profit organisation dedicated to promote and serve the sport of boxing'. Through the efforts of its president Jose Sulaiman, it is the most powerful boxing commission with, in theory, the best champions. Its rivals are the World Boxing Association, formed by a group of Panamians a year earlier and dismissed by most in the know as a corrupt joke, though that has not prevented every major promoter in the world dealing with it.

Pepe Forbes works for Barry Hearn, now a major boxing promoter after making his fortune from snooker, as an agent looking after foreign fighters. He recalls when a visiting World Boxing Association representative was hanging round at the bar of a hotel after the pre-fight weigh-in. 'He asked me if we [the Hearn camp] had a middleweight fighter. I said yes, Chris Eubank. He said, "OK, we'll make him number five". I'm not sure what happened to Chris's rating to be honest. We hadn't done anything particularly nice for this guy, but with those people, give them enough drinks and they'll do anything.'

Then in 1984 another commission was formed, the International Boxing Federation. Based in America and headed by the respected Robert Lee, it has a growing reputation for straight dealing, and trying to ensure the queue for championship bouts is as orderly as possible. 'People were not happy with the way things were with the WBA,' says Jon Robinson, its European president, 'and out of that other things were born.' It is now recognised and welcomed by the British Boxing Board of Control. The quartet of major commissions is completed by the most junior member, the World Boxing Organisation, formed in the late eighties. Each commission governs its own championships, is entirely self-formed and self-appointing, and needs only two things to survive: the recognition of promoters and television, which has paid a cut for the privilege of televising one of the commission's bouts.

But it is a symbiotic relationship: television wants to be able to offer its public as many fights labelled 'world championship' as possible. The more commissions, the more championships, the more viewers. Hence there are now 68 world titles – 17 weight divisions multiplied by four world commissions. Unlike football's world power FIFA, or cricket's International Cricket Conference, boxing has no central control.

There are over 1,000 licensed boxers in Britain. Of those, only 650 are active in any one year; of those, only 50 have a reasonable amount of talent which would put them with a realistic chance of fighting for a British title. Boxing's trade paper, *Boxing News*, in its mid-year world ratings for 1991, listed just 13 British boxers in the world's top 15 among all the weight divisions, and just three champions. (There were 19 American champions.) Only five had world title fights the previous year. And only a similar number are big draws, boxers with a following or a personality that pulls in the crowds; boxers who sell tickets, as they say in the trade, and can make themselves and their managers or promoters rich.

The boxing cake in Britain is a very small one, which is why there are so few major promoters falling over themselves to handle the careers of the few good boxers around. Promoters are often seen as manipulators of boxers – the honourable combatants pushed around like pawns by the money men – but everyone in boxing feeds off the fighters. No good fighters, no good money. A host of smaller operators, working from home or tatty one-room offices, mostly struggle to balance the books, and often have other businesses which subsidise boxing promotion. They form the vast majority of the 78 promoters licensed by the Board in 1990.

Thomas Hauser writes: 'Like gamblers, managers feed on eternal hope. Except for the few who've been financially successful, they scrape and claw, waiting for the next fighter to pin their hopes on. They work nights in restaurants and bars, believing in their hearts that someday they'll be in the gym, they'll look up and the next Sugar Ray Robinson or Joe Louis will come through the door. That's what a manager lives for.'

Harry Burgess is such a manager, and has been for years, for longer than he cares to remember. He opened the front door of his flat off the Gray's Inn Road behind King's Cross Station at 10am on a grey winter morning. Wearing a dressing gown and nothing else, his lined, lived-in, night-time face stared out in disbelief. A cigarette drooped from his mouth. His grey hair was everywhere; his bulging tummy was struggling to undo the dressing gown belt. Would he inadvertently reveal all?

Harry isn't used to seeing this time of the day. Are these people selling something? Or checking on the TV licence? But then he remembers he agreed to an interview. He gestures and grunts for us to come in. Perhaps we could go and have a cup of tea, let him get dressed, and come back in 20 minutes? But he insists, 'no, no I'll get you something', and his pudgy hands wave us in. Big hands. A fighter's hands – the first clue that he has been involved in boxing. The second, perhaps, is his unselfconscious hospitality.

Harry hasn't moved far in life. He was born round the back of Pentonville Prison. He went to live in Essex once, in Loughton, with his first wife. But he didn't rate it and came home. He is a Londoner, a boxing manager, and erstwhile promoter.

'My grandfather John Burgess came from round here and he was one of the best bare knuckle fighters in Somers Town [the area between King's Cross, Euston and Camden Town]. Because of his reputation people used to challenge him in pubs for a few shillings, and he'd fight them outside. My father, Sid, used to hang out with Sam Burns, who managed former British champion Terry Downes.' Boxing is in the blood.

'I used to love to box, but once I had a street fight with a kid and he hit me with one of those skeleton rings that were all the fashion in the 1950s. I got a bad cut, and I couldn't box after that.'

But he had to stay in the game, because he loved it. 'You have to start at the bottom, become a trainer, find a kid, believe in him, apply for a manager's licence. It's like a fish taking the bait, innit? Then you're hooked for the rest of your life.'

Upstairs in his musty living room, his wife, who is out at work, has been allowed to put up pictures of flowers. But the rest is all boxing. Books, videos, and magazines – including 44 years of *Boxing News*. A Sky TV dish is fixed on to the wall outside. An anomaly in such an old-fashioned setting, but it is not there for the films, or to impress the neighbours. Many of the big fights can now only be seen on satellite television.

'It's a bastard sport. It's like being a heroin addict. Who would sit down every Sunday and fill in files of details of every British fighter? I've done that for 40 years. You've got to be a crank to do it. People never retire out of boxing. I've got a friend, Roger Colson, he's 76, and he was at a show last night.

'If you're a manager, you'll be in the gym and one day a kid will come in and ask if he can go pro with you. You'll see him skipping. And he can skip. Nothing brilliant, but he'll do. And you watch him work out, and spar, and you get that buzz.'

But Harry was not content with simply dreaming in the gym. He has promoted as well. 'The taxman asked me why I put on fights? I sat and thought. It's because when the show is over people come up to you and say, "Harry, that was a wonderful show." You don't think of the repercussions. It's really magnificent. The next day you sit down and realise you've done your money – again.' Harry rolls a cigarette round his mouth as if about to sell a pair of tights. He once took a swing at the famous promoter Mickey Duff in the gents' loo at Quaglino's restaurant in Jermyn Street at a boxing writers' dinner. Drunk and staggering, he had had enough of his old friend who had made it to the top of the pile and left him behind. But he was held back before it all got too serious.

Harry's love for boxing wanes in an instant when he reminds himself how the sport has changed. 'Television is killing it. It's a viper. It generates big money for a few, but it's killing the small halls. Eventually it will kill boxing. All those stupid interviews in the ring, microphones in the corner, we can't even swear now. That's not boxing it's show-biz. There used to be fights at places like Hoxton Baths, Mile End Arena, Caledonian Road Baths, Lime Grove, Paddington. Ordinary people used to pack them out. Now shows are on at dinner-dance places, and country clubs. How many are genuine small hall promotions each year? Maybe 15 out of 300.'

What has happened in boxing is merely an example of a more general shift brought on by more sophisticated communications. Like show business, which often shared many of the same venues, boxing has evolved from a predominantly community activity with fighters enjoying a strong local following, to a nationwide one, although at a more frightening pace. In the 1950s and '60s far more people could be small-time stars. Nowadays a boxer is either a television phenomenon or he is nothing.

Burgess flicks through old books where he has kept a record of his promotions. Lewisham Concert Hall, 1979. Hiring the hall, the ring, printing the tickets, and board tax, two doctors, a time keeper, house seconds, an MC and stewards, cost him £940. There were five fights, of varying length, and mainly two-minute rounds, though the top of the bill fighters fought eight three-minute rounds, and shared a purse of £750. The other eight fighters shared £1,000. After ticket sales he'd lost £117. Nights like that have forced him out of promoting.

'If you haven't got a star attraction to get you television money it's bloody difficult,' he says, 'even if you still put on a fucking blinding show.'

These days undercard fighters earn between £400 and £500 for six two-minute rounds. Frank Warren raised the rates in the early 1980s, and other big promoters like Barry Hearn have continued the trend. Word soon spread among fighters of better money to be had, and small guys like Harry were priced out and feel the pinch.

However, the rise in undercard earnings cannot just be put down to television or ambitious promoters like Warren. By 1990, the average wage had risen to £237 a week, and with it higher expectations of what life could offer. Accordingly, a boxer, who puts himself on the line every time he goes in the ring wants and expects between £400 and £500, minimum. As one fighter said, 'what's the point in going through it all for £250 when I get that in a week without being hurt.'

But once, Harry Burgess wasn't dreaming or complaining, or doing money. He got hold of a light-welterweight called Alan Lamb, who came from Lancaster.

'I used to stage his fights up in Morecambe near his home town. The place was packed. People used to hang off the rafters. There'd be a *waiting list* for returns. I nicknamed him the

"Lancaster Lion". The kids used to have scarves with his name on and chanted it like at a football match.' Harry sat there, still in just a dressing gown, clapping, and singing – 'Lancaster Lion! Lancaster Lion!' – his mind swung back to those heady nights in the north-west. Momentarily the disappointments were put aside.

'It was fuckin' *unbelievable*. The adrenalin was going, my mouth was dry. It used to take me three hours to come down. I can imagine a little what it must be like for those rock stars. It was such a buzz. I had the boy fighting for me on my shows, and people used to say "how come Harry Burgess has got Alan Lamb?"

'Anyway, he kept winning, and I was thinking he's going to do it, he's really going to do it. He was knocking down better and better opponents, and doing it in less time than he'd done the early ones. He had a killer punch. I brought over a Belgian boy who'd lost by half a point to British champion Clinton McKenzie. Lamb knocked him out in 23 seconds.'

Lamb was regarded as one of the top prospects during the early 1980s and the most exciting puncher at his weight since Dave 'Boy' Green – who had a world title fight with Sugar Ray Leonard. Burgess had pound signs in his eyes. But firstly, Lamb had to take the British title off Clinton McKenzie, the boxer who Terry Marsh was also aiming for. Lamb and McKenzie met in 1983.

'McKenzie was a southpaw and Lamb had a thing about them,' Burgess recalls. 'He just didn't like them.' (Unlike orthodox boxers, southpaws lead with their right hand, and are notoriously awkward to catch.) 'He said he found them difficult to hit – but it was all in his mind. He was married with two kids and I brought him down here when I should have left him up there and paid for sparring partners. I made a mistake. And on the night, he just didn't box to his capabilities. He lost by two rounds.'

From then on, things began to fall apart for Lamb. 'He got beat in his next fight. I went up there. He was back home and he had a moustache, and a lion tattooed on his arm, and Jack the

Lad clothes. I said to the trainer Bobby Day, "'e's at it, 'e's got a bird." '

"'E reckoned 'e hadn't, but I knew otherwise. Anyway, it turned out it was the woman living opposite him. 'E went out and fought Jeff Decker and he was winning until Decker threw a punch and hit him on the top of the head and 'e just went down.'

'It turned out that the day before the fight 'e weighed 10 stone 12 pounds. The fight was at 10 stone 2. 'E hadn't been running or training or anything, just giving it to this bird. So 'e'd gone down to the gym and 'e'd skipped for three hours non stop. 'E had nothing to eat, and went out running at 11pm, 4am and 8am. 'E took off ten pounds in 28 hours. 'E was like a gollywog. 'E had no strength. 'E couldn't take anything. After that fight, I said that's you finished with me!'

Alan Lamb brought Harry Burgess his greatest nights in boxing, but he is also his biggest disappointment. Lamb made £37,000. 'But it could and should have been so much more. If he'd beaten McKenzie, I had a contract ready to fight the European champion, Oliva for £30,000.'

Clinton McKenzie sees it all rather differently. 'For me, the Lamb fight was just a stepping stone; he had a punch on him sure, but I just wasn't bothered or overwhelmed. I didn't see him as being in the same class as me. I could have knocked him out, but I was enjoying myself. I rocked him time and time again. I remember he caught with me a good body shot, but that was it. That was my time.'

In boxing one man's big moment on which his whole career, and his manager's, will stand and fall, is just a formality for another. Unlike many sports, the little guys do rub shoulders with the big guys. Success always seems so tantalisingly close, but things can go wrong; the momentum is lost, and everything falls apart. Frank Warren was always aware of this. He made sure he had at least half a dozen good boxers so that if one lost, or left him, there'd be another he could pin his hopes on. And he had a knack of knowing which ones to sign, and appreciated the need to have good people working with him. His period of being a small-time manager did not last long after receiving his licence. Then he was off, with fighters who won.

Harry Burgess still has about ten boxers on his books, but he is 61 now and admits to feeling his age. 'I used to love to have a fight myself, but I'm getting on now.' Though he did have a bit of a tussle last year on holiday with his wife in Guernsey. 'Some young bloke in his thirties tried to throw me out of a jacuzzi. It was a draw.'

Harry revealed his plans for the rest of the day. 'I'm off to the bookies for the afternoon to earn a living, and then I'm going to a show tonight.' Boxing people like Harry may not be completely model citizens, but could not be accused of living vicariously. Not for them to stare out the window at passers-by and look forward to *Neighbours* on the television. There are fights to go to, boys to see, rows to be had with the Board of Control, or the board of 'fucking out of control' as Harry is prone to call it when he gets steamed up.

He made his way to the betting shop, still dreaming about what might have happened if the Lancaster Lion hadn't had a thing about southpaws. Harry Burgess' story of the one that got away is common in a sport where only a few dealers hold all the trump cards.

Advancement in boxing is capricious and unpredictable, so numerous are the contingencies. Good fighters can go for years without getting a shot at a title, then miss out through bad luck or an injury to their opponent, while more mediocre performers rise quickly to snatch their chance. As Mickey Duff said once, 'You must remember this is not a sport of morals, a sport where you take your turn to bat. You have to grab opportunities as they come.'

The scarcity of money-spinning talent and major venues in London explains the never-ending disputes between boxing impresarios which can seem so childish to the outside world. But the same might happen if musical producers like Andrew Lloyd-Webber and Cameron Mackintosh only had the choice of two West End theatres and three or four major stars.

The popular perception of boxing's promoters is that they inhabit a shifty, underhand, VAT-free world, with gangsters for friends and police and tax inspectors for enemies. There is no hard evidence of organised crime ever having had a powerful influence over boxing in this country. Criminals and boxing people often come from the same places, with social links of varying strengths between the two fraternities. And it is widely accepted that both boxing and crime offer an escape route from impoverishment. As John McVicar, the journalist and former criminal once said, 'Violence is respected and criminals admire pugilists. A basic ingredient in crime is fearlessness and it is admired in the ring. Fighters want to get out of their background. Boxing is rooted in the sub-culture.'

Criminal types enjoy the mirrored prestige that being associated with winning fighters brings, even more so if they once boxed themselves, and can say they once could go a good few rounds. Like the Kray twins. Both Ronnie and Reggie boxed, Reggie even won the London schoolboy championship at West Ham public baths in 1948, but gave it all up after a few professional fights. One of their nightclubs, the Double R in Bow Road, had a gym above which was opened by Henry Cooper. They used to hang out with fighters like Ted 'Kid' Lewis, British featherweight champion Terry Spinks, light-heavyweight Billy Walker, and Freddie Mills. So important was the reflected glory the twins perceived in the presence of champions they paid the American world heavyweight champion Sonny Liston £500 just to attend another of their nightclubs, the Cambridge Rooms on the Kingston by-pass. For Liston, the evening proved more life-threatening than any of his ring encounters, as Reggie gave him a hair-raising ride back to the Dorchester.

But the days of the Krays have long gone in London. A criminal empire of such ruthless, brutal efficiency has not been seen since. As Duncan Campbell writes in his book on crime, *That Was Business, This Is Personal*, 'gone are the days of family firms who control their territory by fear and coercion. This is an age of multi-national, million-pound, quasi-legitimate crime; a new age of criminals as yet unmatched by new-age policemen.'

Such 'invisible' criminals are not part of boxing. The game's links with the underworld are diminishing fast because crime has moved on, particularly to drug-dealing, which has no place in boxing. But the small-time guys who think they're a bit tasty, enjoy the dimly-lit world of boxing, gambling and nightclubs.

Anyone who hangs around the boxing scene long enough can find people to do any unsavoury jobs required – scare someone here, smash a window there – but the permeating hand of a mob there is not. Unlike the United States, where back in the 1950s a federal investigation was launched into the Mafia's involvement in boxing.

The fight game in Britain is not inherently corrupt. Boxing bosses may wear camel-hair coats, but they don't enter the dressing room before a fight and tell their boy 'tonight ain't your night', that is Hollywood stuff, a misconception sustained by endless gangster movies and the enduring fascination of arch-criminals, and a world of hoods running protection rackets and all-night spielers at down-at-heel clubs and masterminding bank raids. Boxers and gangsters are linked in a romantic sort of way by their names. Just as old-time villains had evocative nicknames, Jack 'The Hat' McVitie, Frank 'The Mad Axeman' Mitchell, so some fighters have also chosen an additional muscular title to add to their reputation: Roberto 'Hands of Stone' Duran, Thomas 'The Hitman' Hearns, or Nigel Benn, 'The Dark Destroyer'.

Inevitably some boxers' careers have actually overlapped with spells of crime. Former champions like 'Smiling' Sammy McCarthy have had trouble keeping out of jail once their fighting careers and the good money came to an end. The news in brief columns of newspapers occasionally reveal former or current fighters facing charges of drunkenness, assault, theft or criminal damage. It is part of life to the boxing fraternity, which is always quick to remind dissenters that without the discipline and character improvement wrought by boxing a lot more young men would be in a lot more trouble.

A trainer, Jimmy Tibbs, was once part of an East End gang whose family solidarity got a little out of hand. His father, James

Tibbs, his uncle, brother Robert and Jimmy himself were at the heart of an eight-man team sentenced in 1973 to a total of 58 years for various violent offences. Jimmy Tibbs received ten years for attempted murder, possessing a firearm and assaulting a policeman. His boxing career, which had begun at the West Ham club and led to him being a decent contender in the middle-and light-heavyweight divisions, had ended by then. Released after three years for good behaviour, he has become a walking advertisement for the British penal system. The Board of Control judged his rehabilitation to be complete enough to award him a trainer's licence. He has gone on to become one of the top exponents of his trade, working for Terry Lawless at the manager's Royal Oak gym in Canning Town, then Frank Warren, and then back to Lawless.

'I got in to a bit of trouble. I turned it all in, did what I had to do, and came back to boxing. Whatever you've heard about my family we was never bad people. Things happened years ago . . . but since then I've always brought up my sons to respect people, and to work hard.' His son Jimmy Junior is a semi-professional footballer, and Mark is a promising, young boxer.

'I've never been really horrible to people. I've had my tussles with people. People do, not just in the East End, but all over the country, all over the world.'

Rogueishly good-looking, with thick black hair and stubble, and a disarming smile, Tibbs looks the part he will never play again. These days he works hard, devotes himself to his family, and worships the Lord. Jimmy Tibbs is a born-again Christian.

Repentance and social rehabilitation were followed by full-blown penitence and a personal rediscovery of life's meaning. 'You can't get away from the truth. When I look back on my life I have had everything happen to me. I nearly got killed a couple of times. One of my sons nearly died in an accident as a young boy as well. I think the Lord has had his hand on me.

'One day I was at West Ham boxing club, and a friend of mine, who I heard was a born-again Christian from years back, was working in the gym. We started talking. I said, "Don't tell me about Jesus, I know all about him. I was brought up as a

Catholic." He said, "What d'you know about 'im?" And I realised I didn't know anything. I asked my friend more and more questions and I knew he was right, and it just changed my life.'

At least once a week Tibbs attends the Elim Pentecostal Church in Ilford – 'you should come down some time, it's great, it gets like a rock concert at times with all the singing' – but stresses it is not how often you worship, but how close you are to God, that really matters.

'I can see clearer now, see the other man's point of view. A small example: one of the boxers – Gary Stretch – hit me on the arm today with a shot in training. It really hurt. I would have gone mad before I was a Christian, called him everything.

'I have got lots to learn. I have only been a Christian six months, and it's not easy. You give your faith to the Lord, and he takes over. My life has completely changed, but I am still Jimmy Tibbs the trainer, this is my living full-time.'

At one stage doubts surfaced over the compatibility of Christianity and a trade where men are paid to belt the daylights out of each other. Then one day he heard a preacher say Christians were needed in sport, and he felt his job, helping fighters stay fit and channel their aggression constructively, was justified.

Shortly afterwards Tibbs says God gave him reassurance to continue in boxing. The morning before a fight he had been praying, hoping for a sign. Just four hours later he was walking to the weigh-in with one of the boxers, Jimmy Clark, when Clark turned round. 'He stopped, and tears were running down his eyes. He said, "Jim I want to be a Christian, I want to know about Jesus but I don't know how to do it." That was the sign. It wasn't just a coincidence,' says Tibbs, his eyes glowing with faith. 'And he won the fight.'

If boxing is not bent, it is inherently sharp-dealing and ruthless. At times it is about irresponsibly uneven matches, or two sets of tickets, one for the accountant and official records, and one to show how the promotion has really succeeded, or money promised to fighters, sellers of advance tickets or other sundry characters that turns out to be less than promised.

However, as the *Sun*'s boxing correspondent Colin Hart says, 'Even in a dishonourable business like boxing there is a certain amount of honour among thieves. It's a cut-throat, vicious business – they've all pulled strokes at some time or another but there are unwritten rules – you do not do this to a fellow promoter, you do not do that to a fellow manager, until it suits you, then you do it. If there's enough money in it you'll do it. But is boxing any different to any other business? Tabloid journalism is now a dishonourable business. The City of London, are they all honourable men? In boxing they are no different, they are just another part of life. But they are likeable rogues, and show great compassion when you least expect it.'

In a sport where the margin between fabulous wealth and fame and a crushing sense of under-achievement can be one devastating punch, nerves are high and tempers are short. It's a small, gossipy world where people make firm allegiances which, when the time comes, are equally firmly broken. Unhampered by the deliberations that an extended formal education sometimes brings, boxers' masters rarely see shades of grey. They would rather be charged with walking through a fence than be accused of sitting on one.

The promoter and manager Frank Maloney is unequivocal about the ruthlessness of his business: 'People in boxing are hypocrites, and they will suck your blood dry. Socially I keep myself aloof from people in boxing, I have been turned over so many times. I'll work with anyone but it's pure business. Loyalty doesn't exist in boxing.'

CHAPTER FIVE

The Establishment

No one has ever, or ever will, monopolise the sport as Jack Solomons did. If the received image of boxing promoters is of men with cunning eyes, big smiles, big coats and fat cigars, it's because several of the post-war promoters like Solomons and his great adversary Harry Levene, actually had cunning eyes, big smiles, big coats and fat cigars. Solomons died in 1979. For 15 years following the end of the Second World War, this nabob of the noble art was dominant, for another ten he was a major player battling against skilful opponents. One of them, Mickey Duff, not given to handing out compliments lightly, describes Solomons as the greatest promoter that ever lived – 'me included'.

Les Roberts, a Yorkshireman, now 71 and retired, was one of the finest matchmakers in the business, working for 23 years for the National Sporting Club at the Café Royal in Piccadilly.

'They've changed it all now,' he says, looking disapprovingly round the Regent Palace Hotel, sited opposite the Café Royal. Now a bland Trust House Forte production, it was once a regular haunt for boxing citizens; the bar would hum with fight chat, as punters mingled with managers, cornermen and boxers, staying over before or after a bout at the Café.

Solomons was renowned for staging rousing fights between evenly-matched boxers in front of vast crowds not seen since. Roberts insists his fond memory of the Solomons' era is not mere nostalgia. 'Solomons took pride in what he did. He wanted to make money, but he wanted to give value to the public. Now they don't care, they charge £20 a ticket and the fight goes one punch.'

Immediately the Second World War was over, Solomons staged the British heavyweight championship between Jack London and Bruce Woodcock at Tottenham Hotspur's White Hart Lane stadium in north London before 40,000, an event timed superbly to exploit the relief of the end of hostilities, an opportunity for the public to enjoy itself in public.

Solomons' gifts for hype and showmanship were uniquely effective in whipping up enthusiasm for his boxing shows. But it was easier then. In 1946–47 there were 1,028 promotions around the country, compared to about 270 a year these days. It was a time when boxing communities, particularly the East End, were bigger and more solid, and small halls were almost invariably packed to the rafters with audiences there to see their local heroes. Fights lasted for longer than now, more blood was spilt in the ring, and house fighters had a harder time of it – though they were always meant to win. It was a time before boxing suffered from the spawning of other leisure industries, and before television created a new generation of less well-informed, armchair fans.

Solomons promoted nine open air shows at the White City stadium between 1948 and 1958. He drew 50,000 there for the contest between Bruce Woodcock and Lee Savold in 1950. He ran sell-out shows at the Royal Albert Hall, sell-out shows at the Wembley Arena, then known as the Empire Pool, and sell-out promotions at Earl's Court Exhibition Centre, including in 1955 Randolph Turpin's victory over the American, Sugar Ray Robinson, arguably the greatest boxer the world has seen. It was a major shock, and one which unfortunately inflicted a fatal heart attack at ringside upon Izzy Cohen, Solomons' brother-in-law. In 1963 Solomons brought Cassius Clay, 'The Louisville Lip' to meet Henry Cooper, the night 'Our 'Enery' deposited his genius opponent on his backside, before going on to lose.

Solomons, known as 'Jolly Jack', was a jocular, raucous, fast-quipping larger-than-life figure. Born in Petticoat Lane in 1900, he was part of the area's poor Jewish community that made up such a large part of the boxing world in the first half of the century and a little beyond. As Jews prospered and spread to other, more comfortable parts of London, their representatives among the fighters' fraternity vanished. The only ones who remained in the game were those on the management side, most notably men like Solomons, and after him Harry Levene, Mickey Duff and Jarvis Astaire. All of them boxed early on in their lives, and all gave it up – in Solomons' case under an ultimatum from his mother-in-law. He began promoting in 1931. At the pinnacle of his career in 1959 he told Brian Glanville, now the veteran but still vigorous football correspondent of the *Sunday Times*, but then writing for the *Jewish Chronicle*, about his sadness at the decline of Jewish boxing.

'Jewish parents today are more concerned with going to the hairdresser and playing cards than having children. In the old days there were nine, ten or twelve in the family. If you came home and you'd been fighting, your father gave you a belt. They [the kids] aren't tough enough today. Look at your 'Kid' Bergs and 'Kid' Lewises, they were grand fighters when they were 17, today they're grand spenders when they are 17. Now the coloured men come under the same category as the Jews used to – the hungry fighters.'

If Solomons' own colourfulness makes him sound like an appealing character, it should be remembered he was a tyrant. As chairman of the Board's Southern Area Council, which controlled boxing in London, he wielded a power unthinkable today, able to give the yea or nay to other promoters' shows, decline licences to people out of his favour, and surround himself with cronies.

Ray Clarke, general secretary of the Board from 1972–1986, says: 'He would sit here as chairman and call up people at his whim. Mickey Duff was up at nearly every meeting on some trumped-up charge or other in those days, so were other protagonists like Ronnie Ezra and David Breitman who used to run fairly big shows at the old Empress Hall. As for the people who sat on the council, most of them worked for him: Mike Milligan, Nat Sellers, who used to sweep his office out. And Sam Burns, who used to sit in his office.'

Mickey Duff worked for Solomons for a time, before they

argued and Duff was released, probably the biggest mistake Solomons ever made. In early 1958 Duff went to work as matchmaker for Harry Levene, who was beginning to rival Solomons. Born of poor Russian-Jewish parents in the East End, Levene first managed a fighter at the age of 15.

After four years working on New York newspapers, he returned to become a boxing manager, building up a stable of fighters which featured Jack 'Kid' Berg. After the war and a spell running Bagatelle, one of the West End's hottest nightclubs, he moved into Soho offices just a stone's throw from Solomons'. Levene was a large, vivacious man, with almost no hair and a famous hook nose, broken in a boxing match when he was thirteen. They called him the 'Bald Eagle', for obvious reasons, and 'Harry the Hoarse' after his gravel-voice worn out by incessant shouting. His contacts, tenacity and experience, coupled with Duff's infectious energy, made a formidable pairing.

When, in the late fifties, Solomons managed, through the Southern Area Council, to force Levene to cancel a show on the same night as one of his, the bell had rung for one of sport's greatest feuds. The two men never talked to each other again. When Solomons died, a journalist rang Levene to get a reaction: he was merely informed of Harry the Hoarse's next promotion. But Levene and Duff could only be formidable once they had removed Jack Solomons from the Board's Southern Area Council, and that could only be done by forming an alliance of anti-Solomons confederates. Of those the most important, apart from Levene and Duff, were Jarvis Astaire and Sam Burns.

Burns, who had worked for Solomons, managed Terry Downes, a boxer with huge drawing power and some ability – he was middleweight world champion for a short time. Astaire also had an interest in Downes, and the three of them grew wealthy, and in Astaire's case particularly wealthy, with a chain of betting shops and Hurst Park Racecourse, exploiting the Gaming Act of 1963 which legalised off-course bookmaking and created a multi-million pound betting industry. Astaire had worked off and on with Levene since the early fifties, but he had worked with Solomons too – agreeing for a time that Downes should fight only on Jolly Jack's promotions. But within a couple of years Astaire and Burns became dissatisfied with the amount of work and money Downes was receiving, and let him fight for Levene. What Solomons termed 'the mob' or 'the syndicate' in a futile effort to disgrace his opponents was then formed by Levene, Astaire, Burns and Duff.

In 1960 they manoeuvred the removal of Solomons from the Southern Area Council, which was replaced by a committee of members with no financial interest in the sport and void of Solomons' cronies. Duff described it as a 'battle of the generations', just as 20 years later Frank Warren would describe his attempt to dislodge Duff and others from the top promoters' pedestal. It was an efficient operation to break one monopoly and before too long replace it with another. Solomons never forgave the Board. In 1966 when it invited Jarvis Astaire to present a prize at a Solomons promotion, Jolly Jack rang up the Board and said, 'Why don't you come over to my place, spit in my face, put your hand on it, and wipe it all over?' In his will, Solomons left a final condemnation of boxing's mandarins – a penny.

At the behest of Solomons, two investigations into the 'syndicate' were launched, in 1960 and 1963. They concluded there were licence holders working together, but that there was nothing the Board could do about it. 'What could the Board do? Ring them up and say, "You must all be independent, you must not speak to him or him"? They knew the Board's feelings, but there wasn't much to be done. Really they got together because they were sick to the teeth with Jack Solomons running boxing,' says Ray Clarke.

Levene's status as the number one promoter was confirmed in May 1966 when he staged the return of Cassius Clay, by now called Muhammad Ali, to fight Henry Cooper at Arsenal's Highbury stadium. Levene staged 12 world title fights in Britain between 1961 and 1977, by which time his powers were fading. From the mid-seventies on, Duff and the others were running the show. Levene, after years of senility, died in 1988, aged 90.

If boxing is directed by strong personalities, they don't come any stronger than Mickey Duff and Jarvis Astaire. Duff was born in Cracow, Poland, in 1929. Seven years later his father, a rabbi, left for England, having told the family it would soon not be possible for a Jew to walk the street without fearing for his life. With his job as a cantor at a London synagogue, he scraped up the money for the family to follow a couple of years later. Young Monek Prager, as Duff was born, arrived in London's East End able to say 'please' and 'thank you'. Monek soon became Morris and was sent to rabbinical college in Northampton. When he showed early promotional instincts, organising an impromptu boxing competition in the toilets, his parents were summarily told there was a shortage of beds at the college. But he had caught the boxing bug. 'There was a kid with two pairs of gloves challenging everybody,' he once said. 'I didn't have the guts to take him on. He was beating the stuffing out of everyone. But I watched and watched and realised that they were swinging at him and he was punching straight. I then said, "I'll have a go", punched the way he did and knocked the shit out of him.'

At an early age Duff had the knack of pulling a stroke here or there to get his own way. Desperate to enter the London Schoolboy Championships on his return to the capital, the 13-year-old Duff faked a letter approving his entry from his school, and changed his name to Mickey Duff, so his father wouldn't find out. 'My father would have killed me had he known I was boxing – literally killed me,' said Duff, who came up with his new name from Jackie Boy Duffy, a character in a James Cagney film. Friends had already begun to call him Mickey.

Duff carried on boxing as an amateur out of the West Ham gym, then lied about his age to become a professional a few months under the limit of 16. He had 69 fights, at lightweight and then welterweight, losing only eight, and at the same time fighting in boxing booths at fairgrounds. Recovering from a bout of jaundice at the age of 19, Duff realised he wasn't championship material. He had always spent time at the gyms chatting to managers and trainers and after managing a friend, decided to be a matchmaker, becoming the youngest holder of such a licence, and quickly getting a job as matchmaker at the Mile End Arena.

Duff had so far done everything young, but at a cost. His father may not have killed him once he found out what young Morris was up to, but never fully forgave him. And relations between the two were soured forever. Duff's father, grandfather and great-grandfather had all been rabbis, now Morris was *mishuga*, and going into boxing, at a time when the family had a successful restaurant up and running.

But having raced fairly recklessly through the preliminaries of his career, Duff then made sure he learnt the game thoroughly from the bottom up, though he progressed quickly enough. Boxing became his life, not just a job; Mickey Duff epitomises the obsessive regard that boxing people have for their sport.

Duff has always remained his own man, not without considerable risks at times. When in the mid-sixties he and others started the Anglo-American Sporting Club, a black tie-and-boxing establishment, the first guest of honour was Sugar Ray Robinson. It was a major event in London sporting life, and everyone wanted to be there, including the Kray twins, whose names were on the guest list of a member. Duff also had an impressive number of Scotland Yard detectives, judges and lawyers coming on the first night. The last people he wanted present were the twins, whose public profile was then at its height. Duff himself went down to one of the Krays' headquarters, the Blind Beggar pub in Bethnal Green, and told them they weren't welcome. They didn't turn up, but they sent Duff's wife a present in the post – a parcel containing four dead rats.

Colin Hart has been friends with Duff for years. They grew up in the same milieu, with Hart also boxing at school in the East End and for youth clubs. 'Mickey's not happy unless he is with boxing people or newspaper and television guys. He is one of the most fascinating men I have ever met. But don't get me wrong. Mickey's got many faults, and he is and has been very, very ruthless in his dealings with fellow promoters, managers, fighters and press men. If somebody crosses him, he is liable to ostracise them, send them to Coventry. If a fighter crosses him, he'll never put him on again. Though he has mellowed down the years. He's unstoppable now but 30 years ago he was incredible. He'd be off on one plane, sign a deal then straight back on to another.'

In a world where bitter disagreement is endemic, one of very few common denominators is the view that Mickey Duff's knowledge of boxing is unrivalled in Britain, if not the world. As Ray Clarke, remarks: 'Duff is in my opinion the most knowledgeable man in boxing over my years with the Board. He makes mistakes, they all make mistakes. But he just lives boxing.' For the last 10 years or so he has had an office in America, finding opponents for British fighters, managing a few Americans.

As a matchmaker, they say Duff makes Cupid look a slouch; he claims he has no equal, and once said of his peers: 'A lot of boxing promoters couldn't match the cheeks of their own backside.'

Duff has earned a lot of money, but declines to call himself a millionaire, preferring to reiterate the phrase of film director Joseph Levine, that he has 'up yours' money. His children went to public school, and he provided a home in Los Angeles for his wife Lily. Like so many other boxing fanatics, the business has cost him his marriage. A betting man all his life, he might have been worth a lot more. 'He used to be a well-known casino gambler in the United States, but doesn't do that any more,' says Hart. 'He gambles on boxing, that's his great love. And because he's so knowledgeable he wins more than he loses.'

If Duff is respected for his learning, he is not particularly well liked, though these days, at the age of 62, he inevitably has a sageness about him which is beginning to smooth out some of the rough edges; but all this is underpinned by an aggressive, irascible will. Five foot nine inches tall, he is a neat, trim figure, who thrusts his snubbed face forward with a look of arrogant determination. No one drives a harder bargain than Mickey Duff, with the exception of his friend Jarvis Astaire, but then no one in boxing promotion has remained on their feet for as long.

The manager and promoter Frank Maloney vividly remembers Mickey Duff's negotiating skills when he worked with

Ambrose Mendy to promote the domestic fight of 1989 between their man Nigel Benn, Commonwealth middleweight champion, and Michael Watson, then fighting for Mickey Duff. Maloney, Mendy and Duff met at the offices of Mendy's solicitor Henri Brandman. But Mendy was obliged to sit in the corridor outside as Duff refused to talk to someone who didn't hold a British Boxing Board of Control licence. By 10pm, negotiations were still not finished, so Brandman suggested they adjourn for a meal at the Phoenix Apollo, the restaurant in Stratford, east London, that doubled as Mendy's headquarters. Maloney remembers: 'Mickey did a lot of shouting and screaming, but once he'd bitten into something that was it.

'We had a meal. In between eating and slinging wine down his throat, Mickey Duff was just shouting and screaming. Brian Lynch [then Benn's trainer] came in and was allowed to sit with us because he was a licence holder, but Mendy was sitting further down in the restaurant.' With Maloney getting up and down to relay the latest score in negotiations, by 3am a draft contract had been drawn up. 'I didn't say much, just let Mickey shout and scream. At one point he stood up over the table shouting at me, pointing at me, that he wanted this clause in the contract, this and that.

'We wanted the fight badly and so we conceded quite a lot of points. But I learnt one thing about Mickey, his tactics were to terrorise you.' Maloney remembers his first visit to Duff's Wardour Street office, where the master sits behind a huge desk, and places guests on an intimidatingly low sofa. 'Being small it didn't matter to me. I said, "Is this some formal way of trying to impress me, because I am having trouble reaching the desk, Mickey." It was good to watch the master at work. I learnt a lot in those hours of negotiations with Mickey Duff. I think at the time Mickey was too good for all of us. It was the master playing with the boys. There were a lot of things agreed to I wouldn't consider now.'

Duff has never been a solo operator. Although he is the best known up-front man in British boxing – holding press conferences, firing off highly quotable comments willy-nilly, appearing in the corner with his fighters – he has always been in partnership one way or another.

The most important of those partnerships has been with Jarvis Astaire, a friend and colleague for over 30 years.

People pause a while before answering questions about Jarvis Astaire, as if he may be listening just around the corner. Often he is referred to as 'the Godfather', or 'Mr X'. Seen by many as the most powerful man in British boxing, in the last 25 years he has given few interviews of any consequence. In terms of publicity, Astaire is so reclusive he has almost become a rumour.

Astaire dismisses this and readily admits he has been involved in boxing for 48 years. 'There are people who jump in the ring when the fight's over and kiss and cuddle the winner, and that has never been my style. So as a result you are thought of as a background, shadowy figure.'

He grew up in Willesden but was born in 1924 in the East End, as his mother Esther preferred the care that could be provided by the family's old local doctor. A grammar school boy, his parents ran a millinery at the Barbican. He was active in Jewish youth clubs and all his life has retained a strong identity in the Jewish community, principally through charitable work and membership of the Marble Arch, Western and West London synagogues. Leaving school at 17 he became a salesman for a pharmaceutical company and for a while he ran a shirt stall in Brick Lane in Spitalfields.

Astaire has never been keen to be associated with boxing, though it has been a cornerstone of his life. He took out a boxing manager's licence when he was just 20, in 1944, making him the youngest manager in the country, and held that licence until 1984. He has held an agent's licence since 1961.

Astaire has never held a promoter's licence, something of an anomaly since he has been behind some of the biggest promotions of the last 30 years, a typical example of the piecemeal way the Board can work. John Morris, the current general secretary, however, doesn't see anything odd about it. 'Jarvis has his faults, but is one of the most straight fellows you will come across. These days Jarvis Astaire is, with others, part of

National Promotions, which holds a licence, and if National Promotions was called before the Board, then Jarvis Astaire would come before the Board. It is no secret he has been part of the promotional set-up, the point is they cause us far less concern than many others.'

Astaire thinks nothing of it either. 'I have been involved in promotion. I am not an individually licensed promoter, I have never had one in my name. I was in partnership with Harry Levene and then Mickey Duff. I have been known by the Board of Control to be involved, nothing was hidden from them. Because one doesn't want to get one's name in lights the whole time does that mean to say there is something peculiar?'

Astaire's largely anonymous career in boxing began shortly after the Second World War when he became manager of Billy Thompson, who soon became British lightweight champion. His stable of prominent boxers included Downes, Sammy McCarthy, Peter Waterman, the brother of actor Dennis, and Terry Spinks.

In 1948, aged 24, Astaire had married Phyllis Oppenheim, daughter of the multi-millionaire Henry Oppenheim, head of Mappin & Webb, jewellers to the royal family. His partner and best friend, Charles Burkeman, married her twin sister, Sally, now a Conservative MP.

When Henry died Astaire and Burkeman both gained an interest in the company, which they sold to wealthy businessman Charles Clore in the sixties. They were an unstoppable duo, opening a chain of menswear shops which ended up as Hope Brothers. They then moved into property, forming Associated City Properties, still operating today. One of his greatest achievements, amid a welter of successful interests, was the Hurst Park Syndicate, the chain of betting shops built up with Downes, which was sold to William Hill in the early seventies for £1,800,000, at a vast profit.

Market-trader directness, social acceptability, and business sense, has brought him millions, but Astaire has always stayed out of the limelight. Until he launched Viewsport – a venture far more high profile and 'respectable' than the mere management of fighters – he was virtually unheard of. It has been suggested the Oppenheims disapproved of his involvement in boxing, which then had probably an even more tawdry image than today. The promoter Mike Barrett says, 'In my opinion she [Phyllis] didn't particularly like the characters in boxing, so he kept his name out. I think it appealed to his vanity to carry on that way.'

In the late 1950s Astaire and Duff met up on a plane coming back from America. They both held manager's licences, and soon were working together. Astaire always allowed Duff to be the front man.

Astaire was never named as a member of what Solomons called 'the Syndicate' until about 1963. Certainly few outside boxing were aware of how extensive and well-established Astaire's activity in boxing had been. He has never liked to be called a promoter, always preferring his association with boxing to be made through his screen ventures.

If Astaire has dismissed boxing as a hobby, it has however taught him the kind of straight-talking, tough dealing that has served him so well in business. Tall and good-looking, Astaire cuts a sophisticated figure, and it could hardly be said he grew up on the wrong side of the tracks, unlike his colleagues in the fight fraternity; but he can talk their language as and when he thinks the time is right.

In 1973 he told a reporter from the *Sunday Times* how he dealt with the sports journalist Dudley Doust, who had reported that the American boxer Floyd Patterson had claimed Astaire had failed to fulfil a promise to pay the boxer's hotel bill. 'I said, "Hello Dudley, how are you? Dudley, I happen to be with a couple of American newspapermen who say that Floyd Patterson is the phoniest prick they have ever met in their lives and I want to tell you that I don't agree because, Dudley, you are." It was controlled anger, you see.'

Like his friend and colleague Duff, it is hard to find anyone with a fond word for Astaire, save for his business skills. Harry Burgess isn't afraid to break the common reticence on the subject of Jarvis. 'If there's a heaven and a hell, he'll go down there as a chief stoker.'

While Duff beavered away securing the allegiances of promising boxers, Astaire was realising a five-year-long ambition – to show boxing on closed circuit television. The first time he did so, in 1964, was the Terry Downes-Willie Pastrano world middleweight contest, which Downes lost. Cinemas were packed. By 1966, the Clay-Cooper fight at Arsenal was shown in 17 locations by Astaire's company Viewsport. Astaire was the first to realise the growing possibilities for profit that television offered. Later he added to his portfolio – film investment, becoming an agent for Dustin Hoffman (until the two split on bad terms), and in the mid-eighties the vice-chairmanship of Wembley Stadium, controlling the big events from Cup Finals to concerts by Madonna. On becoming a director of Wembley Plc, Astaire immediately doubled the rents. 'I knew it would be a good move because they had always undercharged me when I rented their facilities.' He is now a director of over 20 companies, including Mappin & Webb, William Hill, and Anglo-Continental. The highlight of years of charitable work was his appointment as Chief Barker of the Variety Club in 1983; near the time he successfully sued the *Guardian* for libel over a story claiming he was involved in charity principally for personal aggrandisement. While his business life has been one success story after another, Astaire's personal life has been beset by sadness. He has twice been widowed. Phyllis Oppenheim died from cancer in 1974, and in 1986 the same disease killed his second wife, Nadine Hyman, whom he had married in 1981.

By the late sixties Astaire's former contact Burt McCarthy had a stable of around ten boxers but like others felt pressurised by the growing power Duff was beginning to wield. One of his friends was a matchmaker called Al Phillips who was also beginning to feel that Duff was trying to ostracise him. Phillips arranged a meeting of malcontents, which included a manager, Terry Lawless.

'Duff had the contacts, the television; he was the unquestioned boss, with Astaire,' says McCarthy. 'One day Al asked me over to his place in Woodford. Terry Lawless and Morrie Vickers were with him. Al said, "We've just about had enough of

Mickey Duff. No longer are we going to allow him to threaten, bully and dictate to us. We feel if we join on allegiance, and stay together, if Duff tries to refuse to do business with one of us, he won't do it with any of us." With the boys we had between the four of us it would have been difficult to put on shows without us.

'We all shook hands and agreed this pact. About three weeks to a month later I picked up the paper and saw Lawless had Anderson v Cartwright on a Duff promotion. And none of us were supposed to do any business with him. We'd all work with Al Phillips . . . But Lawless went on without us, and that was the beginning of Lawless and Duff cementing a powerful relationship.'

Lawless, who is the most successful manager in the history of British boxing, began to supply fighters for Duff promotions, and gradually seemed to provide almost exclusively for Duff, Levene, or the final partner, Mike Barrett. As part of this group, Lawless, a former East End clerk, has guided John H. Stracey, Maurice Hope, Jim Watt and Charlie Magri to world championships.

However, an informal partnership of Astaire, Duff and Lawless would not have been able to establish a grip on boxing without access to the most popular venue in London; a traditional setting with a strong patriotic atmosphere, the Royal Albert Hall.

Mike Barrett has long been considered by many to be the gentleman of boxing. Others unfairly describe him as a mere minion to Duff and Astaire, the 'tea boy', only useful because he happened to hold the exclusive rights to stage boxing at the Albert Hall, a contract which ended in the mid-eighties. The hall is now open to any promoter who can afford it.

Barrett is from a different social background to his former colleagues. He may have boxed as an amateur, but he grew up in Newhaven, Sussex, and looks more like a tax inspector than a sport entrepreneur. The son of an immigration officer, he joined a land agency after school and ended up as a wharfinger in Woolwich. His first boxing promotion was in 1960 at Epsom

Baths. Two years later he had the Albert Hall contract. Needing a partner with greater boxing knowledge, he called Mickey Duff. The former matchmaker Les Roberts who at the time worked with Duff, remembers how they met.

'The phone rang and the caller asked for Duff. He said it was Mike Barrett. I thought "who?" He was a nobody, had done only two shows. He'd been a wharfinger and the wharf had been taken over. His whack had been £17,000, a lot of money in those days. He said he'd taken an office at Joe Bloom's gym which used to be in Earlham Street.

'Mickey came back later. I told him this fella called Mike Barrett had called and he said, "Who the fuckin' hell is Mike Barrett?" I told Mickey he'd done a couple of shows. Mickey rang him and told me he was going to see him. He came rushing back in an hour and said, "What do you think he's got? He's got the exclusive contract for the Albert Hall, and he wants me to work with him. I'm taking him to a solicitor tomorrow. I'm going to truss him up like a chicken ready for the oven." Those were Mickey's exact words, and he did, because as soon as he [Barrett] lost Albert Hall, they said *on your way*.'

Barrett doesn't quite see it like that. In 1988 he split from Duff and Lawless, principally because he and Lawless were unable to get on; Barrett was paid a hefty sum, perhaps as much as £250,000, to leave their joint company National Promotions and go his own way. With Duff spending more and more time in the United States, Barrett and Lawless were obliged to work together, and couldn't. 'I refused to accept the sort of matches Lawless wanted to put on,' says Barrett. He publicly criticised the fight between Frank Bruno and Chuck Gardner in Cannes, in June, 1987. Gardner, over-weight, out of condition, with his bald head and handlebar moustache looking like a Victorian circus strong man, lasted barely a round. An American, he had been banned from fighting in Britain two years previously. 'Gardner had no right to hold a licence,' says Barrett. 'He looked pregnant. The fight made Bruno look foolish, it wasn't fair on him. Lawless has never spoken to me since that day.'

But promoting boxing on his own didn't work out so well for

Barrett. Now 63, he has lost £100,000 in a couple of years, and sticks to managing around 10 fighters, all of them reasonable but none of them world class. The glory days of promoting the big nights in Kensington are distant now. In the late 1980s, under a new general manager, the Albert Hall trebled rents and increased its percentage of the gate money, leaving Barrett relieved he is not promoting there any more. Barrett had done a minimum six shows a year since 1962. 'It was in the dark and I turned the place on. I saw there was an opportunity to take on Solomons and Levene, and I just hit it off with the general manager Christopher Hopper. I got hold of Duff because he was a smart hustler and matchmaker, and he jumped at the opportunity to come in. Duff can't dot the i's and cross the t's. He needs other people around. I made him a partner and only his megalomania later made him want to be the one and only.'

Clearly from the seventies onwards, the four members of the coalition often worked together, and certainly made sure they never worked against each other. It made sense not to. Astaire, apart from being vice-chairman of Wembley, had the financial clout and was the right man to negotiate the big deals. Duff and Lawless had the boxers, Barrett the Albert Hall. Other promoters were prevented from getting a look in at the sport's two main arenas, Wembley and the Albert Hall, thus condemning the rest to small or medium shows. Promoters in the regions were particularly bitter. Talented boxers in turn thought unless they worked for the cartel, as it came to be known, they would miss the chance of a championship shot or a big pay day.

What rankled most of all was their arrangement with the BBC which effectively shut out other promoters. The more boxing's live audiences declined, the more important television revenue became. For years ITV didn't show any domestic boxing, saying the cartel had all the good fighters, and the cartel was with the BBC.

The BBC has always denied having an exclusive contract, but admitted having an agreement to screen a certain number of Duff & Co shows a year. The former BBC head of sport, Alan Hart, described it as an 'understanding'. If not exclusive in writing, the Corporation's policy was so in practice. Over the years smaller promoters like Les Roberts, Eddie Thomas in Wales or Ricky Porter in the West Country approached the BBC with British championship fights and were turned down. Good fighters managed by the wrong people could go for years before they received any television coverage and the subsequent chance of higher purses. Johnny Owen, who died tragically after a fight in Los Angeles in 1980, won British, Commonwealth and European titles before appearing on the small screen.

Ray Clarke admits: 'The BBC worked with the Mickey Duff group. We tried, over and over again with the BBC to spread out their coverage to other promoters. They said they had tried to do business with smaller promoters but too often didn't get the fight promised. After a while they got frustrated and decided to stick with the group. I have to say the group's promotions were better. They used to put on some fantastic shows at Wembley and the Albert Hall.'

The BBC's current head of sport, Jonathan Martin, declined to be interviewed, but a press officer, Mike Gardner, gave the party line when asked why the BBC had stuck with Duff & Co for so long. 'Because they have the best boxers don't they? What we are after is to present the best of British boxing. The big names will always sell. Over the years they have a good track record of presenting good matches.'

If some of the BBC's money was well spent, some was not. In 1984 it was revealed the Corporation paid £20,000 for Frank Bruno's fight against Philip Brown which was so bad it wasn't shown.

Gardner confirmed there was a contract with the group to do six or seven shows a year, though recently other promoters' shows have been broadcast. When asked how much money is involved he said, 'We never announce how much is paid for something, but one boxer is different from another. We have to keep amounts confidential as other people are after the business. Amounts vary from fight to fight. We try to give as much value as possible to licence payers.'

As the group's grip strengthened, boxing punters began to

question the value for money they were getting. The fights simply weren't as good as they had been. Defeat for house fighters became virtually unheard of, as talented boxers were shielded by fights against second-rate opponents – bodies, stiffs, bums and corpses, as they are called in the trade.

Frank Maloney, who once worked for Duff and Barrett as a matchmaker, thinks they took it too far. He recalls, in particular, one fight he matched between a Duff fighter called Brian Nickels and another boxer called Wayne Weekes. At the weigh-in Nickels was overweight. 'I reckon they put him in the sauna to bring his weight down. On the night, it was March 1987, Weekes knocked Nickels out in round five, and it was Nickels who had sold all the tickets.

'Jarvis Astaire and Terry Lawless were screaming and shouting at me, "you'll never work again" and so on. And I said that they didn't want fair fights, and that I hadn't made Nickels go in the sauna. I may not have had a lot of money but I had a lot of pride.'

Maloney remembers how, 'Mickey Duff once told me in his office that I'd broken a rule – never get a house fighter beaten. The man who sells the tickets has got to be looked after.'

Maloney recognises house fighters are investments for which opponents have to be carefully vetted, even if contests are not fixed. 'But I like to give boxers a 65–35 chance rather than an 80–20 one.'

House fighters have always been meant to win, and been put in the ring against carefully chosen opposition; but in the fifties and sixties they had to work harder for victory. In the seventies the house fighter's chances of winning gradually rose from 70–30 to 90–10. Winning constantly builds up impressive but rather bogus records which are used as a selling device to the public and media, particularly television companies looking for new big names to draw viewers. And promoters go far and wide in search of bodies to put in the ring with their own men, with the United States and Mexico as the most common sources. Between 1972 and 1983, Mickey Duff imported 364 fighters from overseas; only 31 won. On one famous occasion in 1980, the night of the

'Tijuana Tumblers', four visiting Mexicans lasted a mere 16 minutes 20 seconds between them in the ring against Duff and Lawless boxers. Duff was sufficiently embarrassed to more or less apologise on television immediately afterwards. Commercial pressures were reducing the risks managers allowed their boxers to take in the ring, which in turn reduced the sport's popularity with the punters. While a good fight is an exhilarating spectacle, a bad one is an extreme embarrassment. Jabs occasionally flick out but never land, hooks dissolve in mid-air as the two combatants keep their distance, while the crowd grows restless and the volume of general chatter supersedes the usual noises of encouragement.

Attendances at small hall shows began to suffer more and more until the point was reached where only a show which had sold television rights stood to make much money, if any. So it became even more crucial that good prospects were safely guided to a well-filmed career. Duff and Lawless in particular have been expert at that. Lawless is renowned as a cautious manager, though perhaps more out of concern for his boxers' safety and financial well-being (the more fights they have the more money they earn) than commercial cynicism. He has expertly steered many of his boxers to a prominence they might well not have achieved under other managers.

Like all empires, the Duff group became flabby and complacent. Punters grew restless at the lack of decent entertainment. At the same time the world of boxing was being shaken up – with more championships, television coverage was growing at home and abroad. ITV, dormant for so long, in 1980 clinched a £250,000 deal to cover six world title fights staged abroad. The cartel was undoubtedly the best at its job, but on the whole it wasn't making an outstanding job of it.

Barrett is in no doubt when the decline began, recalling that around 1981 shows full of absurdly one-sided fights became commonplace. Half his customers at the Albert Hall had always been regulars. 'They began to say sorry, we have had enough of it. Now there are hardly any old timers who go. I built up the Albert Hall from nothing, as a boxing venue. The downturn came when Duff started as a manager and started doing the same thing as Lawless by matching his boxers against absolute losers. That's when the rot set in.

'I am horrified by the mismatching that goes on just because certain promoters with TV contracts prostitute boxing just for the sake of building up fighters with the easiest possible fights they can find, regardless of the public, who are often thought of as stupid people who don't know anything about what they are watching. These promoters have prostituted the whole business. I object to that, it is utterly wrong.'

By the early 1980s, boxing was crying out for a strong competitor to the Duff group. That competitor turned out to be Frank Warren. Others had tried and failed, but none had possessed Warren's contacts, his fighters, or his daring. Like Astaire, he discovered that doing something simple well could bring success.

Barrett insists there would have been no way in for him had the old powers not made mistakes. 'The so-called cartel was professional people who spent every minute working at boxing. It was a full-time professional business we built up and it did an awful lot for boxing.

'But Duff became very arrogant in the way he was dealing with the Board and wanted to dominate them, and the Board got fed up with it all. Duff is a very bombastic, self-opinionated person who will shout and yell at people if he can't get his own way, and he was responsible for that situation coming about, instead of dealing in the normal way. Warren had been putting on unlicensed shows, and they decided to invite him in as a way of building up opposition to us, even to the extent that Colin Moynihan, who used to be sports minister, and was then a steward on the Board, went to Bob Arum and asked if he could help Warren in any way. Though now it's all misfired and they must rue the day they let him in.'

Through his unlicensed shows Warren had learnt the basics of boxing promotion and realised that crowds wanted good old-fashioned entertainment, real contests between two fighters each with a chance of winning, with new razzmatazz touches on top.

As Warren began to promote his early licensed shows, he realised those formulas would carry on working for him, though at greater expense. Warren's shows were simply more fun to go to; he took more risks in his matchmaking, generating fights which soon produced heated, raucous atmospheres in the arena.

Warren was the ambitious youth taking on the establishment, just as its members had in their time taken on the establishment embodied by Jack Solomons. Though a far more reticent personality, Warren was learning the art of publicity and self-promotion that was a cornerstone of Jolly Jack's accomplishments.

The old alliance of Astaire-Duff-Lawless-Barrett had forgotten how to sell boxing; but then with no competition it didn't really need to. But selling is at the heart of boxing promotion, a fact ignored at a promoter's peril. As Frank Maloney says, 'Boxing's all about bluffing. It's like poker, whoever has got the calmest nerve will win. That's what it boils down to. You bluff in business don't you? It's a matter of how much nerve you've got. How much front you've got. How much you can sell yourself. You have to sell yourself to people you're raising money from, you have to sell yourself to TV, then the fighter has to sell himself to the public. It's about selling, all the way down the line.'

CHAPTER SIX

The Making of a Fighter

During the first couple of years of his professional career, Marsh experienced what it's like to be an also ran fighter, with no hope of television coverage and few straightforward fights. He was not yet being groomed as a future champion, and there was little excitement surrounding his contests. He would turn up, bringing with him a few members of his family and friends, manage an unspectacular win, and then usually go straight home to Jacqui, without celebrating.

At the beginning his performances were far from spectacular. Marsh first figured on Warren's undercard in October 1981 against Andrew De Costa, at the Bloomsbury Crest Hotel. He won on points over six rounds and went on to win his next five fights in the same manner, by grabbing a lead and holding on to it rather than winning with the conviction of one destined to go far. And following his third fight against Kid Murray, he was even taken to hospital after collapsing from exhaustion.

In Marsh's seventh fight he managed only a draw against Lloyd Christie. He seemed to be just another ex-amateur boxer who would hang around for a few years and lose whenever he met someone who could hit hard. Warren decided it was time to test him out, arranging for him to fight a boxer called Chris Sanigar with the fight in Sanigar's home town, Bristol.

'Sanigar was not a man to mess around with; especially when he was fighting in Bristol. Shortly after that Frank sent me out to fight a Frenchman called Didier Kowalski from a mining town, St Arnand. I was fighting the local hero. Now when you get sent over to a little town far away, you know it's not meant to be your

night. I mean, what are they paying money for to see Terry
Marsh beat up their favourite?' Marsh speaks in a high-pitched
breathless, cockney voice; full of nervous energy, the words
tumble over one another, and can sound a little confused, as if he
is not exactly sure of the point he wants to make.

Marsh was not expected to emerge on top from either the
encounter in Bristol or the one in St Arnand, and does not look
back on them with nostalgia. But he survived them, maintaining
his unbeaten record, and moving gradually up the ratings.
Warren now knew his fireman was worth cherishing; there were
no more unnecessarily tough battles in unfriendly towns. But
from 1981 to halfway through 1984, Marsh had to be content
with being just one of several hundred boxers in Britain who
receive little adulation or financial incentive for their efforts. It is
not like being a Third Division footballer, who will enjoy a little
celebrity in his own town, and might sometimes play in a Cup
game against a famous club. At the equivalent position in boxing
there is little romance. The sport is tough, at all stages, but at this
uncompromising level, there are relatively small purses, and
such slim chances of glory.

Virtually all of the 650 active professional fighters in Britain
are unknown to the general public. Even winning a world
championship is not a guarantee of widespread fame. It takes
something extra and it happens to very few, but occasionally, a
man's reputation in the ring spreads widely before he even
manages to get a title belt clasped around him.

A number of people feel ambivalent about their appetite for
boxing. To help justify their bloodlust they tend to need a hero to
have something more than raw aggression and fighting skill. It is
often a complex equation that produces a people's champion,
who gathers a following beyond the hometown support he is
bound to receive, and whose popularity will not necessarily
correlate with his potency in the ring.

Shrewd management and compassionate matchmaking help,
but that can only play a part. Boxing promoters cannot, as the
saying goes, force bums on to seats. A captivating personality in
a fighter can. A man's fighting style in the ring also matters – the

public likes risk-takers – and it helps if he looks impressive when he is stripped down to just shorts; but his manner outside the ring is important too. It is easier for heavyweights to gain fame, because of the status of being the hardest hitters and simply being in the biggest range; but that alone is not enough. Former British champion Gary Mason will never be loved as Frank Bruno M.B.E. was, and to an extent, still is.

'He was just sold to the public. He can't fight. He's a big lump of lard,' says matchmaker Les Roberts. 'If the board was run how it used to be, boxers like Bruno would have to go through eliminator stages to prove his worth. [Apart from Tyson] he's boxed two who were in the top ten – Bonecrusher Smith and Tim Witherspoon – and lost to them both badly.' Roberts describes Bruno's career as 'the biggest sting since Jack Doyle'. Doyle was an affable Irishman; a boxer, singer and immense celebrity, with good looks and a matinée film star wife, Movita. As a heavyweight boxer in the 1930s he had a punch, but little finesse and was never even British champion. On a couple of occasions he threw a fight (something which Bruno would never dream of doing). But he drew in crowds, and Roberts' comparison with Bruno expresses the disgruntlement of a boxing purist that such limited fighters should hog so much of the limelight.

Bruno was the boxer with the broadest appeal in the 1980s. He was too rigid a fighter and he had a weak chin. He was fed some appalling 'bodies', as they are known in boxing. The public loved him because he could knock down these journeyman opponents and looked great doing it. His body was an impressive male archetype. Outside the ring his trusting, 'Yes 'Arry, know what I mean 'Arry', conversations with the BBC's Harry Carpenter were amusing and showed him in an engagingly vulnerable light, exploiting his remarkably deep, simple, London voice.

He had help with lines and quips from scriptwriter Norman Giller, a former sports journalist who has made a living from writing for celebrities. Bruno's initial response when he began being interviewed seems to have been instinctive, but Giller advised him on how it could be developed.

Bruno's first manager, Burt McCarthy, who discovered him as an amateur, believes Bruno's public persona as big, lovable Frank is a façade. He said: 'Frank's never really been lovable Frank. [He] has portrayed an image that is keeping him in very good stead, and good luck to the kid. But Frank Bruno, the naïve, poor boy, is all on the outside, not the inside. He's not as naïve as he makes out. Every post is a winning post for Frank Bruno. The boy is motivated in one direction *for money*, and I think he's achieved what he set out to do, and there's nothing wrong with that. I don't hold it against the kid because there was a time when he didn't have anything. When I first knew him as an 18-year-old he used to look forward to meeting me to have a steak. I got friendly with him. He was a raw but powerful amateur, and he joined up with me. He was very immature in those days.'

Rivals, notably Duff and Lawless, soon got wind of their association. Bruno was the English ABA heavyweight champion and an exciting prospect.

'The moment I was seen with Bruno, Duff & Co felt threatened. It was worth them having a look. Duff came to see him and offered the boy all sorts of things like television. Frank was a bit ashamed to tell me because we had got so close. I said go and speak to them, listen to what they have to offer you. I didn't have any doubt in my mind that they would coax him away, and they did.'

Once again, McCarthy was battling with the Lawless-Duff partnership. In September 1981 Bruno made an application for his first licence with Lawless as his manager. But the Board rejected it because he was too short-sighted in his right eye. His lack of peripheral vision would mean he would have trouble seeing punches coming.

'Frank phoned me and told me that he needed an eye operation to help his myopia. He said he was feeling very depressed, as all he'd ever wanted to do was box. I said, "Frank, are you asking me to pay for the operation?"

'He said in short, "I suppose I am, yes." I asked him if he'd spoken to Lawless. Frank said that he had and that Lawless kept promising to pay for it but would never get round to it. He was having trouble getting hold of him on the phone, and always being told that he'd just missed him. Anyway, I offered to pay. But I made it clear I didn't want to get involved in all kinds of aggravation, and that he should go and tell Lawless. He [Lawless] must have pulled the money up quickly. Frank went off to Bogota, in Columbia, and I got a call about eight weeks after he got back, and he said how he appreciated what I'd been prepared to do for him.'

The operation was successful and Bruno was given the licence. But he was inactive for the next year and McCarthy says that during this time Bruno asked him to sign him up.

'He said to me, I've done nothing for the last 18 months, and my family have done nothing for me, and there comes a time in a man's life when a man's gotta do what a man's gotta do. He actually said that. He had no money and no work while his eyes were repairing. I signed him on a board of control contract and a private contract I'd taken out with counsel. Tony Adams [a welterweight] was the witness to it.'

According to McCarthy a month or so after the contract, in September 1981, Lawless and Duff got hold of Bruno and pressurised him into signing the contract. In his view, Mickey Duff behaved like a gangster without a gun. However, perhaps Bruno made up his own mind to join Lawless and Duff because that represented the most sensible career move.

When Bruno got his licence in February 1982 it was with Terry Lawless as his manager. McCarthy took Bruno to court to try to stop his first fight. 'I was only against Frank in name. Really it was Lawless and Duff.' The judge ruled that Bruno's contract with McCarthy was not binding because at the time he was unlicensed, and did not obtain one within 28 days. However, because Bruno had not given McCarthy the first option on the right to manage him McCarthy could win substantial damages. Eventually, in 1985, he received around £100,000 from his former fighter.

'I think he turned out as good as I thought he could be. Not a world champion, but a European champion and a big attraction.

But I think he might have been a lot better had I been able to send him to the Kronk gym in Detroit for 12 to 18 months just to learn his business and have the confidence to go in with better quality men. And I think he might have been a more accomplished fighter. Because when Lawless first signed him it was ludicrous. He should have gone off sparring with top-class heavyweights. So maybe he lost something, because they certainly weren't going to let him out of their grasp.'

The British sporting public yearns for a world heavyweight champion in much the same way as they long for England to win the World Cup again. Indeed, Bruno v Tyson, and England v West Germany in Italia 90 can boast the two highest ever recorded viewing figures in England.

Bruno was protected right down the line. Jimmy Tibbs, who at one time assisted Lawless in trying to make something of Bruno, has complained that he wanted him to bring in some tough sparring partners to show Bruno what heavyweight boxing was really about. But Lawless, perhaps fearing it would unnerve Bruno, was against it.

This air of artificiality also existed outside the ring. Ken Jones, the *Independent*'s chief sports writer, says there was an aggressive protectiveness, and any criticism of Bruno would lead to telephone calls from Jarvis Astaire expressing his disappointment. But what is undeniable is that he possessed attributes that appealed to British people.

The greatest of Bruno's performances came against Mike Tyson in 1989. At the time, Tyson was considered to be invincible. His fights had been lasting only a few minutes, including a ludicrous defence against Michael Spinks that was all over in 13 seconds.

Bruno, who was paid £1.5 million to fight the world champion, went down in the first ten seconds. But he got up immediately and at the end of the first round he wobbled Tyson. 'And Bruno's hurt Tyson', screamed Harry Carpenter hysterically, 'get in there Frank.' But Bruno did not capitalise as a natural boxer would have done and the fight ended in round five. He had fared far better than most people had predicted he would.

'For what he had, I think he's done very well,' said McCarthy. 'He's projected himself against his real personality, and you've got to give him credit for that. Whether it will last, I do not know. I don't think he will stand the test of time like Henry [Cooper] has done.' Recently it's been pantomime rather than punching for Bruno.

The Irish featherweight Barry McGuigan was a fighter who, at his peak, had a style and look in and outside the ring that gave him an aura of invincibility. He is a charismatic person, though in the opposite way from Bruno. The 'Clones-Cyclone', as he was known, from County Monaghan, is all Irish eloquence and charm. Good-looking, with sleek, black hair and regular features, there is no hint of a squashed nose. His relatively small yet powerful and compact body, that, as Hugh McIlvanney said, delivered punches with a 'percussive, cumulative rhythm . . . invested with a ruthless sense of purpose', was always immensely satisfying to watch. There seemed to be no frailty there. But McGuigan was far more devastating against top-quality opposition than Bruno ever was. In boxing terms, one was the real thing, and the other was not. McGuigan was not given an easy path to the world title. But regardless of their worldwide status, these two men were the most popular and best-known British fighters in the eighties, both having hurdled the invisible barrier called public acceptance.

In 1984 Terry Marsh was a long way from crossing that barrier. He began that year as just another expectant British boxer, one of many looking for the right fight to come along at the right time. He was rated number one contender for the British light-welterweight title behind the champion Clinton McKenzie, and he was number five in Europe, but he did not count in world terms. His professional career was unremarkable so far and rarely publicised, but he was making steady, if unspectacular progress.

In boxing circles Marsh was considered an outstanding ex-amateur who did not have the big punch to equip him against the top professional fighters. He was, of course, managed by the emerging Frank Warren, who as a promoter was likely to help him get the fights he needed.

Sometimes a boxer's time may simply pass by, and he is left to reflect on a career in which his hopes and ability are never quite fulfilled. The British light-welterweight holder whom Marsh was aiming for, Clinton McKenzie, was such a fighter. He had dominated the division in Britain for six years, was a former European champion, and yet he had never fought for a world title. He looks back on it with regret but not bitterness. 'It just wasn't supposed to happen for me,' he reflected from an office in Norwood, where he is trying to make it as a promoter. 'I enjoyed my career tremendously and the only thing I regret is not having fought for the big one.'

Two years before fighting Marsh he had been lined up to fight an American called Johnny Bumphus. But in defending his European title he was disqualified for punching low, and the title fight, which would have earned him around £70,000, was called off.

By 1984 Terry Marsh, the younger, undefeated man, was coming up and looking to fight the British champion. After winning the final eliminator against Tony Sinnott, Marsh got his chance on 19 September 1984. Warren promoted the contest and shifted the venue from the Crest Hotel, Bloomsbury, to East London, at the Britannia Leisure Centre in Shoreditch, an area described by Warren as 'the spiritual home of boxing'. Marsh was fighting near his old club in Cable Street. McKenzie was 29 three days before the fight.

Marsh, 26, was expected to lose. He would be fit, and his flashing left hand would cause problems, but the Croydon southpaw would be too much for him, and a clear-cut points win was predicted. Marsh appeared to be the typical straight-backed, British amateur, with a stiff left jab followed up by a right hand.

'The worst decision I ever made in my boxing life was to fight Marsh,' recalls Clinton. Mickey Duff [his manager] said, 'Don't fight this one. He's awkward, give up the title. You don't need it.'

It went the full distance of 12 three-minute rounds. A fault in the ventilation system at the Britannia Leisure Centre, meant it was fought in strength-sapping heat. A number of men in the audience were stripped to the waist by the close of the fight. Clinton says, 'There was one round when I thought someone had put a match to me. It was like a frying pan in the ring.' In the final round Marsh was ahead on points, and McKenzie knew he would have to stop him to hold on to his title.

'I'd underestimated him. I had no respect for his punching power, and he looked so skinny that at first I thought I'd blow him away. But he kept catching me off balance. I remember pinning him against the ropes in round seven or eight and I let everything at him. He was the hardest bloke I ever hit to the stomach. I could feel my punches sinking in. I could hear him groaning. How the hell he got through that I'll never know. He was a very tough guy.'

The last three minutes were fought to thunderous applause, with the two fighters rooted to the middle of the ring, trading punches. Marsh was cut above the left eye, was swaying and hanging on. All his boxing technique was abandoned, as he held on, driven on by the sounds of the firemen from Tilbury banging their feet in support. Thirty-six hours earlier Marsh himself had finished a shift. He stayed on his feet to win a unanimous points decision. The new champion had to be carried from the ring in a state of exhaustion. Ernie Fossey his trainer was so worried about him he took him to St Bartholomew's Hospital. He had lost ten pounds in weight. Referee Sid Nathan gave it to Marsh by eight rounds to three, with one round drawn. It had been a war.

Marsh had given a perfect display of boxing on the retreat, proving that guts and technique could still prevail over hard professionalism. It was the domestic fight of the year.

Clinton, who was renowned as a 15-round fighter, believes the shortened length of the fight saved Marsh. But Fossey disagrees. 'If Terry had had to go 15, he would have paced himself to do that. If Terry had to go 20 rounds he would do it. He'd go to 25.'

It was a performance that in later years, as Marsh came to be better known, would be seen as a classic Marsh exhibition of how to nullify an opponent by destroying his resilience or as Marsh used to say, by 'breaking the other fighter's heart'.

'A lot of fighters go for the throat – I go for the heart. Go for the heart and you crack the mind. Then you finish the body.'

It was the beginning of the end for McKenzie, who retired soon afterwards. But there was one last hurrah. He came back and fought Lloyd Christie for his old British title in 1989. 'I was very depressed after I retired. My marriage broke up, and I was short of cash. There was only one way back. Life is all about stepping in the ring and boxing is a great education. It shows you that in life if you want something you can fight and get it. It was just like the movies. My last chance, everything was on the line. My little boy Leon was there shouting for me. It went the distance. It was close. I was so tense waiting for the decision. I wanted it so bad. I was there in the ring thinking, have I done enough, have I done enough? The referee put my hand up.'

He recalls sheepishly that he got paid virtually nothing for it. 'I wouldn't even mention it. I'm too embarrassed. It was less than £5,000. All I wanted was my British title back.'

Boxing, though not just a sport, is also more than simply a business.

But if the fight altered an aging champion's career, so conversely for Marsh it was a springboard to success. It was his first real exposure on television; and it not only won him the British title but credibility as a professional. He was asked to do a bit of television commentary alongside Reg Gutteridge – a clear sign that the fighting fireman had arrived.

'It was after that I started to take it all a little more seriously,' says Marsh. 'I thought, if I can be British champion without training that hard, then I might as well really go for it.'

He was Warren's first amateur to make it to a British title and victory was made all the more satisfying for Frank because his rival Mickey Duff had been in McKenzie's corner. In Warren's campaign, a major battle had been won.

Marsh began to receive publicity. As McKenzie noted, he did not have the looks. In the ring he was pale, and his ribs stuck out like a piano keyboard. His tight curly hair was cut in an unfashionable mop. His wiry physique gave no indication of the reserves of courage and strength that had served him so well in the Marines. He often wore a very unboxing-like moustache. He was not hip. He looked ordinary. But this, as it turned out, became an integral part of his image. Like McGuigan he was eloquent and pleasant outside the ring, though with Terry it was as much his lifestyle as his persona that helped boost his appeal.

His growing fame was triggered by being a fireman as well as a professional boxer; it separated him from all other fighters. It seemed as if he was just a regular boy who happened to spar and fight in the evenings to earn some extra cash. His boxing was a romantic form of moonlighting. No one thought Terry Marsh could go all the way to a world title.

He and Jacqui had a baby girl, Kelly. He had his job. His routine was very strict. He used to fit training in to an eight day cycle of two shifts, followed by four days off. When he was on night duty he had to run straight after work, sleep, and then go to the gym in the afternoon. But this overpacked schedule had the advantage of taking the pressure off him. A lot of fighters are forced to live in a state of almost perpetual hype: the gaps between fights have somehow to be filled – and the media are always on hand for any extra stories.

Few manage to bridge the gap of the artificiality and drama of a fight night and an everyday existence, in which the most important thing is to stay in shape. But how can they fill their days? Joyce Carol Oates notes how 'boxers have frequently displayed themselves, inside the ring and out, as characters in the literary sense of the word. Extravagant fictions without a structure to contain them.' It has become part of boxing's mythology that some fighters need to inflict damage upon themselves outside the ring. Hence the tales of fighters who cannot organise their lives, of men who are over-generous with money that only comes to them for a short time, who are beset by women or drink problems. Their existence is seen as being as turbulent outside the ring as it is inside. This tradition goes a long way back. It is personified by men like Jack Doyle who in his eventful life, earned three-quarters of a million in the 1930s, and still died penniless, though thousands turned up for a folk hero's funeral.

Another ruined boxer was middleweight Randolph Turpin who beat the legendary Sugar Ray Robinson at Earl's Court, London, in 1951, aged 23. He lost the re-match in New York, and in a return trip there he was arrested and charged with raping a girl. It was settled out of court. A series of doomed businesses, unexpected results, though not by any means all bad, and domestic problems, ended with him wrestling and working in a scrap metal yard. In May 1966, with little money and four daughters to support, he fired two fatal shots at his second youngest child and two at himself.

The year Turpin beat Robinson, John Conteh was born in Toxteth, Liverpool, and if Turpin is considered to have been the greatest British fighter of his era, so the good-looking, streetwise John Conteh was in the 1970s. In 1974 he won the vacant WBC light-heavyweight title against the Argentine Jorge Ahumada. And yet over the next three and a half years he fought only four times, and had his title stripped from him. He began legal proceedings with his manager Mickey Duff, whom he felt was not paying him enough.

He has written that 'everyone, it seemed, wanted to have a drink with the champion of the world. But whether or not the champion could handle his liquor was his problem not theirs.'

Even in 1979, when he was past his peak, Conteh still put up a brilliant performance against Matthew Saad Muhammad, before losing in the 13th round. Muhammad was later stripped of his title after it had been discovered his cornerman used illegal substances on cuts inflicted by Conteh. Muhammad won the rematch in four rounds. Conteh, aged only 28, was finished as a boxer.

Then came unsuccessful business adventures and an accident driving a Rolls Royce down Oxford Street, in which he collided with six cars, and injured his right hand so badly when he jammed it against the steering wheel that he could never again make a fist properly with it. At this period in the early 1980s his life had become almost a parody of mundane post-boxing crises centred around alcoholism. Ironically around this time he had a brief affair with Stephanie La Motta, the daughter of Jake La Motta, the fighter portrayed by Robert De Niro in the film *Raging Bull*, who was not without problems himself.

Conteh is no longer part of the boxing scene, but he turns up now and again at gatherings of the London Ex-boxers Association, where old fighters joke with one another.

'My boy had a trial down at West Ham the other day.'

'Really, how did he get on?'

'Not to bad. He was acquitted.'

They discuss long-ago fights to tunes like 'It's that old devil called love again', banged out on a decrepit piano.

Conteh turns up more out of kindness than for company. Still exciting people, he seemed happy enough. A reporter once wrote, 'I wish I could borrow John Conteh's body for a weekend,' and he still evokes admiration. These days he's a struggling actor and a successful after-dinner speaker.

An ageing fighter shouted out 'whatever else you do, John, don't go in *EastEnders*.'

'I don't mind what end I go in,' he replies.

'John is still the business,' said an old boy, 'but he should have had so much more. Now he's run out of time.'

A hard, demanding sport, boxing seems often to take a lot more from men than just their time and their strength. It can disrupt their whole existence. And the extraordinary self-sacrifice demanded by boxing is, of course, the last thing a young man with fame and money wants to put up with. So perhaps Terry Marsh was fortunate that a form of sacrifice was already built in to his life. He always had the reality of a responsible job to go back to; and Tilbury Fire Station, Essex, is not a place to give anyone too many delusions of grandeur, even a title contender.

There was, however, a logic in this double life. Fire-fighting is a male-dominated world. You have to be one of the lads, to work in a team, to be able to put up with all the jokes and role-playing that goes with such an environment. Terry was used to that lifestyle from his days in the Marines. Just as a gym full of boxers training can feel like a family from which women have been excluded, so a fire station has a similar atmosphere of male camaraderie and endeavour. The station officer plays an equivalent role to the top trainer. If he is doing his job properly he will have a special macho rapport with his men – often, with the younger ones, he may play a semi-paternal role. And, like boxers, firemen are tough and have chosen to flirt with physical danger. The pace of the two lives is also similar. Most of their days are relatively quiet. Firemen train, rest, drill, eat, check hydrants etc, clean up and go home. Only now and again, does a building burst in to flames. Boxers run, rest, train, spar, shower, and go home. And occasionally somebody tries to knock their heads off.

The mirror image is, however, a distorted one. Firemen are part of a team. But a boxer in the ring is on his own. A trainer handing out half-listened-to advice is not with his man in the heat of the fight, not in the way a fireman would be with a colleague, tracking him through clouds of smoke. While Terry Marsh the fire-fighter's greatest elation came from saving somebody's life, as a boxer it came from knocking the other man to the ground.

CHAPTER SEVEN

Warren Busts the Cartel

Frank Warren was virtually the only person in boxing who believed Terry Marsh would progress beyond a British title. That Marsh triumphed against McKenzie was an indication of how Warren's faith could pay off. Four years as a licensed promoter had taken him, like his fighter, beyond all reasonable expectations.

From their first encounter, the grouping of Duff, Astaire, Barrett and Lawless, knew they were up against an opponent made of firmer stuff than the handful of adversaries who had dared to step into the promotional ring with the champions over the years, only to be dispatched with bloodied noses and injured ambition.

On 7 October 1980 the British Boxing Board of Control called Warren into a meeting at their offices. It was a few weeks before he intended to hold his first licensed promotion.

Instantly, Warren was in dispute with Duff and the others. The young promoter had verbally agreed with the Board to stage his first show on 23 November at the Bloomsbury Crest Hotel. Having gone ahead with arrangements, Warren was informed Duff was promoting a show at Wembley on 24 November. The Board's Southern Area Council had a policy, known as the 14-day rule, which prevented two major promotions taking place within 14 days of each other in London, the declared intention being to avoid live audiences being spread too thinly. Warren protested the Board was favouring the old guard, and was summoned to meet the old warrior himself, Mickey Duff. The two were shut in an office together. Duff told Warren he had three options: to move his date, cancel his show or to make an issue with the Board.

Baby-faced Warren, aged 29, told the most experienced man in the business, Duff, aged 52, that he also had three options: cancel his Wembley date, change the date, or 'go eff yourself'. Duff was somewhat ruffled. 'Listen, you've not been in the business five minutes!' he screamed.

The upshot of the ensuing muddle, indecisively handled by the Board, was that Warren had to move his show to 1 December. Duff was ordered to pay £2,500 compensation, later reduced to £1,000. Warren lost £17,000 on the promotion, claiming the switch had deprived him of television revenue. The Board drew a sigh of relief, but knew the struggle with Warren was only just beginning.

Warren had quickly understood the power structure of the sport and a clear vision of how to dismantle it. He told Harry Mullan, editor of *Boxing News*, that the structure of British boxing was like a house of cards: if the bottom card was flicked away, the whole thing would collapse. The vulnerable bottom card was the simple fact that the whole of the power of the Board and its rules which sustained the cartel was built on convention, not law. 'He was right, and it sounded so simple,' says Mullan. 'Like the man who invented disposable nappies – blindingly simple.'

Throughout his unlicensed days Warren had people around him like Uncle Bob and Burt McCarthy who had helped him to reach the right conclusions, but no one else had the tenacity, courage and imagination to effect any change.

Warren appreciated the needs of a boxing promoter in the 1980s: he needed money up front to pay for promotions and attract good fighters; he needed big name fighters with a following to attract television, the only financial source sufficiently lucrative to sustain promotions, pay boxers decent money and make profits for the promoter. Ideally he needed a 'home' venue like the Albert Hall. That was the way the cartel operated, with its exclusive arrangement with the BBC and its grip on the Albert Hall and Wembley, but in the hands of a monopoly boxing was suffocating. With no competition, virtually everyone in the capital's boxing populace effectively worked with the blessing of the cartel and at prices set by it. Regional managers and promoters ran their own often crumbling operations, but were frozen out of the big action in London. The time had long been ripe for a new face, and Warren was it. He had been to see for himself the increasingly unpopular, ill-attended shows put on by the cartel at their venues, where an occasional decent main bout was the only attraction, following an undercard of uninspiring mismatches. Remembering the success he had staging good scraps with the NBC, he was convinced he could upstage the establishment.

Every boxing promoter keeps his financial cards close to his chest, it is part of the game. The true details of television revenue are rarely released, quoted figures for fighters' purses often vary startlingly with the real sum received. Public records reveal a certain amount, but not the whole picture, and boxing bosses are late filers of accounts. But there is still more mystery about Warren's financial sources than any other promoter, chiefly because he seemed to have so much money so quickly.

Speculation linking him to the underworld was catalysed by his uncle's past, and a gangland label stuck to Warren since the NBC shows – the young lord of an illicit-seeming sub-culture. These days there are still whispers around the boxing halls of the capital that money has been laundered to Warren from other families' operations, though there is absolutely nothing to substantiate such rumours. The gangland label is an albatross Warren has always tirelessly sought to rid himself of. 'Wherever I go I hear that I am supposed to be a gangster, even in the Mafia,' he said in 1981. 'Well all I can tell you is that I am 28 years old and I have never had so much as a driving conviction against me. I am not responsible for the people who attend my shows.'

Four years later he was having to make the same noises: 'In boxing there's been all sorts of rumours about me having some mysterious backers and that's why I've been able to put on so many shows. Even the Kray twins have been mentioned which is absolutely bloody marvellous since I must have been about 13 at the time they went away.'

In 1981 Warren had to deal with a smear campaign. A representative he sent to Rome to lodge a purse bid with the European Boxing Union for the European middleweight title fight between Tony Sibson and Nico Cirelli was confronted with a folder by Signor Pini, the EBU secretary. Though not shown the contents, Warren's man was told by Pini it contained allegations that Warren was connected with the Mafia and that two associates of his, including Burt McCarthy, had Mafia connections in Miami, Florida. Pini had also received a telephone call while the representative was present, telling him he should not accept the bid as it was 'unethical'. Warren complained about the whole business to the Board, whose secretary, Ray Clarke, assured him the folder, if it existed, had not emanated from his office.

It may have hurt Warren to be thought of as a bit of a character, but such rumours didn't do his image in boxing any harm. Coming across as a 'guv'nor' fuelled the perception that he was the man who provided the action. And he did.

Not only did Warren have to endure the slings and arrows of slander, he had to bear the considerable costs of his new metier. Promoting shows and renting an office unalleviated by television revenue, not to mention having to lodge an indemnity of several thousand pounds for his promotions with the Board, as all promoters must, were heavy burdens. From 1980 to late 1982 Warren was presenting shows at small venues like Hornsey Town Hall which even if they sold out would have broken even at best. If he was having to sustain heavy losses, how did he do it? Warren himself has offered a variety of explanations. 'On any given day, he'll say something different,' says Harry Mullan. 'He's a mystery man. Some days it's gambling, others the fruit machines, other days pubs. But he would have needed very substantial amounts to do what he was doing. He wouldn't have made any money from his first three years in boxing.'

2 Jon Robinson, Warren's general manager, says a separate

bank account was opened for each fight at Barclays Bank in Gants Hill. Each fight made enough or more to pay for itself. But he, like others, believes Burt McCarthy lent Warren large sums early on and there are strong suggestions that Warren continued borrowing from publicans, as he had in his unlicensed days.

Warren had other business interests. He moved into property though he he has always been rather vague on the details, ran a restaurant in the Barbican called Barbazon, with one of his former Arsenal heroes, Frank McLintock. It did not last. 'The business didn't work out well. We haven't spoken for a long time,' says McLintock. 'The restaurant didn't end in happy circumstances. It didn't do very well and we just let it go. If I say anything bad it would be libellous but I wouldn't want to say anything bland as it might sound that I like him. Even just a tie between myself and him I would prefer not to have.'

As Warren's career gathered steam it was helped along by a strong current of publicity. That turned into a forceful wind when he persuaded Joe Bugner to come out of retirement.

Warren's trainer Ernie Fossey was not the only one who doubted the wisdom of reviving a fighter who had at best enjoyed limited popularity in Britain. In 1971 Bugner had beaten national hero Henry Cooper on a dubious points decision and been a graceless victor. Hungarian-born, he never held the Union Jack as dear as many of the people who watched him, and when he retired, hot-footed to California. Bugner's defensive fighting style was scarcely attractive, but it saw him go the distance with Joe Frazier and Muhammad Ali in the seventies, and sustained him as Britain's sole world heavyweight prospect, a mantle of such significance that even a character as devoid of charm and humour as Bugner was cherished to an extent. Warren's hunch that Bugner would be a big hit was spot on. Bugner, now 32, packed them in at the Bloomsbury Crest and then at the larger Alexandra Palace as demand grew. The crowd wanted to see him win, but loved to jeer; it was a vaudeville, love-hate relationship summed up by one show at the Alexandra Palace when Bugner's entrance to the ring was greeted by the unfurling of a huge banner which simply said: 'Boo'. Big Bad

Joe's comeback brought four wins, all against carefully picked inferior opponents, and thrived on the publicity of his lifestyle more suited to a brooding film star than an athlete. Warren's headquarters had by then moved from Packington Street to the Bloomsbury Crest Hotel, where Bugner was put in a suite so a close eye could be kept on him. Training as little as possible, and claiming he was on the path to the world title, Bugner lounged around with Marlene, his wife and agent, eating, drinking and self-publicising from a specially-ordered mammoth bed. In nine months with Warren they spent almost nothing and earned £50,000. Boxing purists cringed, but crucially for Warren, ITV did not.

A new executive producer, Bob Burrows, had arrived at Thames TV in 1980, charged with expanding the station's sports coverage. A boxing fan, he made it a particular aim to improve domestic coverage of the sport, which was virtually non-existent. In the autumn of 1982 a letter from Frank Warren arrived on his desk. 'Frank came along with his proposals. He wrote me a very good letter setting those out. I had only heard about him in a roundabout way then,' says Burrows.

Then along came Bugner, and Burrows decided to screen his first fight, against the Welsh heavyweight Winston Allen on 28 October 1982. It was a success. The next fight was bought by five of the ITV regions, the next was networked all over the country. Agreed, as Warren would say.

In May 1983 Joe and Marlene walked out on Warren, arranging fights behind his back in America. It was an untidy ending to a tawdry affair, but Warren was left stronger at the end of it. He had his niche with television. And its money.

But the restraints the Board were placing on him still needed to be dealt with. Warren spent £40,000 summoning the legal gale needed to blow away the bottom of the boxing establishment's house of cards. Burrows backed him, and together they leaned on the establishment; it was tough going but once weakened the whole house fell down. For Frank, going through the courts was the best way to do things, indeed the only way the Board and the opposition could be beaten. He stubbornly pursued clearly sighted goals, fired by an intuitive legal mind gratified by good counsel.

Having been confronted with the vagaries of the Board's 14-day rule in his very first promotion, Warren was resolved to demolish it. To his aid came new fair trading and restrictive practices legislation introduced in 1983 by the Conservative government, the entrepreneurial values of which he embraced with some gusto. Warren wanted open competition in the boxing market place, unhindered by tradition and bureaucracy. His single-minded, 'on your bike', spirit fitted boldly into a significant part of the national mood which followed the Falklands War. Britain was unbeatable, and so was Frank Warren.

In the end, the conflict over the 14-day rule didn't have to do battle in court. Warren's lawyers said the Board's rule was only a policy which had no statutory authority. If it was defended in court it would very probably fall foul of the new Restrictive Practices Act. The Board was advised by its lawyers not to pull on its legal gloves. Round one to Warren.

'We were all members of a club,' says Jarvis Astaire. 'And all of us knew the Board's rules could be challenged but nobody ever did. And Warren joined that club agreeing to abide by the rules, and as soon as he had been admitted he challenged. The Board had a tiger by the tail and the tiger turned. That's what I resented.'

The Board was bitter over this assault on a time-honoured rule, but after several years the then general secretary Ray Clarke can bring himself to say: 'In many ways he had a case, because at the time he came into boxing the only big promoters were the group of Levene, Duff and Barrett who all worked together. They favoured it [the 14-day rule], probably because they could sit down between them and separate their dates by three weeks so no one could go in between. That's why Warren got peeved about it – he felt they were deliberately keeping him out. But now it's a free-for-all and you have big shows on the same night in London.'

Greater freedom in staging shows gave Warren greater leeway

to negotiate dates for ITV coverage. Even then he had to overcome another Board policy that a promoter could only broadcast four shows on the same day in a year. Any other shows had to be recorded and screened the next day or later. The Board had been very content with the cartel's practice of filming on Tuesdays at the Albert Hall or Wembley and broadcasting on the BBC's *Sportsnight* on Wednesdays.

With no competition, the cartel felt no pressure to show live boxing. ITV was rightly convinced live boxing or highlights shown a couple of hours after the event, would draw better ratings. 'Frank drove a coach and horses through the whole set up. Frank had tremendous enthusiasm and commitment to the sport. He loves his boxing and is actually very knowledgeable about the sport. And he has total stubbornness not to give in, whatever might happen,' says Bob Burrows. 'There was this nice cosy relationship, the BBC, with dear old Harry Carpenter and coverage of domestic boxing was almost solely the preserve of the BBC and the deals and arrangements with Levene, Barrett and Duff.'

The Board thought live boxing would ruin the sport by keeping the fans at home. Burrows and ITV knew good boxing would always draw big crowds whether shown live or not. So came the inevitable conflict in November 1983. The Board said Thames were not allowed to screen a Warren promotion at the Bloomsbury Crest Hotel, featuring heavyweights Noel Quarless and John L. Gardner, and threatened to withdraw its officials. Warren issued a writ declaring the Board's television policy was a restraint of trade.

The show went ahead and was screened by Thames. Ray Clarke watched it at home on his television, incredulous at the gall of the foe. Again, the Board's lawyers stated a court battle would be a loser. Round two to Warren. Barely a year after he and Thames teamed up, a full-scale onslaught on the BBC and the cartel was possible. The young promoter had never been blatant about the extent of his ambition, always saying boxing was a large cake and all he wanted was a small slice, or that Duff was running Harrods and should not worry about Warren opening a corner shop next door, smart little analogies designed to curry sympathy and veil the vision he held for his role in boxing. Now the monopoly had been broken, Warren intended to take the biggest slice of the boxing cake for himself. With ITV's money behind him, anything was possible.

Warren's career had developed as quickly as a Polaroid image. He had delivered. He had identified the traditionally popular weights: fly, middle and heavy, and found a crowd puller in each – Keith Wallace, Roy Gumbs and Joe Bugner. He set himself a series of goals, of winning posts: a British champion, which Gumbs became in 1981, a European champion and a world beater. By 1983, he had television, he then wanted to promote at the York Hall, Duff's regular small hall, and at the Albert Hall, the star venue.

Already the cartel's monopoly had been badly cracked, but something still bugged Frank Warren. Like many others in the boxing fraternity he knew the cartel had some sort of working arrangement, but like King Solomon's mine, no one had seen proof of it. He even suspected there was some sort of written agreement between the four, which the Board may even have been aware of. Apart from his own struggle to establish himself, so many people in the game complained to him that the Board bent so far backwards to accommodate the Board's wishes they almost broke the rules. The general secretary, Ray Clarke, had always dismissed these complaints as the bitterness of those who came off second best or worse in the promotional battle.

Warren was not satisfied with this. He felt if he could prove a partnership existed which effectively excluded the other promoters and managers it could bring the opposition down, or at least force them to give him the elbow room he wanted.

But knowing what he was up against and being able to prove its existence were two different things. He used to sit in his office and say, 'Jon, I know these buggers are working together, and I want to show them up for what they are.'

In the autumn of 1984 *Sunday Times* journalist Nick Pitt, who had long held similar suspicions, heard about a document that was in the possession of Mickey Duff's brother-in-law, Henry Simmons and that it might be available. It apparently gave details of a partnership involving Duff and the others. Simmons was now trying to offload it on to the newspapers. The *News of the World*, part of News International along with the *Sunday Times*, had heard about it, but both papers' legal departments were extra edgy about documents. The deeply embarrassing episode of the Hitler Diaries was fresh in the memory, when the eminent historian Hugh Trevor-Roper had endorsed a set of notes which turned out to be fake.

News of the document spread to Frank Warren. He spoke to Simmons. If he could see the document, he might be interested in buying it. Having long suspected something like this existed, Warren could hardly wait for the meeting, fixed one lunchtime for the lounge of the Waldorf Hotel in the Strand. Warren made sure he was accompanied by a lawyer whom he hoped would be able to judge whether the document was legitimate. Simmons had had more trouble than he had anticipated selling the document. If somehow Warren could pass it on and get him some money, that suited him just fine.

Neither party wasted any time. Simmons handed Warren a piece of paper. It was dated 11 June 1979. Astaire, Duff, Lawless and Barrett had agreed to share equally all income from 'promotions, matchmaking, management, production, licensing, television, films (connected with boxing), broadcasting, advertising, sponsorship and the like arising therefrom'. Expenses incurred by any of the four from the above activities were pooled. That was that. Warren looked carefully at the four signatures. He recognised them all.

It was precisely what he had dreamt of reading. Struggling to control his delight, he said he wanted to check its authenticity – after all, remember what happened with the Hitler Diaries. Frank passed it on to his lawyer, who said he wanted to hold it up to the light. The lawyer got up and, peering knowledgeably through pince-nez glasses, raised the paper up to a chandelier. Then he walked calmly out of the lounge and through the foyer, breaking into a gentle jog as he reached the door.

Simmons stared at Warren in disbelief. What about the

money? Warren just shrugged his shoulders and told him not to worry. He got up to leave. There was little the middle-aged Simmons could do. He had tried to stitch up his brother-in-law and had in turn been turned over in a classic stroke by Warren and his lawyer, who was now ensconced comfortably in the back of a black cab with the document. The name of the 'lawyer'? Ambrose Mendy.

Mendy passed the document on to Warren, who gave it to the *News of the World*. A little uncertain of its implications, they showed it to their up-market colleagues. Now vindicated after years of highlighting the ill-effects of Duff & Co's grip on boxing, Nick Pitt and his colleague Chris Nawrat set about breaking the news.

The story of the document's existence broke in the *Sunday Times* on 9 December 1984: 'Revealed: the secret cartel behind boxing.' And in the *News of the World* on the same day: 'IT'S A FIX! EXPOSED: THE SECRET DEALS OF BOXING'S MISTER BIGS'. The reaction from the four was of fury, particularly Astaire, whose role in boxing was finally and indisputably established. Neither story had explained how the document had come into the press's hands, though Astaire in a letter the next week to the *Sunday Times* said it had been removed from Duff's house along with some jewels. Jarvis Astaire is 'still very annoyed. The presentation of the story was disgusting, absolutely disgusting. How could you justify it being on the front page? I am still very angry about it. Very angry. It was presented as a rogues' gallery.'

The story gathered pace. On 16 December, the *Sunday Times* revealed it had documents showing the cartel had an agreement with the BBC to screen a number of shows, mostly at the Albert Hall from October 1984 to June 1985. The BBC had agreed to pay at least £190,000 for six shows, when under Board rules each fight had to be negotiated separately. The Office of Fair Trading said it would investigate the whole affair, the matter was debated in the House of Commons.

The same week the *News of the World* had something even spicier. The Friday following the story, the reporter who had written the story, Jeff Edwards, was parking his car in the garage beneath his block of flats. It was 2am. A tall, beefy, 40-ish looking man approached him.

'Mr Edwards? That's a nice scoop you had last week in the paper. I hope you weren't thinking of doing something like that again.' The man reached into a holdall and pulled out a sawn-off shotgun. 'You know what this is don't you? So now you know I'm not joking.' Edwards was put under round-the-clock police guard.

Mickey Duff said at the time: 'Who would do that sort of thing? I don't know.'

Someone, somewhere, was a bit upset.

The Board was obliged to haul up boxing's gang of four. But after a lengthy inquiry it exonerated them, when some sort of punishment, though hardly that of execution given to the Chinese leaders, was deserved. The Board even went as so far as to praise them in its summing up. Somehow it found the agreement did not contravene their rules, nor the laws of the land. The Board's only real sanction is to withdraw or suspend a licence, and it did not have the courage to do so. It simply ordered that in future all boxers should be informed of the four's arrangement.

Everyone had known Astaire was involved, as a sort of chairman, but Lawless's role appalled the boxing world. He was the most successful manager of the era, with world champions like John H. Stracey, Maurice Hope, Jim Watt and Charlie Magri under his belt. Under the Board's rules a manager must not make any deduction from a fighter's purse 'in respect of extra fees or commission'. But under the cartel's agreement, the lower the purse of a Lawless fighter on a Duff or Barrett promotion, the less would have to be deducted from the pooled income. There was a clear conflict of interests. Henry Cooper said at the time, 'for a manager to enter such an agreement must be unethical'. Bob Arum, the American promoter, said: 'If it's true Lawless was part of the promotional group, it's shocking. How can he properly represent his fighters?'

Charlie Magri reacted angrily in the *Sunday Times*: 'I'm very upset about this. I've worked very hard for them and now I realise that I've been earning peanuts. I know Lawless had good offers for me to fight abroad but he never took them. It seems they only wanted me to fight at the Albert Hall or Wembley.' John H. Stracey also said he should have earned more.

However, after hearing from other Lawless boxers, the Board was satisfied 'with his management and the purses he obtained' for his fighters.

The cartel were due to appear before the Board in early February 1985, but in farcical circumstances after two hours the hearing was adjourned to give the Board time to provide details to the four's lawyers of what exactly was under investigation. The lawyers had already threatened legal action for restraint of trade, arguing there was nothing to stop the cartel's agreement, the argument ironically successfully used by Warren in his particular battles. On 22 February came the exoneration.

The Board's statement was spineless and typical of the lack of authority shown when Ray Clarke was in charge. It found that 'far from being against the interests of boxing, it is considered that without their [the cartel's] very active participation boxing in this country would not be in as healthy a state as it is now.'

The cartel later operated in the different form of National Promotions, with Duff, Lawless and Astaire as directors. Lawless later left, but still has a promotional company with Duff. Astaire comes in for the big fights, like Bruno-Tyson. His hands are full these days with running Wembley and closed circuit television all over the country.

He cannot see any case against the cartel's old domination. 'We have never had more world champions in this country than at that time, which must be a slide rule of some sort, and the Board decided to commend us, they didn't have to, did they? There are always have-nots looking through the window at the haves. We achieved what we achieved on merit.'

At least in the long term the story made the Board more accountable, the whole business of boxing more open and made fighters watch themselves even more carefully.

Before long Ray Clarke was replaced by John Morris. Clarke still maintains the decision not to punish the cartel was fair.

'There are monopolies everywhere you look. Is it a bad thing that soccer is monopolised by about five football teams? At some time or another there has always been one big promoter, from the time of Jack Solomons onwards. You get one man, or group, who are better than any of the others.' He denied ever having been aware of the document.

Morris is thankful he was only press officer at the time. 'The Board in the past – I'm not criticising it because times were different – was an autocratic body that would say "no, we won't do that, no, you can't do this." Ray Clarke fought his own battles and is a great friend of mine. But I'm not Ray Clarke nor am I as close, I am not saying Ray was, to any of them . . . the situation now with more people involved in promotion is healthier.'

Frank Warren was vindicated by the whole business and more power was given to his efforts, which continued at full speed. For 15 years other promoters had been trying to get regular television, now Warren had cracked it in three. In 1984 he signed a deal with Central Television for *Fight Night*, a series of shows covering small hall boxing in the Midlands and the north of England. Again, his friends were a help. Burt McCarthy was managing the highly promising middleweight Errol Christie and one night, watching TV at home, noticed in the credits the name of an old contact, Gary Newbon, who had been a junior reporter when McCarthy was a more active manager. Newbon was now high up in Central Sport. McCarthy called him the next day, after eight years, and by the end of the conversation an agreement to cover Christie's fights had been reached. The series began, with Warren promoting other managers' fighters in the regions.

Newbon and Warren fell out a couple of years later, but Warren's small hall shows in London were then featured in *Seconds Out*, shown once a month mainly in the Thames region, on Tuesdays from late 1986. It was vital bread and butter, and a perfect breeding ground for Warren's young fighters.

In the meantime, ten or so of Warren's big shows a year were shown on *Midweek Sports Special*, usually broadcast by the whole network. There was no contract, no fixed dates for shows, but so happy were ITV with Warren's product that he virtually monopolised its boxing time. A former employee of Warren's remembers him describing television as 'a pig, all it thinks about is its next meal', but the same could be said of a boxing promoter waiting for the next wad of television revenue. Warren and Burrows were virtually a partnership, they would find mutually suitable dates, and suitable fights, though on two or three occasions ITV said no if it wasn't happy with the bill. They worked together to build Warren's fighters through television, as Duff and Lawless had done with theirs on the BBC. Boxers like Roy Gumbs, Keith Wallace, Errol Christie, Colin Jones and Terry Marsh all became regulars. Duff & Co still had the household names like Frank Bruno but Warren was building up his own, and showing more, better middle-ranking contests. ITV was very happy with what Warren was feeding it.

Frank used to provide Burrows and Thames with a full evening's entertainment, which compared very well with some of Duff's shows on the BBC. He kept unearthing more and more talent and providing some great scraps. Like Mark Kaylor's triumph over Roy Gumbs, Warren's first champion, for the British middleweight title at Alexandra Palace. Kaylor seemed finished, he had taken unearthly punishment from Gumbs. On his hands and knees, struggling to get up before the count, he was revived by the ferocious, deafening support of his followers. From some unknown reserve Kaylor summoned his greatest strength of the fight, mauling Gumbs with wild punches and stopping him in the fifth round.

Like Terry Marsh's win over McKenzie, it was the fight of the year, a thrilling, brutal but honourable encounter, which typified the sort of fight Warren endeavoured to stage. In the boxing market place punters wanted to see fights which reflected why they had come to like boxing in the first place. Warren appreciated that in these circumstances here was the only way for him to make money out of boxing. Some nights could be a bit chaotic and rowdy, the music could be too loud, but something always happened. An impetus was created as people knew Warren gave good value for money, the bills were packed with good fights, and often the boxing didn't end until midnight.

Warren redefined boxing promotion, taking it into the 1980s after years of sterility. Early innovations were smartened up: crowd-lifting music as the fighters approached the ring, engaging MCs, tarted-up girls parading in the ring; well-designed programmes, posters adorned with catchy fight slogans like 'Thunder and Lightning' for Andries-Sibson. It was all part of the buzz of going to a Warren promotion.

Frank was in boxing to make money, but at the same time was motivated by a degree of idealism. He liked boxing, cared about it, and his anti-authoritarianism opposed the monopolisation of power; boxers deserved to make as much as they could, and needed help to get it. Frank was creating lots of new work and paying well. The people around him all appreciated his philosophy, particularly his trainer and matchmaker Ernie Fossey, who like more or less everyone else of his generation had worked for the cartel at some point, and like many, was frustrated by the experience. He wanted to train fighters for contests that would give them reasonable tests of their ability. 'One of my biggest moans is that a bit of blood and the ref stops it. People want to see a decent fight. I never worry about cuts. I think punches to the kidney does them much more harm than a flesh wound. I've never seen anyone permanently harmed from a cut, have you? How would you like to train your guts out for years and then get stopped on a little cut?'

Critics of Warren said he often risked his fighters for the sake of a good bout for television. Ringside boxing hacks opposed to Warren used to joke that an ambulance should wait outside the dressing-room of Warren's fighters.

'He ruined a lot of young fighters who had talent by putting them too high, too soon,' says one. 'He had one of the best young fighters I had seen in this country for a long time – Keith Wallace. He was ruined, I'm afraid. He had this obsession Wallace was the best flyweight in the world and better than Charlie Magri. What he [Warren] did was stupid and I told him so. He made

Wallace make the eight-stone flyweight limit when it was so obvious he was a bantamweight. He made him make the weight and he couldn't take the punches to the body. If he'd moved up to bantamweight he would have been way up there.' Fossey says in the end Wallace lacked stamina. Opinions are always divided on why good prospects never make it as far as expected. Wallace indeed moved up a weight late in his career, though he is by no means the only boxer to have done so.

If mistakes were made, there were few grumbles from the fighters. Frank's boys were paid well and fought often – by 1985 Warren was doing 28 shows a year – and could hope for swift progress to a championship shot. He doubled average purses and began outbidding the opposition to promote championship fights. Able fighters kept coming over to the Warren camp, partly through his and Ernie Fossey's good eye for a promising talent, but mainly because of the attractive money. Among men with short careers and limited opportunities, word soon spread fast of better cash to be had. Fossey's reputation as a good trainer who pushed his boys hard also helped. 'He had a very important role at this stage, especially as Frank's knowledge of boxing wasn't that strong early on,' says Mike Miller, now head of Channel 4 Sport, then an LBC reporter. 'Frank could spot a winner and a crowd pleaser, but he couldn't have done it without Ernie. Ernie was always there, the trainer, cornerman, the reliable lieutenant.' A string of fighters arrived from St Helens amateur club on Merseyside – Jimmy Price, Keith Wallace and Stevie Johnson. The stable of around 25 boxers under Warren's management was packed with promise.

It was in his own interests to increase purses, but it infuriated the opposition, who then had to match Warren's inflationary practices. The market was opened up, and boxing was shaken out of its lethargy. And the press had someone new and exciting to write about, aided by Warren's nose for a publicity-attracting stunt – a £60,000 bid for Charlie Magri to fight Wallace, a survey to reveal boxing was the most popular sport on television, a $1 million bid for a Bruno contest, a £750,000 bid for Thomas Hearns, the great American champion, to fight for his fourth title at a different weight in London. Those were attempted coups, but in 1985 he pulled off a genuine one: staging the fight between Colin Jones and Don Curry for the world welterweight title at the NEC in Birmingham. Curry was rated as pound for pound one of the top three fighters in the world: Jones was a talented Welshman with a huge following. ITV paid the highest ever fee – thought to be around £200,000 – for a fight in Britain; 12,000 fans, mostly from the valleys, packed the auditorium, and saw Jones lose, his nose freakishly and hideously split by a chopping punch from Curry.

A Jones victory and subsequent title defences could have made Warren a fortune, but it didn't seem to matter at the time. After the fight Warren was confident enough to announce he had already been the top promoter for the last 18 months. 'And that's not being big-headed,' he said. 'I've always given value-for-money shows. The punters recognise this. I put on the best fights, quality fights. And now I'm getting the big names to fight for me too. I don't want to put the other lot out of business. I think they'll put themselves out of business because of the awful shows they put on. I came into this business because I love boxing and because I wanted to make money. What anyone else does is their affair.' In the rest of 1985, he staged three more world title fights; by 1987, he had staged eight.

Despite missing out on the benefits of a Jones victory, Warren was doing very nicely. The shows were packed out, nearly always on television, and often pulling in £30,000–£40,000 a time. In the same year he moved into a £155,000 detached house in Brookman's Park, Hertfordshire. He had come a long way from the Priory Green Estate. Now his neighbours were stockbrokers rather than street traders. The driveway boasted a Rolls Royce with personalised number plate, 626 FJW, and a new Mercedes for his second wife Susan Cox. Frank had divorced Barbara in the late 1970s and not long after met Sue in a pub. He just went up and introduced himself. The daughter of a Bethnal Green cabbie, she was unpretentious, bright, and beautiful. Ten years younger than he, Sue was already into a modelling career that would take her on to the pages of *Vogue*.

The couple quickly moved into a Georgian terraced house in Danbury Street, Islington, before marrying in 1983. Frank, brought up in a large family, adored children and was keen to start a second family. Two years after they wed, their first of four children, Francis, was born. The only blight on an ideal personal life was the separation of his parents in the early 1980s.

There was little new money crassness about Frank, but pictures of him in a £400 suit resting on the bonnet of his Rolls did nothing to dispel the image of a wise guy on the way up. Warren has never puffed big cigars and glittered with offensive jewellery, but he has never struck a casual image. Mickey Duff always looks like a trainer in a suit, Astaire like a tycoon, Barrett like a tax man, Barry Hearn, a later rival, like the owner of a successful chain of menswear shops, but Frank Warren has always looked like a bit of a 'guvnor'. Never a gangster and never desiring to be one, he has unwittingly found the image seductive. A big, male-dominated family, plenty of kids he is devoted to, a big car, authority over subordinates – several of the ingredients are there. The combination of cultivated smoothness and street-level wit mean he can be articulate, lucid but firm with TV companies, streetwise and paternal with the boxers, and efficient and co-operative with the press.

'I have to say that in all the dealings I have ever had with him he has never let me down, and he has been very fair. He always rings back. To use the old cliché, you speak as you find,' says Ken Jones, chief sports writer of the *Independent*. Other reporters are less complimentary, but they mostly sway toward Duff.

'He was a very smooth operator. He was young, beautifully dressed with a charming manner,' says a boxing journalist who fell out with Warren years ago. 'Incredible charm, no doubt about that, and street wit.'

Harry Mullan from *Boxing News* liked Warren from the moment they met. 'We got on and my wife and he and Sue went out together. He's good company, and he has a good eye for people and tells a good story.'

His conversation is not ruled by boxing. Never forgetting his teenage ambition to be a cameraman, Warren has remained mad on films, and was able to see the joke when once asked his favourite – *The Godfather*. Artists he likes include Van Gogh, Monet and Picasso, and his literary tastes are on the side of F. Scott Fitzgerald rather than Frederick Forsyth; Raymond Chandler, P. G. Wodehouse and Tom Sharpe are among other favourites. A passion for music has remained since his clubbing days as a teenager, to the extent of ringing up friends like Mike Miller just to enthuse about a new band like the Neville Brothers; but for all the catholicity of his taste – Mozart, Otis Redding and Bonnie Rait – Frank's hero is 'Old Blue Eyes' himself, Frank Sinatra.

Even those who have fallen out with Warren or have always been pitted against him, begrudgingly admit to his charisma. Terry Lawless was forced to concede: 'You can't sit on your backside and expect boxing to be the same as it was 20 years ago. He's made my life a lot harder but, personally, I like competition. For a young man to come into the business and be as successful as he has been . . . yeah, you've got to be impressed.'

In the mid-eighties he moved office from the suite in the Bloomsbury Crest Hotel to a four-storey house in Tavistock Place nearby. Frank's stylish office in the first-floor drawing room was graced by a huge walnut desk and matching coffee table, with low-slung sofas all round the edge; old boxing and racing prints lined the walls. The door was always open to his staff, who were now busier than ever. Frank was in his element. Working 15 hours a day, he was calm but assertive, always cracking jokes, but never crudely. He would flit around the offices and go into one-to-one huddles with members of staff, give a few friendly but firm instructions, and tell them to 'sort it out'.

Around him Warren had Jon Robinson as general manager, matchmaker and trainer Ernie Fossey, Leslie McCarthy and Mike Williams on administrative work, and Ambrose Mendy, super salesman and occasional impersonator, working on sponsorship and advertising space. All Frank Warren's men. Jean Lee, Sue's aunt, was secretary. Old family friends like Mary Powell would be around to help sell tickets; Frank's younger brother Robert was often there helping out. It was a happy, tight-knit team, whose members rightly had every faith in their boss.

David McConachie, who came along a bit later as press officer, says, 'Frank is a brilliant bloke to work for, he pays well, he treats everyone as equal and gives good perks. He's a very generous bloke. It was a very exciting time. When he first meets people he is very shy. But when it comes to doing business he's totally different. He can switch it on and off when he needs it. The shy guy is the real Frank. In meetings he's not a shouter at all, he knows what he wants and goes to get that. He won't budge on an issue if he knows what he wants. He would rather walk away and say, "I can't do business with you".

'Most people who really do know him really do like him, it's the people who don't really know him who don't like him.' Or people who have fallen out with him.

Good contacts are vital in boxing, and Warren cultivated them in all the right places, like the press, who mostly supported his stormy entrance into boxing. One such press man was Laurence Lustig, a sports photographer with the *Daily Star*, boxing fan, and best friend of Charlie Magri, a household name and former flyweight world champion who was one of the top draws in boxing.

'In those early days Frank was very publicity conscious. It was an exciting time in boxing, we all felt something new was happening. People like me became quite important to him. The tabloids use more picture space than words for boxing, and a manager needs to have contacts on picture desks,' explains Lustig. 'I had his home number, and his mum's number, where he used to go on a Sunday. In those days I could ring him any time. He used to pull me aside at press conferences and say "what can I do here to get it in the paper", that sort of thing. We weren't friends but had a very healthy working relationship.'

Aiming for a promotional coup to equal Jones v Curry, Warren secured an agreement from the Thai fighter and flyweight world champion, Sot Chitilada, to defend his title in Britain against Magri, an incredibly bold move as the East End fighter was managed by Terry Lawless and promoted by Mickey Duff. Warren was smart enough to use Lustig as an intermediary. Lawless refused to play ball, but that weekend the *Sunday Times* story about the cartel broke. It was a boon to Warren. Lawless, who came out worst from the story, felt obliged to open up his operations a little.

'Terry agreed to meet Frank Warren at the Royal Oak, Lawless's gym,' remembers Lustig. 'Frank said no, if he won't come to my office, I won't see him. So childish, both of them. This is my best friend's final chance to get another world title shot, and a huge fight for the boxing public, and these two are too pig-headed to meet on each other's ground.

'So I arranged for them to meet at Charlie's sports shop in Bethnal Green, on the afternoon of half day closing, a neutral ground, roughly half way between the two camps. A bit like a Western, I suppose.'

So one of the biggest fights of the year was settled in an East End sports shop; boxing works like that sometimes. Unfortunately Magri lost in four rounds.

Throughout boxing the sweetest of relationships can turn sour overnight. People are either in or out. Disputes between a promoter and his staff, boxers or other managers, are rarely talked through, but settled by a snap decision, often leaving both parties swearing never to talk to the other again. Friends are 'perfect gentlemen', while enemies are 'complete bastards'. No in-between. Everyone understands the business is ruthless, though there are more than a few who wish they didn't. It applies to any of the bigshots, but Warren seems to have made more enemies than most in his comparatively short time in the game.

One of Warren's current boxers, Tee Jay, stays away from the fight scene unless he is working. 'Boxing people are two-faced. I know they see me and say "Tee Jay, what a good guy" and as soon as your face is turned they say "what a wanker". But that's how they are. I don't go to boxing shows. The boxers are the nicest people.'

For people who haven't grown up in boxing, the shenanigans can become too much to bear. David McConachie left his job as

Frank Warren's press officer in 1991 for that reason. 'It was an exciting business to work in but it got frustrating. All the managers seemed to be out to screw each other. It is full of backstabbing people, and I got fed up with that. It was very rare you could do a straight deal with someone, invariably someone was knocking someone else for money.

'There is a cliché that it is a dark and murky world, but a lot of it is like that. Obviously it's not full of gangsters, but you do get a lot of managers about who think they are gangsters. We would send contracts out to managers, they wouldn't be signed, the Board of Control would then say the purse offer hadn't been met and we'd lose the fight.' Or other managers would promise to supply an opponent and he would get mysteriously injured shortly beforehand, so spoiling the bill. Duff & Co still refuse good purse offers for their fighters, like £30,000 for Lloyd Honeyghan to fight Tony Collins, because of not wanting to work with Frank Warren, claims McConachie.

'It's in the blood of boxing, you might get some straight people who go into the business, but there's a vibe which you've got to operate by. Every manager has to have two or three arch enemies.'

Another former employee of Warren's recalls incredible grief in the day-to-day business of boxing, particularly dealing with foreign fighters. 'Boxers came over who were the wrong weight, didn't have a licence, couldn't box, turned up a day late, fucked off on the way to the weigh-in. It was unbelievable. There were so many arguments, and there's always three or four sides to every story in boxing.'

Fight management is full of half-truths and broken promises. Just like the combat in the ring itself is full of lies. José Torres, the former light-heavyweight champion of the world, once said: 'We fighters understand lies. What's a feint? What's a left hook off the jab? What's an opening? What's thinking one thing and doing another?' Managers, too, have to feint, duck, and occasionally hit below the belt.

The manager and promoter Harry Holland is widely described as one of the warmest and straightest people in the business. Such is his hospitality that he agreed to talk from his hospital bed while awaiting an operation for kidney stones. Holland is a west London exception in the capital's boxing world; brought up in Brentford he has promotions on his side of town sewn up. Short, stoutly built with grey hair, he has a jovial face and crackling voice that have earned him plenty of work as a bit part actor on *EastEnders*. In between arrivals of about six visitors in his hospital room, including one of his boxers Jimmy Cook and wife, Harry's daughter, and his trainer who entered screaming 'Surprise!' while wearing a plastic mask and beard, Holland expressed his frustration with the business of boxing.

'I don't agree that you have got to be ruthless and walk on people all the time. I hope when I'm finished my fighters will turn around and say Harry was a fair guy, and think of me as a friend, and come and visit.

'People say they're going to work together then do the most ridiculous things. Officially all fights should be arranged by contract, but unofficially it doesn't happen. There's no point signing when a manager can always get his fighter out if he wants to, by getting a doctor's note or a bad back or whatever. So small fights are often not contracted, though big fights are of course.

'Managers will make an agreement to fight in say 28 days' time, and that their fighters won't fight in the meantime. Then you find that his guy has fought, got knocked out and won't be ready to fight your man. It's just part of the business.'

Holland says Warren is the only person he has fallen out with so far in boxing. In the early eighties they promoted together, chiefly at Blazers, a club in Windsor. 'He phoned me up, and I hadn't heard of him at that stage. We met at his restaurant in the Barbican called McLintock [sic]. We got on well, did a few promotions then fell out over something to do with boxing. That was the end. I've only ever fallen out with one person, which is not hard: Frank Warren.'

The next day, an hour after his operation, Holland was straight on the mobile phone constantly charged up by his bedside, arranging details for Cook's European super-middleweight fight in Paris a few days later, which he won.

No one could pretend that the people who work for promoters are all model employees, but Frank Warren is well aware
of his reputation for being ruthless with people he is not happy
with.

Pepe Forbes was his foreign agent, responsible for looking
after visiting fighters, until a fight between one of Warren's
boxers, Tom Collins, and the Dutchman Alex Blanchard, for the
European light-heavyweight title, and he is still bitter about the
experience. Forbes was in Blanchard's dressing room while the
referee checked the boxer's bandages and noticed nothing
untoward. When Blanchard came into the ring he had an
advertisement for some product emblazoned on his shorts, a
cheap, silly stroke of the sort that goes on in boxing more than it
should. ITV stopped its live coverage immediately. 'Frank
Warren blamed me for "gross incompetence". He thought I
should have noticed but he was in the dressing room and could
have seen himself. I had another boxer to look after so I left the
dressing room, and the shorts must have been changed. He was
all right until we fell out. He thought I hadn't done my job
properly,' claims Forbes.

Frank Maloney worked as a trainer in the early days with
Warren. 'We fell out for political reasons and money issues, I
suppose. Where I come from, you don't have contracts, your
word is your word. Sometimes Frank didn't understand that. I
didn't like some of the things that were going on, and the way
boxers were looked after. Frank saw boxing in a different way to
me. I don't think it was Frank's greatest love – he was more of a
businessman – but I was probably still in love with it all.

'Yes he had charm, and once he got his teeth into something he
wouldn't let go. He was a very shrewd operator. And he had
loyalty at that time. Loyalty is the key factor in this game, if
you've got loyal staff around you it really helps.'

Despite having a settled team, plenty of extras had already
passed through the Warren camp, and plenty more would do so.
But in 1985 two of the best left, Jon Robinson and Ambrose
Mendy. Robinson left after a disagreement over how shows
should be organised, feeling he wasn't allowed to run things his

way. He and Warren didn't speak for some time but can say hello to each other now.

Mendy left in more controversial circumstances. While he was on honeymoon in 1985 the police raided his house and searched his desk at Frank Warren's office. 'When I got back Warren said I'd never come back here if I were you. He said it messed things up with the TV company, you're on a wanted list, we better not meet.' Warren, who had given Mendy a job after he had just finished serving a sentence for fraud, sacked him.

No charges were ever brought against Mendy, and a letter from Bishopsgate police confirmed his innocence: 'The documents seized from the Bloomsbury Crest Hotel concerning Mr Mendy's interest in boxing promotions no longer form part of investigations and have been returned to Mr Mendy without question.'

Jon Robinson says: 'Frank was upset that something like that should have happened. He had his reputation to think about. Ambrose had to go.'

Mendy recalls, 'I still carried on talking to Warren until I opened my company, the World Sports Corporation. He phoned me up and tried to tell me what to do. I said don't worry I'm looking out for myself. He said, "You can fuck off"; I said, "You fuck off". I went off up to his office and his arsehole collapsed completely.'

Mendy was a good operator at the Warren office, he was full of bright ideas for publicity and expert at signing up sponsors, whose revenue was vital, like Eubick for the Jones fight and Carlsberg for the Magri fight. 'Mendy was a leading light in the Warren camp and it suffered after he left,' says Robinson. Mendy was to get his revenge when Nigel Benn left Warren and agreed to Mendy being his agent.

By now internal relations were not all they might have been, and some of the less attractive tricks of the trade were being picked up. The fights became more one-sided as concern for protecting boxers' records crept up alongside desire to give value for money. The number of poor quality foreign imports he brought in rose; they virtually all lost, like those on Duff's bills. Some weren't treated as well as they might have been. Reggie

Miller, an American brought to fight Nigel Benn, was told to travel to the Royal Albert Hall by public transport.

The early stars of Warren's stable had faded by 1987: Wallace, Price, Gumbs had not proved to be the world champions their manager hoped for. Worst of all, the middleweight Errol Christie, the brightest prospect in British boxing, fell apart. The Coventry fighter had been discovered by Burt McCarthy and fought on Warren's shows. McCarthy had shrewdly sent him to Emanuel Steward's famous Kronk gym in Detroit, where countless champions had been reared. Steward said Christie was magnificent against the best fighters like Mike McCallum, Mark Breland and Thomas 'The Hit Man' Hearns. 'When I saw Errol I fell in love with him,' recalls McCarthy. 'I knew he was for me. He was my kind of fighter. He had everything, the punch, the moves, the lot. I think pound for pound he was the most talented fighter we've had since the war.'

Christie was the most successful junior amateur ever. He turned pro in 1982, at the age of 19, and demolished his early opponents. Everyone thought he would be British champion within a year and take a world title before too long. He became a champion of nothing. The same generation as Benn, Herol Graham, Chris Eubank and Michael Watson, yet though only 28, it seems Christie is from another era.

In 1983 he was put against Jose Seys, a Belgian fighter who at light-heavyweight was a grade above Christie, a middleweight. That does happen from time to time. Christie was expected to win easily – Seys' track record was nothing special. He stopped Christie in the first round. At the ringside in Shoreditch, Frank Warren's head sank into his hands. Burt McCarthy could not believe his eyes. The unthinkable had happened.

Many believe Christie was never the same again. Having been so superior, he could not enter a ring again without imagining he would be knocked out. More victories followed but the spark had gone, defeats became common. Christie eventually left the Warren camp. After a short rest, he has been fighting under the Barry Hearn banner, training at the Henry Cooper gym in the Old Kent Road.

Christie says he was already heading for a burn-out even by the time of the Seys fight. 'I've had a lot of problems. I've been fighting since I was 15. I went into every championship this country put up. As a kid I was involved in every sport there was – football, athletics, rugby, gymnastics, everything. And outside school – boxing. I started boxing when I was eight. I was very competitive,' he says, his eyes distant, bewildered by the memory of his over-activity.

'I was training all the time, and there was no break. I'm still only young but I've flogged my body to death. I never really took a break. I've only ever had two holidays, each for a couple of weeks. I've always been fighting at the top end. When I was 14, I was sparring with guys aged 18. Big men.'

He pauses, and sinks his head downwards. 'I've had problems with my legs. We never knew at the time what it was. But when I came to London it was all about money. My family, we're poor people. I ain't thinking about a break, I'll have that later, I think. I'm thinking about surviving and getting my own house. I needed money, dosh, spondoolies.

'I used to get in the ring and my legs used to shake. It was overwork. When you look at my style, I was always on my toes, jigging around. It all built up and came to an abrupt ending.'

Another pause. More pain to recall. 'My whole body was dried up. And mentally as well, I was gone. And you know what that was? Not enough sex. Not enough time for women, too much fighting.'

He allows himself a smile. 'What was my hardest fight? The last one,' he grinned, breaking into mock-ragamuffin. 'I can hold my own against anybody. You ask the missus. I mean she gives me a bit of bother, she's learning to bob and weave a bit more. I have to watch for her right cross and her left hook, man.'

The humorous veneer can't be kept up for long. Christie is bitter. By now he could be a sporting hero and a millionaire.

'I don't want to be in the same room as McCarthy. I was having problems and I shouldn't have been fighting then. I went through the pain barrier. I tried to block it out. I'd been to all the physios and they couldn't do anything for me. So I carried on, which was a big mistake. Instead of going forward, my whole style of boxing changed. I lost my flair, my charisma in the ring. I was just a flat-foot. All my attraction as a fighter came from my style, not my chat.'

At the time the boxing public thought of the Seys defeat as an aberration – anyone can get caught cold after all. Then in 1985 Christie fought Mark Kaylor in a final eliminator for the British title. The build-up was marked by controversy, as the two scuffled in the street, for which they were both fined by the Board, supposedly because of racial incitement by Kaylor, who had a considerable National Front following. That was real enough, though the fight was simply over-boiled rivalry.

Christie was counted out in the eighth round. 'I had been sparring, and I damaged my nose. I could hardly breathe. I couldn't eat. I was 11 stone at the weigh-in [six pounds under the maximum]. All my power had gone, it was only a matter of time before I blew out. They kept saying it wasn't going to go more than three rounds. So I came out like a bat out of hell, and after five rounds I blew out. I was a young, stupid kid who wasn't taking any notice of what my body was saying. It was saying to me take it easy. Now I'm wiser.'

McCarthy remembers the whole affair with sadness. 'Something went wrong with Christie. With all that tremendous talent. After he lost to Kaylor we realised something was up. We spent a lot of money trying to find out what was wrong. He went to top specialists, from his feet to his head, dieticians, neurologists; he had three scans, the lot. We couldn't find anything wrong but I knew there was something and I asked him not to box again.'

After a long rest for his legs, Christie still believes he can make it. His new trainer, Howard Rainey, is worried if he doesn't become British champion, he will have problems coping with life after boxing. Boxing cognoscenti always sigh 'if only' when his name is mentioned, sharing the disappointment and understanding the pain and humiliation the boxer himself has been through. After Errol had left, someone said, 'I think that was good for him, it does him good to get it off his chest.'

So, despite all Warren's success, by 1987 he still hadn't found a real winner, a boxer who could win a world title and string together a series of defences. Colin Jones lost, Dennis Andries won but then lost. But there was one hope, one fighter who had so far defied all expectations, the fighter he was closest to and had most faith in, Terry Marsh.

CHAPTER EIGHT

A Promoter's Dream, Almost

Marsh began 1985 with a victory against Peter Eubank of Brighton, (an elder brother of Chris Eubank who beat Nigel Benn). Ten months, and four fights later, in October 1985, the deceptively frail-looking fireman took himself off to Monte Carlo to fight for the vacant light-welterweight title of Europe.

Alessandro Scapecci, like Marsh, was 27, but he was a more experienced fighter, having fought 34 pro fights to Marsh's 20, winning 31 and losing three. But he had put in a poor showing against former European champion Patrizio Oliva in July in which he had been heavily outpointed and had barely won a round. He had reached the most frightening stage in any fighter's career, and one which eventually catches up with almost all of them: he dare not lose. Unlike, for instance, a tennis player or a footballer, for whom the end is usually more gradual, Scapecci could not at his age dismiss 1985 as a bad season, have a break, and start all over again.

Marsh, as usual, was quietly confident and not expected by many people to win. However, the fight did not go as anyone had envisaged. After two convincing opening rounds by the challenger, Scapecci's glove split and the fight was stopped for four minutes. In round three, a gash began to open above Marsh's right eye after a clash of heads. But he persisted with his attack, accumulating points steadily, and survived an inspection by a ringside doctor at the end of the fifth round. He fought the sixth round with an even greater intensity, which was out of character; maybe he felt his cut might not survive another round. He drove Scapecci to the ropes near the Italian's corner and he beat him to his knees without, it seemed, having landed any particularly big punches. The fight ended in rather a confused way. Scapecci got up at six, but with his back to Marsh, looked over to his corner, drained, and he waved to his seconds that he had had enough. The referee counted him out, and Marsh had won by a technical knock-out.

'I knew' said Marsh, 'that once I stepped up the pressure he would not last.'

People who feel life has not always treated them fairly cope with it in different ways. Some switch off, perhaps sub-consciously giving up a little, settling for second or third best with an inarticulated acceptance. Some rage against the system and its iniquities. Others resort to humour: they make people laugh, they send things up. People who know Marsh always say 'Terry's a bit of a joker, he likes a laugh.' Marsh sees hypocrisy everywhere, and ridiculing things is one of his defence mechanisms. After one of his more important victories he stood, sweating in the middle of the ring, and said 'There's only one word to describe how I feel now – voluptuous.' A feeling of sensual gratification was not an answer the interviewer was prepared for.

Terry Marsh appears to be very open and light-hearted, but is actually rather an impregnable and private person; friendly to everybody, but close only to his family. Always with a smile, a wink and a joke, and a silly pose for the tabloid photographers, he rarely gives an insight into his feelings, and tends to steer clear of arguments.

Back home the British public were beginning to warm to Marsh, and he now felt that bigger things were in store. The two British boxers who in very different ways carried the burden of being loved had both suffered shattering defeats that summer. Frank Bruno's bid to become a world heavyweight champion ended when he was knocked senseless by 'Terrible' Tim Witherspoon in the eleventh round at Wembley. To add insult to injury, the American did not even look as if he'd bothered to get in to shape to fight Bruno – who never recovered any realistic hopes of becoming a world champion, but who remained as popular as ever.

Barry McGuigan lost his featherweight title to Steve Cruz in the boiling afternoon heat of the Nevada desert, in America, after he had begged his manager Barney Eastwood to postpone the fight, because of ear and ankle trouble.

From there the relationship deteriorated into one of the bitterest disputes between a manager and a fighter. It emerged that Mickey Duff had been paid hundreds of thousands of pounds by Eastwood for agent's services, without McGuigan's knowledge. When McGuigan beat Pedroza to win his world title, £308,337 of the proceeds went in 'agent's fees'. The *Sunday Times* revealed the profit of £448,211 was shared with Mike Barrett and Mickey Duff, while the official purse for McGuigan, lodged with the Board, was only £100,000, less than a third of the 'agent's fees'. McGuigan took legal action over what he considered to be Eastwood's strange financial arrangements. The manager paid his fighter an unprecedented one million pounds to prevent their full details ever coming out in court, but McGuigan had to come out and say that everything was fine and fight two more times for Eastwood. He was never the same fighter after the bout in Nevada.

Meanwhile 1986 had brought a surprising world title victory for a Bermondsey welterweight called Lloyd Honeyghan who defeated the undisputed champion, Don Curry. But outside the ring Lloyd was boastful without putting much fun into what he said, and too brash to be really popular. Feared by opponents for his right hand, and respected by the public, he was not loved. Britain needed a new boxing hero.

Frank Warren's more obviously professionally styled fighters for whom at one time he must have had great hopes – men like Roy Gumbs, Keith Wallace and Jimmy Price – all fell by the way when their big chance arrived. But Marsh had kept going. He was not 'hungry' in the boxing meaning of the world – he was not using fighting to make up for an acutely socially disadvant-aged background, but he was desperate to succeed, relishing a challenge as much from pigheadedness as inborn aggression. He was strong for someone fighting at ten stone and he possessed a varied attack – throwing punches with his left, jabbing, hooking, and using the uppercuts. He could switch to southpaw (leading with the right), but he did not have the force to finish a fight quickly, and also tended to flick his punches rather than moving in with his full weight behind them.

In January 1986, Marsh defended his European title against Tusikoleta Nkalankete at Muswell Hill. 'It was my hardest ever fight, because Nkalankete punched harder than I'd expected,' says Marsh. The contest lasted 12 rounds. He held on to win on points. Another successful defence followed. His challenge for a world title was gathering momentum.

At the end of 1986 it was agreed that Terry Marsh would fight Patrizio Oliva in Monte Carlo for the WBA light-welterweight Crown. Unfortunately the fight was called off because of an injury to the challenger that only he could have sustained. Marsh broke his nose at Tilbury Fire station in an accident with a hose.

Oliva was later beaten by Ubaldo Sacco, and Gene Hatcher's name was also mentioned as a possible Marsh opponent, but nothing came of it. However, British fighters are generally lightly regarded in the US, and with the help of a good purse of around £130,000, Joe Louis Manley, who held the IBF version of the title, was persuaded to come to Britain to defend it.

Gibraltan Pepe Forbes has lived in England since 1956. He speaks five languages, an unusual ability for someone in the boxing world, enabling him to work as an agent for foreign fighters. Mickey Duff and Frank Warren can find a Mexican roadsweeper, but they can't speak to him. Forbes has been an agent for eight world title fights, including the Marsh v Manley encounter. He recalls that Manley and his entourage arrived two weeks before the fight, and set up a camp at Basildon's Festival Hall. 'They thought he would win easily,' recalls Forbes. 'They were very confident – perhaps too confident.'

But the Americans underestimated the role Marsh's home crowd would play. There was no venue in Basildon big enough to stage the contest, so Warren spent around £35,000 importing a circus tent from Italy that seated 6,000 people. It was a typical Warren coup.

Terry Marsh fought Joe Louis Manley for the IBF world light-welterweight title on 4 March 1987 – his fifth wedding anniversary, and his daughter Kelly's third birthday, in a frenzied atmosphere of screaming, raucous home town support, providing a potent mix of aggression laced with racism against Manley. This was what people mean when they refer to Essex Man. White, affluent, Thatcher-supporting, aggressive, West Ham shirts, union jacks and lager; drunk men, who'd been in the pub for a couple of hours getting ready for the biggest sporting night in the town's history. 'We love you Terry, we do! We love you Terry we do! Oh, Terry we love you!'

What had they really come to see? Most of them had never heard of Manley, and had little knowledge of the boxing politics that meant this was the IBF version of the title. They had come to see one of their boys, and a good one at that, fight a black man from across the Atlantic. If ever there was an occasion when a small town closed ranks, and gave their man invaluable vocal support, this was it, the national anthem has rarely been sung with such ferocity. Marsh recognised a lot of people in the crowd. The stewards contributed to the chaotic atmosphere near ringside, with people with £60 tickets being strong-armed back to the £25 seats.

For Manley it all came as a nasty shock. He had been told Marsh had little drawing power. As Marsh entered the ring, just minutes after playing with his daughter Kelly in the changing room, he had the familiar feeling churning around inside him, one that was with him in all fights.

'I experienced total fear,' he says. 'There is no other word for it; but I enjoyed defying the odds.'

In Northern Ireland with the Marines Marsh remembers an underlying trend of fearfulness. 'But above that came such an excess of adrenalin, that the fear was lost, unlike in boxing where it never went away. Why that is, I don't know? Perhaps it is because in the ring I was seeing the whites of their eyes in a way that as a marine I was not.'

On this occasion there was even more fear because of who Manley was, and the importance of the fight. Marsh abandoned his classical, upright British style and gave an uncharacteristically aggressive display. In fact the meanness of his attack – the holding, the butting and the elbowing – showed a new dimension. After the months of waiting, and the disappointment of having had one chance cancelled, Marsh was more desperate than usual. At one point Manley's manager Stan Hoffman shouted out, 'Damn it, ref, what is this, a wrestling match?'

Marsh won the all-important first round. Clearly Manley was only human. The noise intensified. The challenger was on top almost throughout the fight, waving and winking at the crowd after each round. Manley had entered the ring looking a compact, well-balanced fighter. At five foot nine inches tall he was shorter than Marsh, and looked as if he might be stronger. But he became unsettled by the onslaught, from the jabs that turned in to upper-cuts and he lost his rythm. It was almost as if Marsh's desire for the title overwhelmed him. Manley was floored by his opponent with a left hook in round nine. After 20 seconds of round ten referee Randy Neumann stopped the fight.

As Marsh performed an ecstatic somersault in the ring, Warren stepped in to it. This was his big night as well. Frank hugged Terry, Ernie hugged Frank, and Terry hugged them both back. The two men lifted him up on to their shoulders for the hysterical crowd to cheer. After all the fighters who had missed out, Warren had landed the big one. A world champion. Essex roared its approval.

Joe Manley was reported afterwards to have been 'close to death'. Pepe Forbes claims that Manley got diarrhoea 48 hours before the fight. 'His weight went from 10 stone quarter of a pound, to nine stone 11 pounds. No one could work out how he caught it, these things just happen. In my opinion he was not 100 per cent, but that is not to take away from Terry, who did a very good job.'

The fighting fireman had made it. But he did not neglect his responsibilities. He wanted to get back to Tilbury Fire Station the next day, but he was besieged by press and had to wait another 24 hours, so losing a day's holiday.

Manley had fallen for Warren's game plan: lure the champion on to hostile foreign territory with a tempting purse, don't let him box, and rough him up. It had worked before in boxing and it would work again. But the home man has to be good enough to play his part, and Marsh had been up to it.

'You can protect a fighter to a certain stage,' says Barry Hearn, 'but there comes a time when you have to throw him in the deep end, and that was the case with Marsh. There he was, undefeated, and he was put in against the world champion. But what was surprising is that he won. You have lots of situations with fighters when you don't know really how good they are. Marsh's battle with Manley was really one that shocked a lot of people.'

Frank Warren had a world champion after six years of battling for supremacy with Mickey Duff and Terry Lawless. 'Terry and I have a close personal relationship,' he said. 'If he wanted to pack it in today, I would respect his wishes. Whatever he wants to do will be his decision, and he will have my full support.'

Comparing fighters of different weights and eras is always difficult. But it is safe to say that compared to the best British world champions of the last 20 years, Marsh was rather limited. He was not as impressive a fighter as Ken Buchanan, John Conteh, Maurice Hope, Lloyd Honeyghan, Barry McGuigan, John H. Stracey or Jim Watt. But he was as good as Charlie Magri, or Dave McAuley and probably, if pound for pound comparisons are worth anything, better than Dennis Andries, Nigel Benn, Cornelius Boza Edwards, Chris Eubank or Glen McCrory.

'I wasn't the greatest fighter this country has ever produced, but I was one of the cleverest,' says Marsh. He was never the type of boxer to scream and boast about what he was going to do to his opponent. His preparation would begin by convincing himself he was entering the ring with the real threat of losing his unbeaten record. 'I'd form an image in my mind of someone far superior who I was actually fighting, and I thought the better the opponent, the more I'm going to get bashed up and hurt, which in turn stimulated more adrenalin and fear, which made me train even harder.'

Marsh knew he did not possess the one attribute for which every fighter yearns: a knock-out punch. And yet perversely, this may have helped him. There are boxers, and Frank Bruno was one, who do not need to work on their technique because if they get in to trouble in a fight, they can finish their opponent in one glorious, decisive moment. But they tend to find that as they near the top of their profession, they come up against men who can withstand everything that is thrown at them. It is then that the years of not really learning to box, to move around the ring, and to defend oneself, catch up with them.

Marsh used everything else he had – his balance, speed, flexibility, stamina, guts and intelligence to maximum effect to compensate for his weakness. For a man who did not have a big punch, and who cut easily, Terry Marsh was some fighter. He gave several charged-up performances, reaching an intensity that some boxers never manage, and which others achieve once but cannot replicate. The early years when he was small for his age, when he used to get in to street fights in the East End defending his elder brother Jimmy against bigger boys, when he was denied his rightful place in the Moscow Olympic team, when he had to leave the Marines because he did not have enough qualifications to become an officer, only to get them and find out the standard had been raised, have never quite left Marsh. There was an anger in him, a competitiveness, an extraordinary desire to prove his manhood to himself.

'My competitiveness is always against myself,' he says. 'It's a bit like a runner running against the clock. In boxing the opponent had to metamorphose in to that clock. I know it sounds a bit surreal, but I can justify it in my own mind. After I'd won it wasn't a feeling of elation, but smugness. I'd feel very smug that I'd defied the odds yet again.'

The feeling of camaraderie with ex-opponents, common among many fighters who feel a deep, inarticulated respect for men whom they have fought with, whose blood they have felt on their own body, whom they have finally embraced after a fight, surrounded and separated from the noise and lights all around them, is not a feeling Marsh experiences.

'I'm not in touch with any of my old opponents. They're just rungs on a ladder, and once they're past, that's it. I get a little embarrassed if I see one of them. If I've beaten him it seems I'm superior to him, which is ridiculous, because it doesn't make me a better person than them by any stretch of the imagination, but I'm judging them by my own standards. If it was someone who'd beaten me I'd always feel in their shadow. I'd want to get a rematch or compete again in one way or another.'

In March 1987, it looked as though Marsh might be able to hang around at the top for a while. His career had reached unexpected peaks while avoiding any boxing-style controversy. Drinking, assaults, drugs, night clubs, crashing cars – you name it, he wasn't doing it. Marsh was the perfect advertisement for British boxing, and a weapon against the British Medical Association's view that it should be banned. It was as if he breezed almost cheerfully through life, accepting disappointments when they came, and grasping any opportunity that arose. There were none of those bust-ups with his manager that often occur when a fighter is kept waiting for his big payday. He and Frank seemed to have a good working relationship. They did not pretend to be like brothers, they kept their distance, but they could have a joke together. Frank could always rely on Terry to make the weight.

'He never cheated on his training,' says Ernie Fossey, 'and it's hard. Sometimes he'd come in after a weekend looking a bit tired, and I'd say "what's up?" He would have run a half-marathon on the Sunday without telling me beforehand. But once he got going, he'd set his mind to what he had to do, and he was brilliant. Mentally, he was too strong for most fighters; and he became a better puncher as he got older.'

'Terry was good at publicity and always thinking up ideas,' says Mike Miller. 'He used to go out selling his own tickets. He was a promoter's dream, well, almost; if he'd had a big punch, he would have been a promoter's dream.'

In a world marked by acrimony, jealousy, financial squabbles, and unreliability, Marsh seemed above it all. A bit of a Mr Clean, it was almost as if he was trading on his ordinariness: a hometown boy, who lived 10 minutes from his parents, a husband and father, but also a boxer who could cope with the best when called upon. But a man, nevertheless, who would be found coming out of the fire station in the early hours as opposed to being seen leaving Stringfellows.

Marsh's cleancut image extended to his local community. As a member of an athletic club, Pitsea Roadrunners, he used to run to raise money for charity. His consciousness alerted by his elder brother's condition, he was involved with Ashleigh Centre, a place for mentally handicapped people, whose appeal he set up in 1985. He would dress up as Father Christmas for the children there. He gave up his world title boots to be auctioned for muscular dystrophy. In May 1987 he was awarded an RSPCA medal after rescuing nine trapped horses from freezing mud, as part of his fireman's duties.

A local Labour councillor Dave Marks, who has known Marsh since he was a teenager, and who signed his papers, first for the Marines and then the fire brigade, recalls, 'if we were walking down the street, he would always be stopping. Not just to say hello, but to talk to people. I used to have to say, "Come on, Terry, or we're never going to bloody get there." '

The town named their sports centre after him. Just three days before his fight with Manley he was out in Basildon town centre collecting for the Fireman's Benevolent Fund. Basildon's Number One Son, the evening paper called him.

A few months later on 1 July 1987, Marsh was back in the ring to defend his title against a Japanese boxer, Akio Kameda. Kameda was ranked at number 8 and had 27 wins out of 30. He was 31 years old, and it was considered that Warren had found his fighter a relatively straightforward first defence of the title. Marsh topped the bill at the Royal Albert Hall.

It was at this time that Dr Ray Watson, Chairman of Natural Vitality, a health care company co-sponsoring the fight said: 'He [Marsh] has the characteristics of a physiological freak. His heart rate at rest is only 32 beats a minute – about half of anyone else, and he also takes in about double the normal amount of oxygen.'

Things did not go to plan against Kameda. Marsh won the first round convincingly enough but then received a deep cut in the second after a clash of heads, and it appeared he would lose his title. After another clash in round three, blood was streaming into his eye, impairing his ability to see his opponent's punches. But he stepped up his performance. Kameda could not stop the champion from coming forward throwing punches with both hands. In round six Kameda slumped to the floor and took a count of eight. At the end of the round the tough challenger from Japan was so disorientated that he staggered to a neutral corner instead of his own, leaning over the ropes in confusion and exhaustion. The referee stopped the contest. Terry Marsh had broken another heart. 'Mr Clean's' star was rising.

Clinton McKenzie still seems a little shocked by it all. 'Marsh came from nowhere. He had a couple of fights and all of a sudden he was the man. When I fought him I'd been going 10 years and never really got recognised.'

'Terry Marsh used to get pushed to his limits in boxing,' says Frank Maloney, 'and the few times when a fighter went close, Terry could dig deeper than anybody would think.'

'His popularity really only came after the world title,' says Barry Hearn, 'and with his gutsy performance [against Kameda], when he got cut and carried on. At that stage he was probably capable of being built up in to a national hero. He was at that point and there was a void in terms of stars, and then all that other nonsense happened.'

CHAPTER NINE

Things Fall Apart

The Wolfman knocked at the door. Terry Marsh answered. Neil Wallis, a reporter from the *Sun*, given his nickname on account of his broad frame and bushy beard, was calling at Marsh's ordinary, 1950s, semi-detached house in Basildon new town to conduct an interview. Wallis wasn't to know he would walk out a couple of hours later with a story that ended Marsh's career as a boxer.

A few days earlier Wallis had received a tip-off about Terry and Jacqui having marital problems, had phoned Terry and put it to him. Marsh instantly began thinking of the implications. He knew he could string the *Sun* along, and then, if they got their facts wrong, or exaggerated them, he would have no qualms about suing them. But thinking about it a little more, Marsh told Wallis that if he really wanted an exclusive story, he could have one – at a price. Terms were thrashed out. Marsh was to receive a five-figure sum on condition that he did not speak to any other newspaper. A deal was struck, but there were a few days before the story went out.

The next week Terry Marsh and Frank Warren went to Thames Studios in Tottenham Court Road where a press conference was held to announce that the world champion was to begin working as a ringside commentator on Warren's televised boxing show, *Seconds Out*. The two men were in good spirits, photographed together with a microphone and head-phones – Marsh dressed in a suit but with gloves on – playfully sticking a fist on his manager's chin.

Terry had a bit of charisma and ITV were happy to start

involving him in their shows, initially paying him £6,000 for 12 programmes. 'He was a good talker and a nice personality,' says Bob Burrows, of Thames. 'He had a lot of potential as a television star. He was launched here, in commentary terms, as the new Henry Cooper.'

A campaign was mapped out for Marsh. Burrows and Warren saw him having a couple more IBF defences and then going for another title against a champion from another commission. ITV would follow him all the way in what would be a series of money spinning ventures. Then he would retire gracefully, and slip in to television, where he would have already had some experience.

'I don't think Terry quite appreciated what people were trying to do for him, whether it was television or Frank Warren, which is why it's all so sad,' said Burrows.

Marsh had come back from the brink of defeat in his last fight, and was at the peak of his popularity. He had often mentioned how he would like to get out at the top. But after beating Joe Manley he said, 'At 29 I could easily think about retiring. But I owe it to my manager Frank Warren to defend the title at least once.' He had done that. It is relatively easy to be philosophical about boxing, to talk about ending it all. But how many fighters really finish at their peak? The world championship brought a higher profile than before, more adulation, and even greater respect. Marsh had always had an equivocal relationship with the sport, saying once, 'I hate it, and I love it, and I can't wait until I've finished with it.'

Had he ever thought he would get so far? He was there, a champion who had defended his title; the money was on the table for a fight against Frankie Warren. Alternatively there had been talk of a fight with a Puerto Rican boxer, Hector 'Macho' Camacho, for which a purse of half a million dollars for Marsh alone had been mentioned. Terry Marsh had become a lord of the ring. And yet despite exceeding almost everybody's expectations, he had never had a big night against a really renowned opponent to prove how good he had become. He seemed to want this. If the price was right. One last fight before retiring and concentrating on being a fireman. He spent the rest of the summer pondering his future and by September a second defence looked imminent.

A few days after the Thames press conference, on Sunday, 13 September, Marsh left St Pancras Amateur Boxing Club and went to his trainer Ernie Fossey's house in Potters Bar, Hertfordshire, where he met Frank Warren. Rightly or wrongly, Marsh had been anticipating more money that he had eventually received for beating Manley, which was £30,665, inclusive of VAT. The trainer's fee of £2,500 was the only deduction.

'I felt pissed off with him after the world title fight and I signed the receipts M. Mouse.' For his defence against Akio Kameda, Marsh's purse was £146,667. After deductions for managerial and training fees, sparring partners, and IBF and Board of Control taxes, he collected a net payment of £94,532.

'I only wanted to fight again for $500,000,' says Marsh, 'which at the time was £350,000. I was not going to compromise myself for anything less. The only chance of getting that was if the contest went to purse offers [a situation where a number of promoters bid for the right to stage the fight]. The deadline was on the Monday. Lo and behold the day before Frank arranged to meet me. I thought he had got wind of the *Sun* story, so I thought I'd tell him about it.'

But Warren knew nothing about the newspaper deal. He had a contract for Marsh to defend his title against the number one contender, an American called, just to be difficult, Frankie Warren. Marsh was to receive £157,000 gross, from which deductions would also be made. It was by far his biggest payday. But it was still nowhere near the price Marsh believed, as an unbeaten champion, he was worth.

'He came in and slapped a contract in front of me for $250,000, and it fell in to place why he wanted to see me, because of the deadline. But it just wasn't enough money; so I thought OK, you're going to get a surprise in the morning, and I never told him about the story in the *Sun*.'

For half a day Warren thought the fight was going ahead. He would promote the show in December, was looking forward to a big night, and a chance to become better known across the

Atlantic with the American promoters. Fossey was also excited, and stood to earn around £15,000, which would have been the most he had ever taken from a single fight. 'Terry signed it at my house, and I haven't seen him since that day,' says Fossey.

'I was resigned to not fighting again,' admits Marsh, 'so even if there had been purse bids I wouldn't have fought. But Frank wasn't to know that. As far as he was concerned he was trying to fob me off with a contract for a quarter of a million dollars.'

But then came the *Sun* for which Marsh was paid far less than he would have received for fighting Frankie Warren, but caused more of a sensation than he had ever managed in the ring.

The *Sun*'s front page for the first edition on Monday, 14 September, read JACKO THE £100 MILLION MAN, and told how rich pop star Michael Jackson was to become after his marathon world tour. Hardly big news. But this was simply a dummy story, an old Fleet Street trick, to stop rivals the *Daily Mirror* and *Daily Star* from cashing in and printing a spoiler. Although it is only four years ago, the story and the whole tone of the paper already seem quaintly old-fashioned. Thatcher boasts about going on for ten more years, 'Dirty Den' from *EastEnders* rules the pages, and Gazza has not yet been invented. A *Sun* reader delights at how he has made £50,000 simply by selling his council flat in Croydon. Marsh made £25,000 for selling his story, and a further sum for what he desribed as on-going news items.

The headline in the later editions read: WORLD CHAMP TERRY HAS EPILEPSY. Just 76 days after he had successfully defended his title against Akio Kameda, Terry Marsh had retired from boxing because of epilepsy, with the *Sun* claiming that he had hidden the fact for two years.

The story told how he would never be able to fight again, and that, following one of the most closely-guarded secrets ever in boxing, Marsh was facing the biggest battle of his life, as his career as a fireman was also almost certainly over.

The following day Marsh claimed in the paper that his first blackout took place in 1985 while he was having a Chinese meal with his wife and a couple of close friends. 'I slumped over the table and all hell broke loose. When I came round my wife Jacqui was sobbing her heart out and the waiters were panicking. A mate was trying to revive me. I felt absolutely nothing – it was as if someone had snipped a five-second slice out of my life. My first thought was: how will this affect my boxing? I made my best pal swear to tell no one. Whatever it was, I couldn't put my boxing career and job as a fireman at risk. So I made myself burst out laughing and pretended it was all a practical joke. Because I'd pulled stupid pranks before – I once had Jacqui in tears on holiday when I faked a drowning – she believed me.'

Marsh said he had promised his friend he would go to a hospital but hadn't. 'I had just won the European title. The good money purses were starting to come my way, there was talk of a world title shot. There was no way I was going to risk anything jeopardising that.'

He admitted that in 1986 he had suffered an attack. 'Before the Manley fight I kept putting the brain scan off, but eventually was forced to go through with it . . . in July 1987 I was driving through Basildon minutes after dropping my daughter Kelly off when another attack started. Luckily it wasn't a busy road, and I was able to pull over safely. I was just a heart's beat away from passing out. I knew it was serious this time, so I went to see my GP.'

Jacqui Marsh also appeared in the paper under the headline SEE A DOCTOR OR I'LL LEAVE YOU. It was claimed she had given an ultimatum to her husband after he'd had a fit in a department store, which had left their daughter Kelly asking, 'Is my daddy dead, is my daddy dead?'

Typically the *Sun* provided some light-relief, explaining epilepsy to their readers. It claimed that Napoleon, Julius Caesar, and Socrates had all suffered from the same problem as poor old Tel.

The story damaged the credibility of the sport and reinforced prejudices against it. Marsh had showed a lack of regard for the reputation of boxing in Britain. What kind of medical procedures could have allowed Marsh to slip through the net? Needless to say, the newspaper failed to mention that most epileptic sufferers' conditions cannot be diagnosed from brain scans.

But it was not simply the contents of the article that precipitated the rows, the breakdown of the Marsh-Warren relationship and the end of Marsh's cast-iron credibility – it was the manner in which the seemingly incorruptible, seasoned fighter had conducted his affairs. Even if selling the story exclusively to a tabloid without informing his manager or trainer of his intentions did make financial sense, it was not a gentlemanly way of going about things. It was not Terry Marsh's style.

The story did not show Frank Warren in a flattering light. It implied he had acquiesced in allowing an unfit fighter to box. Warren read the story over breakfast at his office in Tavistock Place. He kept saying to Mike Miller, 'But we've just signed the deal for the next fight, we just signed it – what is all this?' He said later, 'Terry's defence was to have been in London in December. At 3pm he signed for it, but the contract is now just a piece of toilet paper.' The story dominated the papers and television for days.

Warren's first instinct was that his fighter had been ripped off. 'They [the *Sun*] have told me the terms they have agreed with Terry, and I have told them those were not satisfactory and I could not stand by and see Terry short-changed after all we have been through in boxing. Accordingly, I asked for an extra £10,000, and they have agreed. As normal, I do not take, nor have taken, any part of his earnings outside the ring. I hope this will help Terry in the months ahead.'

Warren's life was continuing in much the same way as always – fixing up fights, battling with the press. The pressure he put on the *Sun* was the last thing Frank Warren ever did for Terry Marsh. Their working relationship was over. However, Warren was not yet finished with the *Sun*, and sued, claiming the articles had implied he had known of Marsh's condition and still allowed him to box. At the end of the year he received £40,000 in an out-of-court settlement, plus a printed apology. He also won damages from the *Sunday Express* magazine, which had repeated the libel.

It is unlikely the *Sun* were too concerned about the pay-out to

Warren. They had outdone their rivals with the biggest boxing scandal for years. After running it for three days they switched to another story, claiming Scotland Yard wanted to see their 'file' on singer Elton John's 'rent boys'. It was a disastrous move. They were never able to prove their story, they lost circulation, printed a front page apology, and gave the singer one million in an out-of-court settlement. The articles had been written by Neil Wallis among others. He later became the paper's features editor.

The events leading up to Marsh's deal in September 1987 are strange, even by the standards of boxing. They are strewn with coincidences, contradictions and confusion. On 29 June 1987, two days before his title defence, Terry Marsh filled in a medical examination form, which is obligatory under British Boxing Board of Control regulations. To a question about whether he had suffered at anytime from headaches, blackouts, or fits, he answered no.

In August, in a characteristic charity outing, he went on a walk to help raise money for a five-year-old boy, Andrew Smith, who came from a village called Ramsden Heath, where one of the firemen Marsh worked with lived. Andrew suffered from a form of epilepsy and had the mind and impulses of a 15-month-old toddler. Next month, Marsh announced that he was prepared to defend his title for £350,000 against Camacho. He also approached his GP for a medical certificate because he needed to take a heavy goods vehicle driving test as part of his job in the fire brigade. He told his doctor that he had suffered blackouts and was referred to a consultant, Dr Leslie Findley, at Harold Wood Hospital, in Essex.

Dr Findley says Marsh was a very straightforward patient. 'He seemed keen to sort things out. I think it was really his wife who had made him come. She seemed terrified.'

Marsh told him he had been suffering from blackouts, fits, and had once wet himself. On the basis of this consultation, Findley diagnosed the condition as epilepsy. 'They were not just minor conditions either, he had had a major collapse.'

Terry Marsh, the boxer, the ex-marine turned fireman, was in trouble. There are more than 300,000 people in Britain who suffer from epilepsy, but Marsh had more to lose than most of them, both financially and emotionally. It is a condition which has not been able to free itself from prejudice and superstition. It is linked in the popular mind to violence and madness, to mystical or demonic powers. Yet it is a physical and not a psychological condition. In medical terms it is defined as an occasional excessive and disorderly discharge of nervous activity.

Dr Simon Shorvon, medical director of the National Society for Epilepsy, and a consultant neurologist at Queens Hospital, London, said: 'During an epileptic attack the brain acts in a peculiar fashion on a transient basis. There is difficulty with diagnosis because it is based on the patient's own account, plus those of witnesses, of their attacks, and the doctor will be on the look-out for characteristic patterns of behaviour. Most patients will be perfectly normal between seizures. There is no test which you can give which provides a yes or no answer. An EEG test [which measures the brain's electrical activity] is not absolutely conclusive. Marsh's EEG test was clear. There are many different types of the illness. But putting it simply, with around 50 per cent of sufferers the whole brain will be affected during an attack. The rest suffer from less serious partial seizures.'

These two kinds of epilepsy are referred to as *grand mal* and *petit mal*. It is the symptoms of the former which have helped to surround the illness in mystery. Dr Adrian Whiteson, chief medical adviser to the British Boxing Board of Control described them. 'With *grand mal*,' he said, 'the victim feels an aura, a strange sound or smell occurs. Then they lapse into unconsciousness, and shake, frothing at the mouth, before falling to the ground and then sleep.'

He spoke from his consultancy rooms in Wimpole Street, London, an unlikely place to be discussing boxing. However, Dr Whiteson works as a medical consultant to boxing authorities all over the world. He is a GP, who with the help of specialists, sets the medical parameters for boxing. Unpaid by the Board, he is a medical magistrate, making decisions based on other people's opinions. He makes no bones about simply being a GP, but points to 26 years experience in boxing. Dr Whiteson is bound to annoy people from time to time because he is at the centre of a perpetual conflict between commercial and medical considerations.

'*Petit mal,*' he says, 'is just a momentary change in consciousness.' As far as he is concerned, Marsh's symptoms indicated *petit mal*. When he underwent an electrical tracing of the brain, in which images of the brain are examined under X-ray, his scan was normal.

'It is impossible to prove by brain tests whether Marsh has epilepsy,' said Dr Whiteson. 'All we can go on is what he has told doctors. In Findley's opinion, based on what the patient had confessed to him, Marsh suffered from momentary changes of consciousness. He told Dr Findley he was going vacant, pale, and stopping midway through conversations. These episodes, which he described, and which his wife had witnessed, were clearly a change in his mental state.'

While this does not have a devastating effect on most people's lives, it does for a boxer. Dr Whiteson explained: 'If you are in a ring and you have a momentary loss or change in consciousness, and you don't see a punch coming, you could be in real trouble. It's bad enough when you do. If you have an underlying brain problem to start with, and you take punches around the head, it's going to make it worse.'

What is very clear is that Marsh had decided he was going to take a break from boxing. But he wasn't going to go quietly, or unrewarded. He has an acute awareness of how to attract publicity. Barry Hearn says, 'Marsh was always thinking in terms of publicity and PR. I remember once he came to see me at my office with his solicitor. He said, "Oh, I've worked it all out, how to get in the public eye. I was being interviewed the other day, and I fell off this brick wall half way through the interview on purpose because I knew it would get in *It'll be Alright on the Night*." I thought, this guy's crazy. But he was right, it was on that programme, and you could see him just lean back and throw himself off.'

Chris Horrie, co-author of *Stick It Up Your Punter: The Rise and Fall of the Sun* says Marsh belonged to the *Sun*, even though no contract was signed. 'He was part of an established process. The paper saw him, in part, as a *Sun*-created hero. Celebrities and sportsmen are spotted fairly early, after initial success, and then turned in to characters in the soap operas created within the pages of the paper. The tabloids feel they have to be seen by their readers to be friends with celebrities – the *Sun* going out with the stars. The characters picked up are not usually megastars – David Bowie, Paul McCartney, or Mike Tyson – but second division ones like Bros or Terry Marsh. The paper has always identified with Marsh – a white champion. They used him to hand out competition prizes or give his opinion on up and coming fights. It worked, but as usually happens, the *Sun* began to tire of their "hero".'

For years Terry Marsh's public persona had been that of the witty, tough, down-to-earth guy, who did not take his fame very seriously. A man who fought to earn a few bob on the side for his family, and who had little expectation of much else. But more recently he had sometimes seemed to be more ambitious. The boy who had shown early promise as a chess champion and was accepted by Westminster City School now seemed to be revealing again a complexity that had gone underground in the intervening years. It was as if he was belatedly trying to assert a claim to be one of life's leaders – a role which the young uncommissioned marine, the fireman and the boxer had not been able to fulfil.

As Marsh needed an HGV licence for work and could not get the medical certificate unless he kept quiet about his attacks, he must have been aware that his time at the fire brigade was running out, and that if they made him redundant on health grounds, he would lose his boxing licence. This would explain why he suddenly seems to have bared all to the *Sun* on the verge of his biggest ever payday. If he hadn't, Essex County Fire Brigade would have, and he wouldn't have made any money out of it. 'If I'd been working for myself I wouldn't have told any one about the epilepsy, but I did have an obligation to the other firemen I was working with. This was the dilemma I faced. I could have just retired from the fire brigade and told no one about the epilepsy. But if I'd done that, they would have said "as soon as he got a few pennies, all that crap about how he liked his job was bullshit, now he's got a few bob he's given the fire brigade the elbow." I resent the suggestions that I knew about the epilepsy for two years because it suggests I was putting my colleagues at risk.'

This is his explanation as to why he did not sell his story until after the next, most lucrative fight. He denies there was real pressure from the *Sun* to provide them with something. 'They were just lucky coming to the door at the right time with the story about me and the wife.' Maybe the *Sun* knew, somehow, more than they should? Or perhaps Marsh felt that sudden, temporary retirement was the only way he could free himself from Frank Warren, who as a manager had done well for Marsh, but who as promoter had become inconvenient?

'There is no logic in boxing,' says Colin Hart, the *Sun*'s chief boxing writer. 'He may have wanted money desperately or quickly. There could have been all kinds of theories. But if you want logic from people in boxing – you can forget it.'

However, this was not just any boxer telling a strange story. This was Marsh, one of boxing's honest men, admitting he had lied on medical certificates. He had confounded his admirers. Even in Basildon, where he was worshipped, there were murmurings of discontent about his behaviour that days before would have been regarded as heresy. This was a new Terry Marsh, and the beginning of a very different stage in his life.

Once again, it was Maisie Marsh who spoke up for her son, just as she had when he had missed Olympic selection seven years before. Speaking to the *Basildon Evening Echo*, which in a leader article accused her son of having let people down, she said, 'He walked out of the specialist's office with the diagnosis and knew all the doors were closed to him from that moment. Terry conned no one.'

Replying to criticisms that he had failed to tell his colleagues at Tilbury Fire Station she answered: 'Two weeks before the announcement Terry signed on the sick. He covered himself and did not have to put the lives of colleagues at risk.'

'It's a great shock,' said Terry's father Jimmy, 'but I'm not surprised he kept it to himself. That's the way he is. He is a very sensible, responsible man.'

For Terry Marsh everything was over. Once he had told his story, he was just another ex-world champion, and after enquiries by the county medical officer, he wasn't a fireman any longer either.

For any professional sportsman the end is not an easy thing to cope with. It comes at such a relatively early stage in their lives, usually in their early to mid-thirties when other people are maybe on the verge of making a breakthrough. The big media attention, the spine-tingling ovations and the rigorous routine that sport brings to a person's life are almost impossible to replicate in any other activity.

Marsh had hinted in June that he would miss the ring. 'Boxing is the ultimate test,' he said. 'Pitting your will against the opponent. When the other fella gets through, your life is on the line. The adrenalin is immense, like being in a cage with a lion.'

He worked for a while as a model for a mail order catalogue and bought a couple of betting shops in Gants Hill and Romford with his brother John. 'There is lots of wheeling and dealing in boxing. Now I am glad I am out of it,' he said. 'Perhaps the epilepsy has saved me from being conned.' But anyone who imagined that he'd just slip away to run a pub, with black-and-white pictures of his fighting days over the bar, and perhaps a couple of small hall fighters to train in his spare time, was mistaken.

Everything Marsh has done since his retirement has been characterised by an air of uncertainty. For the rest of 1987 he remained a topic of conversation in boxing circles, for annoying and verbally attacking Frank Warren. After their relationship collapsed, Warren wanted Marsh banned as a ringside commentator on *Seconds Out*. Marsh worked on three programmes, but his contract was then cancelled and he was replaced by Barry McGuigan. In December Marsh turned up at a show at the

National Sports Centre in Cardiff disguised as Father Christmas and accompanied by a man claiming to be his lawyer. He went up to an ITV producer at ringside, removed his beard and posed in front of his lawyer – who turned out to be a *Sun* photographer. After he started taking pictures of Marsh, a scuffle broke out and both men were thrown out.

A bemused Frank Warren said: 'Terry now seems to be determined to destroy everything he has built up in boxing and I don't want any part of it.'

In November, Marsh spoke out at a boxing writers' club lunch. When he was asked what changes he would like to see in boxing, he said he wanted managers and promoters to be separated, and that the boxer-manager contract should be revised in the boxer's favour. He claimed he'd only earned £10,000 for his first four years as a professional boxer and that his fighters were treated as 'slaves' by their managers if contracts were taken to the letter. 'The way things are now boxers can't pick their noses without their manager's permission.' This was reported on the front page of *Boxing News*.

Warren invited the paper's editor Harry Mullan to look at his accounts for Terry Marsh. 'Everything was receipted by Marsh in his own handwriting,' says Mullan. 'There was no dispute. It established that Marsh had earned £250,000 from his 27 professional fights. Considering he was never a big commercial attraction I thought it was phenomenal money.

The receipts indicated that for a British final eliminator against Tony Sinnott and for the British title fight against McKenzie, Marsh received a total of £9,472. For the final fight of the four year span for which he said he earned £10,000, the accounts indicated he received £6,000 for defeating Alessandro Scapecci for the vacant European title.

Marsh replied in January, and explained, among other things, that he had meant he had earned £10,000 net, and not gross. Marsh's own figures were significantly lower than the ones signed by him and submitted by Warren.

Marsh also alleged that Warren's managerial deductions were

quoted in *Boxing News* without including the VAT payments that the boxer normally pays. 'That makes my purse appear far greater than it in fact was,' said Marsh, 'and the managerial percentage lower than it really was.'

Percentages figure prominently in boxing purses and are often a source of disagreement. A major bone of contention, and one which may have finally ended the relationship between the two men, was whether or not Warren had promised to pay £22,000 VAT that was outstanding on the Kameda fight.

Amid the arguments about what, exactly, Marsh got paid, one sentence in *Boxing News* stands out: 'My gross earnings were almost £250,000.' Well what would you expect after winning the British, European and world title, not to mention successful defences of the latter two titles. It begs the question, why did he not take issue with Warren earlier? However, once Terry Marsh has made up his mind about something, he is incredibly stubborn. If he believed he hadn't been getting enough money, it would have been virtually impossible for anyone to persuade him otherwise.

'No one ever knows the whole truth about money,' says John Robinson. 'Accounts mean little. You have to be there at the time. All sorts of things get promised such as money for tickets, and training expenses. Maybe Frank made promises he didn't keep? Yet I can never remember Terry complaining at the time.'

It is not difficult to understand Warren's annoyance with his former fighter. Boxing dissipates friendships as swiftly as a champion at his peak dispenses with challengers, and the classic boxing relationship which breaks up is that between a manager and a fighter. By tradition the fighter is a straightforward, honest human being, who has been exploited by his calculating, self-seeking manager. This is a picture that Marsh has tried to peddle. But in his case it just does not work. There is unanimous agreement, among neutral observers, experts and even enemies of Frank Warren, that Warren did a very good job for Marsh.

'These days you could fill Wembley Arena with people who hate Frank Warren,' jokes Frank Maloney, 'but to give Frank his due, he did well with him. Terry had a unique but successful

1. The men Frank Warren had to take on as a promoter (clockwise):
Jarvis Astaire, Mickey Duff, Mike Barrett, Terry Lawless.

2. Frank Warren circa 1977 at a topless pool tournament at a north London pub to raise money for local charities.

3. Warren, boxing promoter and businessman, a few months after he was shot in November 1989.

4. The good times between Frank and Terry, plus Errol Christie, once Warren's brightest prospect.

5. Barry McGuigan united all Ireland as he became a world champion but never recovered from his fight in the desert.

6. Frank Bruno, Britain's most popular fighter in the 1980s, gave it everything in training, but could never live with top American opponents.

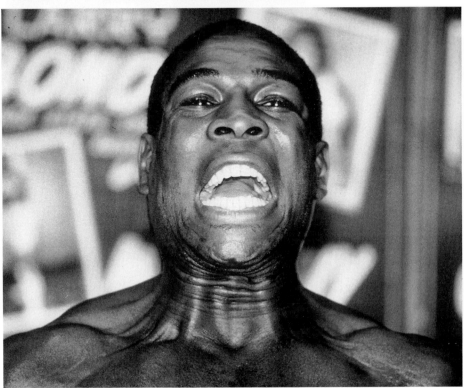

7. Terry Marsh near to collapse but victorious
after winning the British title.

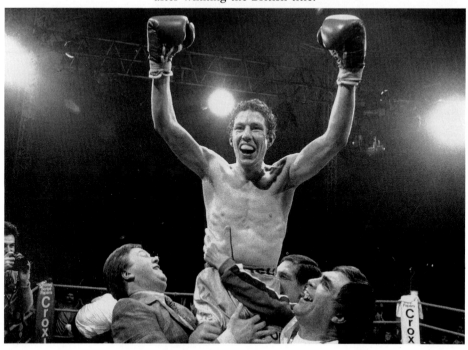

8. And the greatest night of his life . . .
winning the world title.

9. Frank Warren ties the knot with Sue Cox, with brother Robert and friend in attendance.

10. Frank Warren, best man to Ambrose Mendy, 1985.

11. Barry Hearn –
'I will monopolise British boxing.'
He is well on the way.

12 and 13. Boxing's car boys show off their style . . . Frank Warren outside the London Arena with his Bentley, Nigel Benn and Ambrose Mendy sitting on the Porsche.

14. Terry Marsh, the actor, on the set of the ill-fated *Tank Malling*.

15. Terry Marsh on his way to magistrates court,
charged with the attempted murder of Frank Warren.

16. Ecstasy for Chris Eubank, despair for Nigel Benn,
as he losses his world title.

style, yes. But he wasn't a remarkable fighter. He wasn't too popular with fans at first. People used to come to see him partly because it was Terry Marsh and partly because they knew of Frank Warren. And then Terry began to catch on.'

Jon Robinson said: 'Sometimes becoming a world champion is not merely about how good you are, but the chances you get, and Warren worked hard so that Terry got those chances.'

'He was a decent fighter without ever being remotely top class,' said Ken Jones, of the *Independent*, 'and you have to credit Warren for taking a moderate fighter to a world title fight and winning.'

'Terry had a fantastic deal boxing-wise,' says Barry Hearn, 'and for what he achieved, he got well paid.'

There have, however, been suggestions that as Warren diversified his business interests during the 1980s, he ignored many of the people who had helped him on the way up, and became more remote. Lawrence Lustig, the photographer, who has worked with both men, believes there was a gradual but steady breakdown in communication. 'You could say that the way their relationship soured was symptomatic of Warren at that time – losing touch with many of his old boxing allies. In those days when he was after as much publicity as possible we were in touch constantly. Now I cannot get hold of him. Robinson, Mendy, Mike Williams, everyone is gone from the original team. Only Ernie Fossey has stayed.'

Warren, it seems, was growing more self-conscious about his money and reputation, and more selective about whom he confided in. He was also becoming richer by the day, and inevitably was a focus for a number of other people's jealousy.

Whatever Marsh was earning, it was far less than Warren, who was living a much more luxurious lifestyle. For when Warren arranged a fight, money from the huge sponsorship revenues of companies like Natural Vitality, who invested in the Kameda defence, was not simply going in to Frank Warren Promotions Ltd. It was also going to the Sports Network company. So while Warren might technically have 'lost' money on a promotion, in practice he was still easily make an overall profit. Fighters resent purses that look good but have a habit of shrinking. There is the manager's cut, the trainer's 10 per cent, the VAT, the tax on the gross. This becomes an obsession with a man who is toiling away in the gym. The fighter, the one who pushes himself to unprecedented limits to reach the perfect balance between weight and fitness, will always have a sense of injustice against the man who seems to make more money than him simply by talking on the telephone or sitting in meetings. While an outstanding VAT payment of £22,000 on the Kameda fight was the catalyst of their disagreement, and the story in the *Sun* its crisis, the underlying causes ran deep.

If Marsh felt patronised by what he had received, it was in the context of what Warren now had. The older, less well-educated man, appeared to be heading for yet greater fortune, while Marsh, at just 29, was nearing the end of his peak earning potential. It was fine for Warren and his television contacts to sit down over lunch together and hatch plans for Marsh; but they did not have to go through it all in the ring.

While all Marsh's earnings came from himself, his boxing and his fire-fighting, Warren had other fighters, and other interests outside the sport. Marsh was just part of the equation – crucial as a symbol of Warren's abilities as a manager and promoter rather than as a foundation of his financial empire. In bigtime boxing, fighting, television, and money come together to form a potent mix. It is a combination that has forced apart many close alliances.

One of Frank Warren's fighters, a former British cruiserweight champion Tee Jay, says, 'Your manager is your livelihood – your life is in his hands. The relationship is underlined by mistrust. The boxer is always thinking, "Is he getting the right fight for me, or is this just one that suits him? And is the money fair?" Basically they do your thinking for you. Your life is in their hands. When they make a decision, you have to take it or not, but basically they make the plans.'

For the first time in their six year association, this ambitious, intelligent pair had divergent ideas about the way they wanted their careers to go.

'By that stage Terry and Frank's relationship was a game of chess,' says Jon Robinson, 'and Terry fucked Frank [by announcing his retirement in the *Sun*] before Frank fucked him in the end. I believe Terry knew he could not beat Buddy McGirt or Frankie Warren. He's a clever boy Terry. He looks at things, not like most fighters – the average boxer would fight King Kong. Terry and Frank were too clever for each other. Warren was on a mission to be the top promoter . . . and wanted Marsh to fight on. But Terry didn't fancy it. And Warren wasn't used to having a boxer as clever as him.'

Marsh had previously been known as a character, a joker, a fitness fanatic and as the most intelligent boxer in Britain; a paradoxical figure. But it is as if his sudden, enforced retirement warped his judgement and made him bitter about some of his achievements. The disappointment that his time at the very top had passed by so quickly, compounded by the end of his career in the fire brigade, made him angry that he had not had full control over his earnings. After all, what did a fighter like him need a manager for, taking his 25 per cent from the purses? A trainer and a promoter might have sufficed.

He also grew reckless as to what he admitted. He finished the year by revealing in a Sunday newspaper that he had backed Joe Manley to win their world title fight. A third party had apparently put on a four-figure stake on the title holder, leaving Marsh with an extra £5,000 if he had lost. He told the *Basildon Evening Echo*: 'It was like going to Lloyds and insuring myself against defeat.'

There was no suggestion of throwing the fight as the rewards were clearly greater to win, not only for the purse, but for the future fights it would ensure. However, the British Boxing Board of Control did not look charitably upon this revelation. Assistant secretary Simon Block said: 'There's nothing in the regulations concerning betting but in cases where a boxer bets against himself, questions must be asked. This would come under misconduct and the penalties vary from a caution to a boxer having his licence taken away.' Of course Marsh, who no longer had a licence, had become exempt from such punishment.

At the beginning of 1988 Jon Robinson, by now working as Vice-President of the International Boxing Federation, called Ambrose Mendy, Frank Maloney and Terry Marsh in to his office in Hackney Road. 'They had all been out of boxing for varying lengths of time and for various reasons, and I felt they could join up and get back in to it. They had flair. The World Sports Corporation was resurrected. My friend Art Pelulo had "Terrible" Tim Witherspoon in the States and wanted to get him work.'

Marsh & Co were able to announce that Witherspoon, a former WBA heavyweight champion who was well known for having beaten Frank Bruno, would be fighting at York Hall, Bethnal Green. A packed house ensured a successful promotional debut for Marsh. But he did not retain his interest in promoting for long.

'Terry was a crusader. He got a manager's licence, and he wanted to use different techniques to manage fighters,' says Maloney. 'But I think Terry needed excitement and it [promoting] wasn't exciting enough for him. We used to talk and joke, as friends do, but really we were on different wavelengths. Terry saw himself as a saviour of fighters – he wanted to involve them more in decision-making – but it's very hard to break traditions in boxing.

'He was always doing other things. He could have brought in a lot of good ideas, been a breath of fresh air in promotion, but he wasn't stable enough. Sometimes he was out of touch with reality, but that was the nice thing about him. I never saw a bad side or violent side. He always had time to talk to people, to sign autographs.'

By May 1988, Terry Marsh was back in search of the limelight, seeking permission to fight again, and beginning an acting career. He began claiming his illness had been mis-diagnosed, suggesting that his blackouts had been caused by a nutritional rather than a neurological problem. After fights he had binged on Mars Bars, eating up to eight at a time. This massive intake of sugar led him to black out, and since he had stopped doing this, his attacks had ceased, he said.

'I love food, I'd have to go without before a fight, and then I'd really binge. Also I'd stop my training, my body clock would alter. I'd be up, late nights, flavour of the month and all that sort of thing, and it's the equivalent of coming from a hot climate to a very cold climate, from high altitude to low altitude in a short period of time. So I went to see Dr Findley, and he said, "No, it's definitely epilepsy, and there's no point having a second opinion." '

However, Marsh was undeterred, and went to see a Dr Fenwick at the Royal Post Graduate school at Hammersmith, who gave an opinion that epilepsy had not been the correct diagnosis.

Marsh submitted this evidence to the British Boxing Board of Control to indicate that he was not an epileptic, including a letter from a Dr David Ryde of Beckenham, whom he consulted at the end of the year. Ryde wrote: 'I saw Terry in December 1988 to review his epilepsy diagnosis. However, to me his story strongly suggested hypoglycemic attacks, brought on by chocolate binges, in which he would consume six to 10 Mars bars at a time. Though I considered the glucose test as largely irrelevant (and provocative) because it could not duplicate the cause, I felt discretion was the wisest course and had the test performed. In the event it was normal, but so far as I am concerned the clinical diagnosis remains as hypoglycemic attacks. Curiously Terry himself felt the trouble might be related to his binges but he kept his thoughts to himself until I gave him my opinion. I have put him on a sensible diet, and he remains well. He is training for his challenge for the European title.'

In February 1989, Marsh had his request for a licence turned down by the Board. 'We had a hearing,' recalls Adrian Whiteson, 'and Terry said that the reason for him having these attacks was that he had a low sugar level and he was gorging and therefore he produced an attack. So the Board carried out an enhanced glucose tolerance test where you starve the subject for eight to 16 hours, then load it with as much sugar as it can take.

Then the blood sugar levels are checked. Terry Marsh's test was absolutely normal. Terry said he ate eight or nine Mars bars,' said Whiteson, 'and they are big things. I marathon run and I can't eat more than two or three. And he said he had eight. The volume would be impossible to get down; and it wouldn't make any difference to body sugar levels as they have their own regulatory mechanisms.'

However, Marsh's statements about his health that he had made back in 1987 were not cast aside as easily as he imagined they would be. For the hearing he brought his own neurologist [Dr Fenwick] who supported him, but at the end of the day, the question posed was, 'Is Terry Marsh, on his own evidence, more at risk of repeat attacks than the average person?' Though neither his brain scan nor his EEG revealed anything abnormal, Marsh had suffered attacks before, and Dr Fenwick said that he was.

Has Terry Marsh ever in fact been epileptic at all? The question remains open. He remains frustrated by the Board's refusal to let him back in the ring. 'There are all these fighters who don't train, who come in late. Some of them would not pass a magnetic resonance tests, which examines cross-sections of the brain.'

Unfortunately, Marsh had not waited to see if he could fight again, but had already spent several thousand pounds on his comeback fight. He had planned it for Basildon, on 4 March 1989, the second anniversary of his world title triumph. His new trainer was Brian Lynch, who at the time was training Nigel Benn.

'Marsh had everything booked,' recalls Lynch, 'a tent in Basildon, posters printed, all that sort of thing . . . he'd laid out the money. I don't know how much deposit he'd put up, but it was quite a lot of money. He was doing it all, that's the way Terry is, and then it all fell apart. He came up to me, and said, we ain't going to be able to do it Brian. And that was the end of Terry.'

But it was not only the comeback that failed. *Tank Malling*, a film about an investigative reporter's fight to uncover a corruption ring, was not a success. Marsh played the part of a bent copper called Curly McGann. It was filmed in the East End and starred two other ex-boxers, Jimmy Batten, a former British light middleweight champion, and former light-heavyweight champion John Conteh. Sean Connery's son Jason played a villain. The distributors went bust and the film never got out on the streets.

'None of us got paid in the end,' said Jimmy Batten, who has also appeared in the Krays' film and is now an actor when he's not a labourer. 'It was a gamble and it didn't come off. If you put Kevin Costner on at the Albert Hall to box you would not fill it. Generally people want to see actors acting and boxers fighting.'

After the highs of 1987, followed by the trauma of his retirement, the two years since the *Sun* story had been very difficult for Marsh. The difficulties in his life increased at the beginning of 1989 when he went on *Midweek Sports Special* on Thames Television as part of his planned comeback. When asked who had known about his epilepsy he replied, 'everyone who needed to know, knew.'

Warren issued a libel writ. As with the *Sun* article, it was claimed Warren had known about the epilepsy and still let him fight. The two men may only have drifted apart, but stood toe-to-toe exchanging legal punches. Mutual respect and need had given way to mistrust, competing ambition, the intimate resentment of one-time allies, and finally, hatred.

Later that year, in March, Jacqui asked Terry to leave. Jacqui was pregnant, and six months afterwards their son Carl was born. Jacqui had said that Terry's personality altered after he appeared in *Tank Malling*. 'The so-called glamour turned his head. He even wanted to call our son Santino after a character in his favourite movie *The Godfather*. I ask you, Santino Marsh from Basildon.' She also claimed the couple were short of money because of her husband's gambling.

Terry Marsh now divided his time between a flat in Wapping and his parents' house. His personal debts were piling up. Terry Marsh Promotions, run by his younger brother John, was not working out, and had debts of around £30,000. Nothing he had undertaken since his public split from Warren – his betting shops, the promoting, his acting, his proposed comeback in the ring – had succeeded. He remains adamant that this was not a difficult time for him. 'I've always got irons in the fire, there's always a contingency plan. I can always go and fight in America.' However, he does admit that he had bigger debts at the end of 1989, than he had had two years before, when he first embarked on a new career away from boxing and the fire service. For the first time in his life, Terry Marsh was not excelling at what he had chosen to do, and, in keeping with late eighties excessiveness, he was spending more money than he was earning. But while it may have been of little comfort to him at the time, he was not the only one.

CHAPTER TEN

The Shooting

Bob Geldof, Paula Yates and an entourage of six pushed through the ringside security cordon to take their seats. Like all good celebrities they were arriving just minutes before the main event, in this case Barry McGuigan's comeback fight. Geldof, embarrassed by the heads turning his way, tried to hide himself behind his Jesus-like locks. Anyone who was anyone was there.

It was 20 April 1988. Frank Warren had persuaded McGuigan, by now absent from the ring for two years, to continue his career under his promotional banner after the legal wrangle with McGuigan's former manager Barney Eastwood was resolved. The atmosphere inside the Alexandra Palace, recently re-opened after a near-devastating fire, was such that occurs only rarely in a British boxing hall – the special intensity of several thousand people sharing a highly charged expectancy of a sporting spectacle, in this case dilated by the fierce partisanship of a crowd dominated by the Irish, to whom McGuigan was a national rather than simply a sporting hero. As he emerged into the arena, the noise swelled to a deafening level sustained throughout his four round win over Nicky Perez.

At ringside Warren watched nervously as McGuigan, now his number one fighter, brawled his way to victory, without ever looking in danger of losing but without looking entirely convincing. Nevertheless, the 'Clones Cyclone' and former world featherweight champion was back. It was a major coup, and a much needed boost after the tribulations with Terry Marsh.

Worries about Marsh must have been a long way from

Warren's mind on such a night, when the main support bout featured another boxer with a dedicated following: Nigel Benn.

The West Ham boxer won the Commonwealth middleweight title against Abdul Amoru Sandu in a fashion living up to his nickname 'The Dark Destroyer'. In a wild flurry of punches he buried his opponent, who looked relieved when the referee stopped the contest in the second round. Dozens of Benn's supporters tried to storm the ring. Just as a few were clammering over the ropes Warren turned and screamed, 'THAT'S ENOUGH'. The intruders backed off. Frank Warren has his shy side, but if necessary can call upon a temper to impose his authority.

After the show Warren entertained at the San Remo Restaurant in Highgate Hill. His regular boxing contacts noticed plenty of new faces. They were introduced to non-boxing people, people from the property world and the City. Things were changing.

McGuigan's next show was also a huge success, cleverly staged by Warren at the football club in Luton, where direct flights from Ireland arrive. McGuigan won well. But problems beset his following bout in early 1989 against an Argentine, Julio Miranda. Following objections by the local borough, the fight had to be moved from Mudchute Farm in the Isle of Dogs, to Pickett's Lock in Edmonton, a hall holding only 2,000 for the biggest draw in boxing. It was like Arsenal playing at Barnet. Warren faced his biggest ever loss, of £120,000. McGuigan was unhappy at boxing there and nearly lost the fight, only his big heart carrying him through.

The cracks in Warren's boxing operation opened by Marsh's untimely retirement were widening. By now, he had already lost for the first time in a legal battle with the British Boxing Board of Control. The International Boxing Federation had declared its world title fights would remain at 15 rounds, whereas the other governing bodies had reduced theirs to 12; the Board had followed suit, for medical reasons, declaring all fights under its aegis should be at the lower number of rounds. It threatened to outlaw the contest between Tony Sibson and the American Frank Tate for the IBF middleweight title by withdrawing its officials if Warren went ahead with a 15-rounder. The promoter responded with an attempt to get a High Court injunction to force the Board to approve the fight. It failed. The fight went ahead at 12 rounds.

Having lost what had been his main prize-fighting asset in Marsh, Warren could scarcely afford to lose another. But the night before the show at Luton, when he was due to fight the main support bout, Nigel Benn walked out on Warren. Benn was dissatisfied with the purses he had been getting from Warren and the quality of his opposition. 'Herol Graham, Michael Watson – those are the fights I really want. That's what the British public wants. Value for money – not these Yanks nobody's heard of. I really want to get on,' the fighter said at a press conference. On either side of him were the solicitor Henri Brandman and Ambrose Mendy, his new agent.

Benn issued a writ against Warren, and called for an investigation into sums of money allegedly due to him. Warren issued a counter writ for breach of a managerial contract and loss of earnings, claiming he was due a percentage of all Benn earned since his departure. After three years, the case had still to be heard. The whole business would have been far simpler were it not for the legal fog that surrounds the Board of Control's manager-fighter contract, the biggest single source of disputes in boxing. The contract, normally signed for three years, appears to make a chattel out of the fighter – the manager can release him whenever he wishes, the boxer can't go if he chooses. If the boxer wins a championship, the manager can automatically renew the contract. But as the Board has no statutory power, it has been questioned whether the contract is worth the paper it is written on in terms of the law.

In February 1989 the Court of Appeal refused to award an injunction sought by Warren attempting to restrain Mendy from acting as Benn's adviser and compelling the boxer to perform under his contract with Warren. Nigel Benn was thus free to box for himself, with Mendy as his agent.

Some sort of precedent for future manager-fighter conflicts was set by a High Court decision in March 1991 in favour of

Michael Watson in his case against Mickey Duff. The court decided that Duff's dual role as Watson's promoter and manager was a restraint of trade, as it denied the boxer's right to have someone to negotiate on his behalf. 'Mr Duff could hardly negotiate with himself,' said Mr Justice Scott. 'Every pound received by Mr Watson by way of purse or television receipts would reduce the promoter's net receipts.' The judgement was hailed as a triumph for boxers, who had for years declaimed the servitude the Board's contract submitted them to. The court's decision is likely to have a profound effect on the sport's future; the immediate result was that the Board was forced to go back to the legal drawing board.

Members of the old guard like Jarvis Astaire see the court's judgement as the beginning of the end. 'The Duff-Watson case has very serious implications because it virtually leads to chaos. Boxing is a unique sport and a unique professional situation. I am not necessarily in favour of promoters being allowed to manage, but the facts of life are, that if a manager is neither a promoter nor tied in with a promoter, then his boxers are not going to be successful. Boxers will be going constantly to the highest bidder and no one will be able to develop their careers. It becomes a question of "what have you done for me lately?"

'No one will be able to manage and promote. Board regulations will have to prevent that, because as soon as a boxer can produce evidence that his manager is in some way involved in promotion, he will be able to terminate his contract.'

All fighters, knowing their careers are short and could end with a single punch, are notoriously impatient, for big fights and big money. Nigel Benn, as impatient as any other, related better to Ambrose, who promised him bigger things straight away. Benn wasn't let down.

Soon Warren was hit by the departure of another of his star boxers, Gary Stretch, who had gladly joined Frank from one of the cartel, Mike Barrett. Stretch, from St Helens in Merseyside, is a reasonable fighter, winning the British light-middleweight title in 1988. The fact that he was reared on a fair selection of nobodies was an indication of how Warren was settling into the patterns of the establishment he had broken into: finding weak opponents to build up a talented fighter for a television audience. But certain elements, namely young girls, in Stretch's audience would have come to watch him fight a koala bear. His attraction, and marketability, are model looks and matching finely sculptured body. Not only that, he is white. While the Terry Marshes and most other white fighters of this world tend to look like upright prawns under the harsh ring-lights, offset unfavourably against the the darker skin tones of black opponents – compare Frank Bruno to Joe Bugner – Stretch is tall, dark and handsome. It is not every British light-middleweight champion who gets offered modelling contracts or chatted up by Page 3 girls in Stringfellows. Gary Stretch was a lover and a fighter. He was meat and drink – but mainly meat – to the tabloid press, always short of a minor celebrity to fill space. His personal life had suitable – and quite genuine – heartbreak twists; the boxer's mother left his father and three sons when Stretch was just 12, and he has never seen her since. Then his brother Roni was sentenced to three years for planning a robbery, serving a year before another man confessed to the crime.

Stretch, a diffident character and somewhat irked at being boxing's beefcake beauty, can of course do nothing about his looks and is bound to take the money offered to wear a suit for a morning, but boxing took too much of a back seat to the hype. Living beyond his means, he jumped on the whirligig of London night life, having a series of highly publicised affairs with *inter alia*, Lionel Blair's daughter Lucy and the 39-year-old Pretenders singer, Chrissie Hynde. He was stripped of his title for failing to defend it within a year. In September 1990 he left Warren, despite having earned reasonably well in his fights – £20,000 to defend his title, and £15,000 for winning the WBC international title. David McConachie, Warren's former press officer, suspects Stretch started mixing with Terry Marsh and his actor friend Glenn Murphy. 'They probably swayed his opinion on Frank which persuaded him to leave. Every time we offered him a fight he pulled out unexpectedly, for reasons best known to him.'

Predictably enough, the two sides were soon at legal logger-
heads, with Warren suing Stretch for breach of contract, and
Warren's business partner suing the boxer for £20,000 he
allegedly guaranteed in a £59,000 bank overdraft. Since
October 1990 Stretch has been managed by Giant Promotions, a
wing of a company run by entrepreneur Alan Lacey, and
returned to the ring in April 1991 against Chris Eubank to
contest the WBO middleweight title. Trying hard to shed his
playboy image for that of an earnest pugilist, though probably
too late to satisfy boxing purists who see Stretch and his cohorts,
vodaphones and gushing lady publicists *et al*, as an unwelcome
intrusion into their sweat and sawdust world. The intrusion did
not last too much longer, after Eubank demolished Stretch in the
sixth round. As a ringsider said in *Raging Bull* after Jake
LaMotta had destroyed the features of pretty-boy fighter Tony
Janeiro, 'He ain't so pretty now.'

Stretch's departure was another aggravation for Warren, even
worse as he and Stretch had been close, socialising together,
visiting each other's houses. It was the sort of headache that had
led Frank in 1988 to threaten to quit boxing promotion, and
work simply as a manager. 'You wake up so many mornings
wondering what you're doing all this for,' he said. 'It's daft
because I'm not down to my last few hundred quid and there's
plenty of other fields, including property, and putting on all sorts
of events apart from boxing. All I'm getting out of this business is
a massive bill for Anadin.'

No more was heard of his intention to retire, but Warren's
headache wasn't improved when Barry McGuigan lost to Jim
McDonnell in May 1989. The Irishman announced his retirement at the end of the fight. Both Warren and McGuigan made a
lot of money out of the venture, with McGuigan able to buy a
large house in Kent mortgage-free, but the trail to regain a title
was over, and the jewel in Warren's fading crown had gone.

At times Warren's knack of spotting a winner was letting him
down. One day Chris Eubank went to see him with a video of
himself; he wanted to be taken on. Warren sent him to Ernie
Fossey. 'He sparred with Tony Collins, and Tony nearly took

him apart,' recalls Fossey. 'Frank said what do you think? I said I think he's very limited.' Limited, perhaps in sparring, a difficult character, yes, but Eubank's unorthodox gifts later brought him a world title.

As he began to tire of boxing Warren turned his attention briefly to snooker. In the autumn of 1987 it was announced he was on the verge of signing seven of the world's leading players to form a stable to rival that of Barry Hearn, the millionaire snooker promoter. At his first serious attempt, and much to Warren's chagrin, Hearn had recently promoted boxing in a big way with the most over-hyped fight between Frank Bruno and Joe Bugner at White Hart Lane, a contest which Warren had tried to put on four years earlier. Nothing ever came of Warren's snooker stable, though in a brief alliance with Hearn a year later he promoted one tournament, before deciding that snooker was dying as a TV sport.

A more substantial collaboration had begun when he met a solicitor, John Botros, in the mid-eighties. Botros, a couple of years older than Warren, was educated at Trinity College, Oxford, and grew up in a comfortable middle-class background in Derbyshire, with his English mother and Egyptian father, a doctor. Besides his reputation as a hard-nosed lawyer, he had had a couple of small businesses, been a partner in the Napoleon casino in Leicester Square, but was not particularly well-known or connected in the City. As Warren began to mix outside boxing circles, Botros was just the sort of person he was meeting. At the time they first encountered each other, both had recently made a healthy sum of money – Warren from the Jones-Curry fight, Botros by resurrecting a company, United Guarantee Corporation (UGC), and getting its listing back. Botros, with the looks of a poor man's Omar Sharif, a smooth manner with a leisurely, gentleman's club drawl, a hard liver and often cruelly witty man, hit it off immediately with Warren.

Having proved himself as a boxing promoter, Frank Warren wanted to be something more. While liking the sport, he was never a boxing man through and through, had never boxed himself and was never the sort to pore over back copies of

Boxing News and put his feet up in front of a fight video. Never seeking to justify the sport, he just liked it, and saw he could make money from it. 'You can't justify two people punching each other. You can't do that,' he once said. 'I mean, it's not a fight to the death, and there is a lot of skill involved . . . but there must be damage. Somebody actually punching another person in the head has got to cause brain damage.'

In 1987 he told Lynn Barber, 'I tell you, boxing people are all right. Obviously they tend to be working class, so maybe they seem a bit rough, but they're great people really, full of heart.' But he had grown more than a little frustrated by the smallness of the boxing world and the exclusive company of its denizens, who he might have felt were often less intelligent than him. He loves recalling the moment in a TV documentary where Frank Bruno walks into an Italian restaurant and greets the waiters, '*Adios amigos*'. 'He's trying to say hello in Italian and he says goodbye in Spanish – it creases me up every time.'

Warren was certainly more urbane than his rivals. Ken Jones of the *Independent* remembers taking his friend Alan Watkins, political columnist with the *Observer*, to his first boxing promotion – McGuigan's comeback. Warren kindly got Watkins a seat behind Jones. 'Alan didn't need any introduction to Warren, who knew exactly who he was. I think Alan was surprised at that in a boxing promoter.'

Like many workaholics, Warren had come to have few friends outside work. Isolated from a normal, easy-going social life, his spare hours were more and more taken up with business lunches, dinners with contacts and spending time with his family.

He became ever more motivated by the trappings of success. Almost everybody appreciates very expensive things, but many are not desperate to have them. Warren craved them. 'There is nothing he likes better than driving along the sea-front in the south of France in a Rolls Royce,' says Jeff Randall, City editor of the *Sunday Times* who has had a good working relationship with Warren for years. 'If you are socially mobile it is very hard sometimes – I have found this a bit myself – you become a social voyeur. You leave your own background, either through education or money, but you are never quite accepted in, or accept, your new environment. You see your old environment as a bit rough, and someone like Frank can't go back and mix with the boys from the snooker hall. But he is not going to be fully accepted, or want to be, by the gin-and-tonic set in Hertfordshire.'

A displaced member of the working class, Warren felt that *the* working class sport – boxing – could not alone sate his ambition for power, money and a more captivating life. He had broken the monopoly of the cartel, and pulled some big boxing deals, but his rivals survived. Always spurred on by the thrill of a deal, he needed a fresh challenge. Now it was time to swing some new deals – his favourite word after all, was 'agreed'. As he had a habit of saying to his staff, 'Bottom line, I'm bored.'

In the autumn of 1987 Warren announced he wanted to become the most powerful figure in British sport by putting together an organisation to promote, manage, stage and televise its own events. The aim was to perform all aspects of a sport event and then give television a finished tape for broadcast at the end. 'By controlling all aspects of a sporting event I will be master of my own destiny. We will be chasing the best of British in all the top sports. I want a company which compares in quality with Marks & Spencer.' On the boxing side Warren privately maintained Frank Warren Promotions and Sports Network (UK), which received the television fees from his promotions, while in 1986 Warren and Botros had formed a joint company, Loxway, as a basis for new ventures.

On the strength of his boxing promotions and Botros's coup with UGC, in 1987 the pair persuaded CitiBank and the Royal Bank of Scotland to lend them £2.2 million out of a 29.9% share worth £2.8 million that gave them a controlling interest in Rex Williams Leisure Ltd, a publicly-quoted company with interests in gaming machines, snooker and pool table manufacture and sports promotion. Frank Warren was in a manner of speaking back where he started – installing machines, except now he was the first boxing promoter with a listing on the Stock Exchange, and he now had that special, albeit vague, status of a millionaire that put him on a different plane to his boxing rivals. Frank Warren had moved out of the ring and into the boardroom.

Rex Williams, the snooker professional and former world billiards champion, had begun the company in 1974. It was a nice, tidy operation making about £200,000 a year. Warren and Botros approached Rex Williams and the chairman, John Wardle, and it was agreed the newcomers would buy their way in as part of a plan to raise £5 million in new shares. Almost overnight the company was transformed. It was an audacious step, typical of the peak of the Thatcherite era, the boom time of post-Big Bang and pre-Black Monday, when the creed of moneymaking was paramount, when the City was seen as financially indestructible. Having grown slowly over the years. RWL decided to expand rapidly by acquisition. The old directors admired what Frank had achieved in boxing and the tenacity with which he had tackled the sport's establishment. Warren had followed the message of the new Tory party he had always voted for and got on his bike, in some style. The combination of two well-known sporting figures in Williams and Warren, the dynamism shown by Botros's success with UGC and a new wad of capital made it all seem a great move.

At a time when home ownership was regarded as the most important personal aspiration, Warren bought a £1 million mansion in Tewin Wood, Hertfordshire, where he was often photographed with his wife and growing, happy family. Many people have been crassly placed under the Thatcherite umbrella, but Warren really did fit the image of successful, self-made man. It seemed nothing could stop Frank Warren. Boxing tribulations such as Marsh began to seem like irritating punches which were easily avoided.

'I must confess at first I was totally excited by it,' says Rex Williams, still plying his trade on the snooker circuit. 'Frank was an amiable enough bloke to have a drink with, an amiable, babyfaced type of bloke.'

Rex stayed up in the Midlands while everything was happening down in London. John Wardle quickly resigned as chairman, to be replaced by Warren, while he and Botros introduced new faces to the board.

With astonishing speed, RWL swallowed up a number of other companies. About £1.2 million was invested in Space Adventure 3000, a futuristic theme centre in Tooley Street, London Bridge, which had the world's largest flight simulator. It was the brainchild of Ted Dove, a former BBC executive, who was appointed manager. Either it was poorly run or badly conceived, but certainly it wasn't promoted very effectively. Forecast to make between £150,000 and £200,000 a year, it closed in June 1990, two years after opening.

RWL invested £600,000 in Dalton Watson, a classic car publisher, and James Tindall, who had recently left Penguin, was appointed in charge. A previously small concern, it never took off in the way projected, and had collapsed by early 1989.

A video duplication company, Silvertape Ltd, trading as Harlequin Video, was bought for about £800,000 in late 1988. Eighteen months later it too had collapsed with debts of £2.5 million. Botros called in the Fraud Squad to investigate financial anomalies that could have cost the company £300,000.

Privilege, a corporate entertainment company begun by Warren, never took off, lost money quickly and was closed down.

Barry Hearn once said Frank Warren knocked down doors before looking to see if they were open. Warren and Botros together had moved too far, too fast. In the spirit of the age, they had bought up businesses and tried to make them profitable too quickly. It was a scatter-gun approach and none of the targets were properly hit. Both were on new ground. Warren was a talented promoter of a sport which was part of his milieu, but now ignored the principles of sticking with what you know and of using tried and trusty contacts. He didn't know much about what he was getting into, and didn't really know the people he asked to run them.

Black Monday, 22 October 1987, didn't help: it wiped £3 million off RWL's share value. Warren later admitted his mistake to Lynn Barber. 'I was a bad judge of character. I let myself down. Normally I go with my gut feeling, but I was trying to please all these City institution, go along with the City mentality, and they're not great supporters. There's a big snob element, it's just bullshit. I don't think I'll go back to the City.'

RWL, having shown pre-tax profits of £225,000 in 1987, the figure the next year made £18,000. Shares plummeted from a high of 88p to 15p towards the end of 1989. By then five directors had resigned, including Rex Williams himself. John Botros was forced to admit that 'a number of the acquisitions have proved most unsuccessful'.

'Everyone thought they were good ideas, and decisions were taken by the board, though Frank and Botros essentially made the decisions,' says a former employee of Warren's. 'I think they are both deal-makers but not managers of businesses. Although they may come across as ruthless, they [Warren and Botros] were always prone to romanticise, they were always starry-eyed about the next deal. They used to joke about making a film called 'The Promoters', a kind of boxing version of Mel Brooks' *The Producers*. Nothing ever came of it, but it amused them.' New companies, like Loxway Travel, were formed, then became dormant.

The key element in Warren's grand vision was the London Arena. As early as 1980 Warren had talked of building his own venue, even of constructing a rival to Wembley. All the other major promoters had their 'home' venues, and it was Warren's dream to have a power base from which to promote his own boxing shows and a star-studded variety of other events.

Three parties backed the Arena, for which cost estimates vary from £18-£25 million, raised on the site of an old banana warehouse in London's Docklands: Loxway, the pop promoter Harvey Goldsmith, and the Labour peer Lord Selsdon. Before the Arena opened, Loxway bought out Goldsmith's £4 million-pound share to take a 70 per cent stake in the project. The Arena, seating 12,500, was to stage boxing, pop concerts, a variety of indoor sports, exhibitions and community events. Like his bullish purchase of RWL, the whole concept of the Arena fitted the prevailing economic big thinking. As the East End is boxing's heartland, it made sense to have a major venue in that part of town, rather than in Chelsea or Kensington, areas that have not produced black heavyweight prospects.

Jon Robinson, forthright as ever, swears he first suggested Frank move to the Docklands. 'I'm very possessive of my East End, I come from Limehouse, and all my family worked in the Docks. And when they were being built up again I saw all these new buildings. I couldn't believe it and I sent away to an estate agent at the top of Cotton Street off East India Dock Road and got some brochures on units off the Canary Wharf, and I said, "Frank this is going to be the place of the future, you should get a place down there". My idea was to have a gymnasium with mezzanine floors and an office overlooking it. You paid no rates for ten years and all that type of thing.

'Frank said, "I don't fucking want to go to the East End, there's nothing good down there".'

But down there went Frank and opened the London Arena in February 1989. It became his new headquarters, with the boss now resident in an expansive modern office with his precious walnut desk and prints moved from Tavistock Place. Things were buzzing. Warren would hold five-minute meetings with his staff, working off a bit of paper with twenty points. He would say 'you do this, you do that, come back tomorrow and tell me how you got on'. Always in early, and always last to leave, in between he skipped around London – to a boxing meeting, to a business lunch, back to the Arena. A fax machine was installed in an office at home. 'A lot was happening,' recalls David McConachie, his former press officer. 'But he never shouted at anyone, and he commanded loyalty. Frank knows what he wants and gets it. He was just a really nice bloke to work for. If you're young like me he treats you like a brother or a mate, he doesn't act the boss. We were always having a laugh.'

But ten months after opening, the Arena needed refinancing, in other words, a loan. Warren had no choice but to go back to the City's banks. At the same time Rex Williams Leisure was faltering, though no one outside the company knew things were not all they had promised to be. Warren invested his real

confidence in Botros, and on the boxing side of things, in Ernie
Fossey. To those two he was extremely close. With others he was
always personable, but aloof. Problems couldn't be discussed
openly *en masse*. 'In management meetings we weren't allowed
to talk about money, but everyone wanted to say, look we don't
have any money. It was daft. The situation continued with debts
not being talked about or tackled,' recalls a former employee.

Warren's entrepreneurial image grew: he now drove a Bentley
and in October 1989 the 'millionaire boxing promoter' helped
organise a charity ball in Park Lane which raised thousands of
pounds for needy children, where he danced and chatted at
length with Princess Michael of Kent. It was all a long way from
unlicensed fight nights in Finsbury Park.

Boxing had evidently become a lesser concern, though Warren
still had a healthy number of TV dates, featuring the by now
regular shows at the Arena and at smaller venues like the York
Hall. Occasionally he would do a small hall event without
television, and had such an evening arranged at the Broadway
Theatre, Barking, for 30 November 1989. The bill featured an
up and coming boxer promoted by Warren, the featherweight
Colin McMillan, who was due to be fighting Mark Goult, from
Wisbech. The evening was designed to keep Warren's fighters
busy and give them a payday before Christmas. Good support
was guaranteed for McMillan in his home town, but it was to be
a low-key affair in a 600-seater municipal theatre, with an
audience primarily made up of the boxers' friends and relatives.

As sometimes happens, the main opponent, Goult, pulled out
at the last minute and had to be replaced, by a New Yorker,
Sylvester Osuji. It was a nuisance Warren could have done
without as in the days preceding the show he was preoccupied
with meeting bankers to secure the loan for the Arena. A meeting
on the day itself had run late and it crossed his mind not to go to
Barking but, as ever, Warren was determined to attend his show,
due to start at 8pm.

As fans arrived at the Broadway in dribs and drabs, one figure
stood on his spot, about 50 yards in front of the theatre. Several

people noticed him, hands in pockets of his hooded parka jacket, shifting his feet about, occasionally looking around him. A few kids thought he looked funny – it was dark but not particularly cold – and dared one of their number to go and ask him the time. It was ten to eight. A few minutes later the youngster returned with a friend to tease this odd figure with a scarf tied around his face a bit more. They asked what he was doing, and were told he was waiting for a friend. He gave his name as Paul. Giggling, the kids left him.

Later than planned, at ten past eight, Warren arrived with John Botros, straight from a business meeting. His driver Harry Whiting pulled up the Bentley in a side road to the left of the theatre. The crowd was settling down inside, waiting for the first bout to begin. The hooded figure approached the car as it slowed down. When Warren and Botros got out of the car, he moved within six feet of the vehicle, and stopped. As Warren reached in for his jacket he heard a bang, a noise like a firecracker or a car backfiring. Startled, he straightened himself and saw the hooded figure who, arms extended, was pointing a gun at him.

They faced each other for four or five seconds. Another 'firecracker' went off. Warren felt a pain in his side and knew he had been shot. The bullet had entered his chest near his armpit, went into his left arm, and out the other side. Despite the pain, his survival instincts made him run away, even zig-zagging up and down a grass embankment to make himself a more difficult target should the gunman fire again.

A woman screamed. Botros shouted at the gunman as he charged at him, head first, pushing him against the car behind the Bentley, before the gunman broke free and sprinted athletically away across the large common in front of the theatre. He was too fast for Botros or Whiting to catch. Someone in a car which pulled up alongside asked Warren if he was all right, he said he had been shot, sank down on one knee and was consumed in agony. There was a strange gurgling noise as blood filled his lungs and he lost breath. His shirt and waistcoat became drenched with blood. He told himself not to close his eyes, or he would never open them again.

Frank's brother Robert was working in the box office of the theatre. He heard the noise of the shots, also assuming it to be a car backfiring. Someone ran in and said a man had been shot. Robert rushed out screaming 'Someone's been shot!' Seeing his elder brother holding his stomach and chest he screamed in horror, 'It's Frank, Frank's been shot!' Warren said, 'I've been shot, I'm OK.' Robert laid his brother on his side, while a boxing fan who had been waiting for a late friend put his coat over Warren, now shivering with cold. Robert ran back into the theatre to call an ambulance, but a police van arrived first, and took Warren to Brook Hospital in Shooters Hill.

Inside the theatre, the crowd was told the first bout would be delayed while Board of Control doctors helped with an 'accident'. Those spectators who rushed out saw several police cars, officers huddling together and constables cordoning off the area around the Bentley. They were ushered back inside, and the show continued in order that everyone could be questioned afterwards. McMillan stopped Osuji in four rounds.

Meanwhile someone at the theatre had put a call out to the newspapers. In newsrooms throughout London the simple message was received, 'Frank Warren has been shot, Broadway Theatre, Barking.' Knowing nothing more, not even whether he was dead or alive, reporters grabbed their coats and notebooks and rushed to the scene.

They arrived to find confusion. Dozens of police officers were unable to say anything about the shooting. Scores of people were milling around; everyone in the audience was interviewed by police and then swamped by reporters anxious for an account of what had been seen. Few had anything to say. People poured out of the Barge Aground, the pub adjacent to the theatre, and were treating it all as a bit of a joke – it wasn't every day someone got shot in Barking. A teenager came up to a couple of reporters and said he had seen who had done it – Clark Kent.

More senior officers kept arriving, to be informed in furtive huddles with their juniors of what was happening. It was not until 11.30pm that a brief statement was made at Barking police station, just round the corner from the theatre. It was clear no one had got a good look at the gunman, who had indeed escaped. The briefest of descriptions was given: the gunman was white, between 5 ft 7 ins and 5 ft 11 ins and wore a hooded jacket. One bullet had struck Warren, who had survived. Meanwhile Warren's wife Sue had been informed and was already at the hospital, where her husband was recovering in intensive care.

The story dominated the newspapers. Over the next few days speculation mounted about the shooting. Detective Superintendent Jeff Rees said the assassination attempt had clearly been carried out by a professional using a semi-automatic pistol, that there were no wasted shots. It was later realised one shot had missed and one bullet been expelled from the gun without being fired.

Workmen at Warren's house revealed they had seen five men dressed in smart suits staking out the residence only hours before the shooting; the *Sun* claimed it received a call from someone who said: 'Tell him I missed him last time. Next time I won't.' Scotland Yard received several phone calls from people claiming they knew who was behind the shooting, and said it was following several lines of inquiry, including interviewing top sporting figures. According to one report, police received a tipoff that a second attempt would be made on Warren's life and soon moved him from the Brook to a private hospital where high security would be easier.

The boxing world was quick to disown the incident. Even Warren had once rubbished that sort of thing happening in boxing: 'Nah, boxing is supposed to be this big, heavy Mafia number, but if that's the case, why hasn't Mickey Duff shot me, or why haven't I got him shot? I've had some silly phone calls, idiots, but gangs of heavies, definitely not.'

Mickey Duff, ever quotable, said: 'I am absolutely positive no one involved in the sport has anything to do with it,' adding tantalisingly, 'we all make enemies in boxing but Frank Warren makes 'em easier than most.' There were murmurs that a personal or business dispute may have led to the shooting.

As Warren recovered in hospital, his Uncle Bob spent every

night by his bedside. Frank's family pulled together to help itself and their boy through a traumatic experience.

Jimmy Warren, another uncle, says: 'We are a very close family, very loyal. None of us could believe he got shot. It was terrible someone shot him, he was trying to kill him, you know, they shot 'im in chest. You should just shoot someone in the foot. And 'e was just getting out of his car, it was a surprise like the movies.'

A day or two after being shot Frank was taken off the respirator and was able to talk to his wife, then two months pregnant with their fourth child. Police officers interviewed the victim at his bedside, but were frustrated that he could not identify his assailant.

As well as the family, Ernie Fossey, John Botros and a couple of journalist contacts, visited regularly. After only a few days Warren, incredibly, was sitting up in bed and giving orders to his staff. After surgery he had half a lung missing, was weak and losing weight and just wanted to forget work and go and spend time in his beloved south of France.

'I felt angry about it. A couple of days after it happened I would cheerfully have taken a gun and gone for revenge – and I know that if I'd had a gun at the time I would have shot back. I am very bitter. Who would have looked after my children? I would never have seen my new baby.'

Warren showed extraordinary courage, ignoring his pain to pay attention to work. His staff, under strict instructions to maintain secrecy, were taken by police to Warren's hospital bedside, where they would quickly fire questions at him, get briefed and go back to the office.

Just 14 days after being shot, and against the best medical advice, Warren returned to public life, calling a press conference at the London Arena. With his brother Robert by his side and all his boxers behind him, he recollected the shooting, even managing to entertain as he did so, 'I can tell you it wasn't a publicity stunt'. No, he couldn't think of anyone who might have wanted to kill him, and yes, it was life back to normal. Out of the blue came a strange question. Did he know a flower girl from Romford? 'What kind of flower? Flour as in Homepride, or flower as in *My Fair Lady*?' joked Warren. The subject was left there.

As a hands-on boss, and with considerable problems to deal with, Warren saw he had no choice but to recommence working as hard as ever. It was proof of his gutsy reaction to a traumatic event, one which he described with intelligence and sensitivity. 'The most humiliating experience in my life was the shooting,' he said in *The Times*. 'You see I wasn't frightened, I was embarrassed more than anything else. That's what I felt in hospital, embarrassed because, let's face it, I personally want control of the situation.

'The worst thing you can do is humiliate someone. It's worse than pain. I had my clothes off and I was naked and it was weird because I was lying on a table and I couldn't catch my breath and my lungs and the blood and then I would disappear and come back and I kept thinking, this is a farce.'

Some of the papers treated the shooting with less sensitivity. The *Daily Mirror* ended a feature, 'Frank Warren started in the gutter – and almost ended up there.' The *Sunday Express* speculated he was shot by the same gunman who had shot two drugs dealers. Frank was soon back in legal action – and was later awarded £10,000 against the *Mirror*, with Express Newspapers paying £47,500 in an out-of-court settlement. The *Sun* coughed up £40,000 out of court after suggesting Warren knew Terry Marsh had epilepsy. Soon the *Mail on Sunday* paid £37,500 as it alleged Warren broke Stock Exchange rules. A host of other writs have been issued against the paper which has continued to probe the finances of Warren's companies.

Frank has done well out of libel cases, perhaps as well as £200,000, a figure his libel lawyer, Steven Heffer, says 'wouldn't be far out'. A cynic might suggest libel settlements have been Warren's easiest means of making money over the past few years, but remuneration alone cannot be the sole motivation. Some of the stories about him have been ludicrous, but his reaction to others suggest an over-sensitivity to adverse comments that approaches paranoia. The offending words in the

Daily Mirror article were buried at the end of a gushing profile, for instance. Then a host of smaller actions, £1,000 settlements and awards here and there, have been brought. In 1985 the *Sun* paid a similar figure after suggesting Warren had deceived the public by announcing a projected fight for Joe Bugner when he had not mentioned it to the manager of Bugner's opponent, Tex Cobb.

Does Frank Warren get a buzz out of litigation? 'I don't know,' says Heffer, who works with Binks Stern. 'I don't think he does particularly, I think he gets very aggrieved if someone says something he doesn't like. The main thing from his point of view and the advice we always give, is that you have got to go for them [the newspapers] otherwise they are just going to keep doing it.' It has worked. The mere mention of an article on Frank Warren can send a newspaper lawyer into a paroxysm of panic. Frank has always used the law to get his way, initially, when breaking the cartel, for specific, constructive purposes. But these days it seems, as his old general manager Jon Robinson says, 'Frank Warren doesn't have a shit without talking to his lawyer.'

Much as Warren wished life could return to normal after the attempt on his life, it could not. Getting shot unfortunately increased Warren's celebrity rating immeasurably. Everything he did came under closer media scrutiny, including his business, by no means the only struggling enterprise in London. The only benefit was that during his stay in hospital a tumour was found, and removed, on his thyroid gland. Pope John Paul II, himself the target of an assassination attempt, sent a simple message, '*Paenet*', 'Let it be repented'. At least Warren's sense of humour wasn't wiped away; when later asked what his motto in life would be, he replied, 'if in doubt – duck'.

Like a draught, whispers continued circulating around the boxing community, genuinely shocked but intrigued by the shooting. Those who bore serious grudges against Warren thought he had something like this coming, though trying to bump someone off was a bit much.

'I'd be surprised if anyone got shot,' says one manager. 'But I didn't shed any tears. I must be truthful, I think I even had a smile on my face. I believe your life is fated. Whatever's going to happen is going to happen, especially in boxing. If you take things for granted, you upset a lot of people . . .'

But no one suspected that anyone who had boxed for him might be under suspicion.

Then Terry Marsh was arrested at Gatwick Airport on his way back from America on 16 January 1990. He had travelled there with Ambrose Mendy and Nigel Benn, hanging around, pulling practical jokes or finding silly things with which to occupy himself like running about the hotel wearing a huge rubber hand, chatting to journalists and keeping Nigel cheerful before his fight against Sanderline Williams. There was talk of meeting Bob Arum and fixing up a three-fight deal, of getting a licence to box in New Jersey. Lawrence Lustig, the *Daily Star* photographer, was with him the night before they returned to England. 'He was talking about going to Florida to arrange his comeback, and the next minute he was on the plane home.' It was hard to pin Terry down to anything definite.

As they arrived at customs, Mendy and Benn were stopped and searched while Marsh passed through. He laughed and shouted, 'I see the white man gets through.' Then five men approached. One said, 'I am D.I. Wiggins of the Murder Squad and I am arresting you for the attempted murder of Frank Warren.' Marsh was handcuffed and taken to Gatwick police station, where he stayed overnight.

Though a charge had been made, Warren's life continued with the strange accessories of the threatened man, like security guards on constant guard at his home.

And the stigma of being shot increased because Marsh's arrest was such a surprise. Despite the epilepsy episode, the former champion's integrity and wholesome image had remained largely intact. The suspicion that he had shot Frank Warren made some people think, what had Warren put him through? But then, perhaps his arrest was another piece in the jigsaw of his money problems, marital difficulties and the impending libel trial. Either way it seemed an extraordinary sequel to an extraordinary event. The shooting fulfilled public fantasies of boxing as a murky, violent, seedy underworld. It became a testimonial for an era of gangsterism which no one was entirely sure had passed by. In fact the crime was rather un-English and certainly unique in boxing. In Italy or the United States, countries where guns are widely available and organised crime prominent, shootings are more common. But in England, people do not just get shot in the street every day.

Whatever was being muttered in the pubs, boxing halls and newsrooms of the capital, Warren's future depended on what was being muttered in the high-tech offices of the City of London. Bankers do not like customers getting shot. It reveals a slight unreliability. It was not only bad for his health, but bad for his image. As Jeff Randall says, 'The effect was devastating. The whole thing about Frank Warren was that he was trying to change his image from a London spiv to a serious businessman, and how many serious businessmen get shot in the street? Bankers quite rightly started asking questions about the sort of man they were dealing with.'

The refinancing of the Arena, very close to completion on 30 November, began to dry up. By 3 January, RWL's stockbrokers, Brown Shipley, stood down by 'mutual agreement'. In April the company went into administration, its shares suspended at 10p, with total deficiencies of £3.1 million. Warren resigned as chairman and Botros took over. A new managing director, Jeff Williams, was brought in to look after the company and try to come up with a revival plan along with the administrators, Stoy Hayward. The shareholders, including Rex Williams, who held two million shares, were dumbfounded.

'We were a nice successful little company and this happened. That was my retirement. And now I'm looking for other things to get involved in. I think there were just bad acquisitions, simple as that. It has been a very distressing time for me. Very upsetting. And people that backed me have also lost their money, probably, and people that worked for the company for years have lost their jobs. The whole thing has been a tragic episode in my life,' says Williams.

Warren and Botros weren't delighted with the way things had turned out either. Then they were hit by a small printing firm claiming Warren owed £15,000 for posters and programmes for fight promotions, and the head of the security firm which protected Warren after the shooting sued over £24,000 it claimed was outstanding. The promoter's lawyers claimed the bill was not paid because 'goods and services were not properly supplied'. Warren responded: 'When you have been shot and you have been lying around for a while it's hard to pick up the pieces.'

Later in the year he admitted: 'We've been very close to going under on a couple of occasions and we're still fighting our way through it.'

A crucial stage in the fight was the refinancing of the Arena, finally secured in May 1990. Loxway's bankers, Security Pacific, led negotiations for a loan of around £4 million.

'I'm not going to roll over and see my dreams die,' said Warren at the time. 'The Arena is the first to be built in London since the 1920s, and I'm determined to see it through.' He gave the Arena until 1992 to work. The venue had its highlights, such as concerts by Luciano Pavarotti, Duran Duran, and Frank's hero, Frank Sinatra, but continued to struggle. To compound matters, the Arena had been hit by costs which according to Warren ran into 'millions of pounds' on new stadium safety requirements which followed firstly the Bradford fire and then the Hillsborough disaster, as well as an over-run on building costs.

What went wrong with the London Arena? It has suffered particularly from the poor transport and infrastructure which has affected the whole area. It can take hours to get there, and there is only a small car park. Leaving a show by public transport means a 20-minute walk off the island. Taxis are nowhere to be found. Some performers were reluctant to play at a venue they had never heard of and their fans couldn't get to. Situated between an office development, Harbour Exchange, and Glengall Bridge, 'a business village', it is functionally designed: a rectangular block, about the length of three football pitches and the width of two, with a grey corrugated-metal outer wall, with a band of yellow and one of blue running all the way round. Essentially the Arena is a multi-purpose aircraft hangar. It can be split up, rows of the 12,500 seats can be shifted around at the touch of a button; anything can be staged there, from Pink Floyd to fishing exhibitions, from basketball to boxing. It struggles to create the atmosphere for separate events that a single purpose venue can, it can't recreate the raucous atmosphere of the York Hall or Royal Albert Hall for boxing, or Hammersmith Odeon for pop. It is like watching football in a purpose-built, municipal stadium after years of standing on the terraces. Frank Warren boldly intended it to be the flagship of entertainments in the Docklands, with him at the helm. It was a battle to prevent it sinking.

After the Docklands boom, came the Docklands crash. The hangover after the champagne years. While the Arena struggled on, other ventures collapsed. Tobacco Dock, a £70m shopping complex in Wapping, went into receivership, as did Butler's Wharf, a luxury residential development by Sir Terence Conran, and Burrell's Wharf and Bow Quarter, owned by Kentish properties. They were all led into the ring by over-optimism in the Docklands and floored by the recession and the sterile property market it brought with it.

As interest rates rose and it became harder to borrow, a lot of big names got into trouble; Frank Warren was not alone. The Levitt Group, Polly Peck, Brent Walker, Stormseal as well as thousands of other small businesses began to suffer. Suddenly it was bad news all round. Even for Barry Hearn, by late 1989 firmly committed to boxing promotion.

'That's Thatcherism, innit? You borrow money and worry about it later. Listen, it all depends on your *gearing* – the percentage of what you borrow against what you own. If you get your *gearing* wrong, and you get caught in that high interest spiral which eradicates the rest of your gearing, then the rest is history, you know.

'It's tough out there at the moment, we have all suffered. You think of some of the names that have been in trouble. What about Roger Levitt? He done TWENTY TWO MILLION QUID! And he looks well on it!

'It's a sign of the times. The strong ones get through it, I mean we all take a bashing, don't get me wrong, I mean, fucking 'ell sometimes you have to work for nothing or less than nothing – in the bad times – and you hope to make money in the good times. But I mean the *quality* people, the proper players, get through, and the others don't. That's what life's about.'

Heavily geared, the Arena had to work quickly, and it didn't. The shares Warren and Botros had in Rex Williams were now frozen. The debts on the Arena were mounting. Neither had a personal fortune to offset their problems even a little.

It doesn't appear Warren was ever a millionaire in cash terms, though few are. It is as if he simply decided to be rich. As Jeff Randall says, 'With a little bit of front, a little bit of money and a lot of hard work and confidence you can go a long way. A lot of people have gone a long way on a little backing, hot air and hard work. I see people like that in the City all the time.'

Public records on his companies don't indicate massive profits, though they don't paint a full picture of his financial history. In June 1987, Loxway's assets of £302,619 were only just higher than liabilities. Frank Warren Promotions in 1983 made a net profit of £2,984, in July 1985, £85,713, and a year later, £3,971, on a turnover of £1.1 million. In 1988 it had a debt of £2.3 million which involved the share purchase in RWL. At one stage it was threatened with being struck off the companies register for filing late accounts. Sport Network (UK), which received the TV fees for fights, lost £12,682 in 1985 on a turnover of £658,852 and made a net profit of £14,518 in 1986, and had liabilities of £4,342 in July 1988. By late 1989 an overdraft guaranteed by Warren and his wife of £800,000 had built up with the National Westminster Bank.

For all their problems, Warren and Botros had the London Arena, or a 70 per cent stake in it. That achievement was undeniable. Mistakes had been made with the RWL acquisitions, but if the Arena worked, they could keep their heads above water. More dramatic developments were to come.

Just to pile on the agony of the previous few months, in May, Frank's younger brother Robert was charged with grievous bodily harm after a night club brawl. Robert, a bouncer at Ra Ras in Islington, had always worked on and off for Frank, as well as doing a bit of scaffolding.

The promoter's fighters suffered badly from the shooting. With a business to save, there was less time to devote to boxing. Things started to go wrong, sponsors pulled out, shows were cancelled or re-arranged. The stable was whittled down to about 10, the number of shows on TV to half-a-dozen. One of Frank's trainers, Jimmy Tibbs, left and took his boxers with him. 'Frank had a rough couple of years, the boxing scene went a bit dead, and I had six or seven young lads around me who needed work,' says Tibbs. 'It was nothing personal. Shows were getting cancelled and boxing's my living. I liked Frank Warren and still do like him. I have always found him a very polite man.'

Tee Jay was as shocked as all Warren's fighters were by the shooting, but without wishing to sound selfish, he was also deeply worried about his own future. 'I couldn't believe it. When he got shot, for a few hours I was thinking that my life was over, you understand? If your manager's dying, what are you going to do now? He was just on the verge of trying to get me a world title fight and it never crossed my mind I could get another manager. For those few hours I thought my life was finished, that's how much dependence there is, you get to rely on your manager so much. I was praying he lived for myself, for my career.

'After he got shot he had a lot of problems, things weren't working so well for him. The office became disorganised, you would phone in, no one would know what was happening. Before he had everything under control but after he got shot suddenly everything became haywire. The atmosphere wasn't the same and hasn't been the same up to now.'

A few months on from the shooting, Warren said 'After being shot, everything's a breeze. After that, I'm alive, that's the main thing.' Unfortunately, a foul wind was blowing just around the corner: the trial of Terry Marsh.

CHAPTER ELEVEN

Trial and Error

The Old Bailey lies within the confines of the old City of London at the top of Ludgate Hill, within shouting distance of St Paul's. It was completed in 1905 and built on the site where Newgate prison once stood. A number of the prison's stones were used in making the lowest storey of the Central Criminal Court – the principal Crown Court for the London area. Until 1861, public hangings had taken place outside Newgate; today it is not the hangman that lurks outside, but the pack of press photographers, whose numbers multiply like amoebas whenever there is a major trial. The Crown v Terry Marsh was such a trial, the most publicised attempted murder case since the former leader of the Liberal party, Jeremy Thorpe, was accused of conspiring to kill his friend Norman Scott, in 1979. Case number T900715, Marsh, opened on 22 October 1990 in court two. The ex-boxer was accused of the attempted murder of his former manager Frank Warren. The media gathered *en masse* for the trial of the year, and boxing's trial of the century.

The dock in court two is big enough to hold a dozen defendants, but from the custody area below, the sole, slim figure of Marsh stepped alertly into it at 10.30am. Dressed in a double-breasted blue suit, a striped shirt, and loosely knotted tie, he was jumpy and twitchy, but not looking unduly worried for a man in his position. As he was to do over and over again during the 12-day trial, Marsh smiled up at his family and friends in the crowded public gallery, which included his mother Maisie, brother John, business agent Ambrose Mendy, and friend and fictional counterpart Glenn Murphy, who plays

the part of a fireman and amateur boxer in the BBC series
London's Burning.

Marsh had faced two charges prior to his trial: attempted
murder and illegal possession of 10 rounds of 9mm ammunition.
On the first morning the judge, Desmond Fennell, ruled the
second indictment should be taken separately, after the
defendant's counsel submitted that the minor charge would
prejudice the jury's treatment of the main one.

As the jury were sworn in, Marsh took all their names. It
would be a strange person who did not follow his or her own
trial, yet there are degrees of concentration; every trial, however
captivating, has moments of relative tedium. After extended
periods of motionlessness, Marsh would relax his under-used
muscles, straighten his back and turn his neck like an animal
who might pounce, but throughout his trial, the defendant
followed proceedings with unusual intensity.

The clerk of the court read out the charge. 'How do you
plead?'

'Not guilty,' replied Marsh in his high-pitched East London
accent. A murmur of expectation went around the court, but the
show got off to a false start as the rest of the first day was taken
up with discussions on the admissibility as evidence of documents of Marsh's relating to the libel case Warren had brought
against Marsh.

The next day the contest started in earnest. In the prosecution
corner, Ann Curnow, QC. Looking down from the public
gallery, Ambrose Mendy might have recognised her as the
woman who had in 1972 prosecuted him as a 17-year-old for
robbery, to which he pleaded guilty and was given a suspended
sentence.

Miss Curnow bears more than a slight resemblance to former
Junior Health Minister Edwina Currie MP, but there the
similarity ends. The wife of Old Bailey judge Neil Dennison, she
could easily be taken for the product of a wealthy, well-to-do
shire family, so correct is her speech, and so confident her
manner. Throughout the trial she was a competent combatant,
though never appearing particularly familiar or comfortable

with the game in which she found herself, perhaps not surprisingly as she had only been given the case three weeks beforehand. The language of boxing seemed alien. It was hard to imagine her ringside at a big title fight. 'It doesn't matter not having an interest in boxing,' she said after the trial, 'provided you can learn what you need for the trial. I'm not that interested in guns either.'

Ann Curnow, however, was not born into the Establishment. Her father, who had been managing director of a failed clothing business, died in the Second World War. After the war was over, her mother decided Ann should not grow up in a home without a man, with little money coming in. She managed to find her daughter a place at St Hilda's Anglican Convent School in Whitby, North Yorkshire, a private school which kindly allowed her to be educated for next to nothing. She shone academically, taking her 'A' Levels at only 17 and entering King's College London to study law at the end of the same summer. 'It was the only place that would take me so young, and the only subject – law was not such a sought-after thing in those days.'

Miss Curnow's services as a barrister were not in great demand in her early years as she struggled against an institutionalised sexism which was barely beginning to erode. There were only five to six other women at Gray's Inn when she joined in the late fifties. 'We didn't feel we were flavour of the month. I was given no work in chambers for years, and survived on dock briefs.' She was one of a band of female pioneers, and is realistic enough to admit that after a while it was an advantage being a woman. 'Being reasonably competent, people recognise you, whereas there are lots of men who look the same.'

Rising through the ranks of the profession, she took silk in 1985, and is now one of the leading prosecutors in the country, working with the thoroughness and orderliness that a convent education is expected to bring, augmented by her intelligence and underlined by a resilience born of a struggle against early adversities.

Her opponent in the Marsh trial, Richard Ferguson, QC, is

probably the best cornerman a defendant could have. A six-foot Irishman, who could pass himself off as a former light heavy-weight, he is a big enough fan to have been at Queen's Park Rangers football ground in West London to see Barry McGuigan win the world featherweight title in 1985. Like Curnow, he comes from an unconventional background for someone so prominent in the legal profession, but a more down-to-earth one which Ferguson makes no effort to disguise. Ferguson is a Protestant from Enniskillen, Northern Ireland, but dispels any whiff of religious bias by emphasising immediately that he is married to a Catholic. After reading law at Queens' College, Belfast, and taking an arts degree at Trinity College, Dublin, he qualified as a lawyer at Gray's Inn chambers in London, and is now at Temple chambers. In his time as a Union MP on the liberal wing of the party, three terrorist attacks were made on his home. He resigned from politics, moved to London and became one of the leading criminal law advocates. Ferguson defended members of the IRA, acted in the Birmingham Six appeal rehearing, represented Kevin Taylor, the Manchester businessman and friend of John Stalker, in his aborted trial, unsuccessfully but very skilfully defended Ernest Saunders in the Guinness trial, and as soon as that was done, he began preparing his defence of Marsh. Although Ferguson is a man with impeccable legal training, his background spares him the standard English public school accent of so many of his profession. His loud, confident, Ulster voice, allied to his imposing physique, and rugged features, lends a touch of streetwise sass to his craft, which seemed in perfect accord with this case and its protagonists. A man whose hobbies are listed as drinking Guinness and 'playing around at being a farmer', he says, 'I like sport, like most Irish people I think, and I was intrigued by it all.'

On Tuesday, 23 October, Miss Curnow opened the case for the prosecution. She told the jury there was no positive scientific evidence linking Marsh to the gunman. 'The Crown points to motive, the descriptions of the gunman, the coat recovered and his possession of similar calibre ammunition. One thing that is crystal clear is that the gunman intended to kill Mr Warren and only just failed by a few centimetres,' she announced in her careful, round-vowelled tones.

She succinctly outlined Warren's career, and described how Marsh and his former manager had most recently come to grief over the interview on Thames Television's *Midweek Sports Special* in January 1989, when Marsh implied Warren knew about his epilepsy.

The prosecution alleged Marsh feared the libel case would ruin him financially. If Warren carried out his intention to sue, and won, Marsh was threatened not only with bankruptcy, but with the loss of his personal reputation, Curnow said. Even in defeat his legal costs would be enormous. 'He would be exposed as a cheat and a liar. Bearing in mind Marsh's high media profile during his very successful boxing career, he was facing personal humiliation of a very high order.'

On the third day, Frank Warren was called to testify. There is something about his very name that engenders a sense of trepidation. Maybe it is a combination of the wide-open 'Frank' with the suggestion in the surname of the dark underground. When his name was called, the courtroom tensed and murmured, as if the trial proper could only begin with the arrival of the victim. Warren entered, dressed in a blue blazer, striped shirt and unfamiliar glasses. The two men who had hugged each other in the middle of boxing rings all over England stole a nervous glance at one another. Warren looked rather serene. Marsh looked more thoughtful than ever, as if with the appearance of his former manager and promoter, the reality of the trial was really touching him for the first time.

Miss Curnow led her witness gently through telling the court of his business interests, how he had come to manage Marsh, and how they had stopped speaking to each other after Marsh had announced his epilepsy and retirement in the *Sun*, and Warren had ensured his former boxer was dropped from commentating on *Seconds Out*.

Warren then gave a graphic account of how he had narrowly

escaped death in a soft voice so barely audible he often had to be asked to speak up so the jury could hear.

The courts have generally been good to Frank Warren. He is notoriously litigious and has lost only twice in 35 or so legal cases. Any inaccuracy, however small, that might irritate most people for a day or two, but which they would then forget, Warren does not. He will be straight on the phone to his solicitor.

But this occasion was different. This was not a case of Warren's choosing. Being shot at had not improved his standing as a businessman. He said in an interview with Lynn Barber in the *Independent on Sunday* published the day before the trial, that he could have done without it – the time in court, the negative publicity and 'the aggravation'. A few days later, on 25 October, under cross-examination from Ferguson, Warren suffered unforeseen aggravation. It turned out to be one of the most humiliating of days, probably the second worst day of Frank Warren's life.

Ferguson's questions had begun tamely enough the afternoon before. Yes, the only people who knew he was going to Barking were his business partner, chauffeur and personal assistant. Yes, he had known Marsh for nine years, and had often seen him train with his face partially covered by a protective headguard. As for the Thames interview, Warren said he had been reluctant to sue as the channel was his 'bread and butter', screening his small to medium shows. But Marsh had continually been making statements that Warren had known about the epilepsy and that 'something had to be done'. Warren denied Marsh had told him about the epilepsy before the contract to defend his world title had been signed in September 1987.

Ferguson threw a body punch: 'I suggest to you that you did not want to take on board the fact that your prize fighter was telling you he had epilepsy, because you were more interested in getting him to sign a contract for his next fight. You had exchanged telexes. You didn't want to hear anything that would put the fight at risk.' The end of the day – it had been vaguely uncomfortable for Warren, but the worst was yet to come.

He arrived for round two the next morning in a charcoal grey double-breasted suit and red tie, looking relaxed and unaware of the revelation about to break. Warren admitted the shooting had a bad effect on business. Ferguson pushed the point further: towards the end of 1989 Warren's financial empire was crumbling. It was common knowledge in the boxing and business worlds that he had overstretched himself. But now everyone would know. He glanced at the press, eagerly jotting down every damaging detail. He was forced to admit that his company, Rex Williams Leisure Ltd, had gone into receivership with debts of £3 million; that another company, Frank Warren Promotions, had been warned by the Inland Revenue for not filing accounts and been threatened with being struck off the company register, that the Fraud Squad had been called in by John Botros to investigate an RWL subsidiary, Silvertape, which was wound up with debts of £2.5 million, and that there was a loan of £800,000 from the National Westminster Bank guaranteed by Warren and his wife. The promoter admitted his debts were £4–4.25 million, against assets which covered that, and denied he was under financial pressure from sources other than the banks.

But Warren had lost the coolness of the day before, the coolness that had always characterised his public persona. He twitched his head a bit, fiddled with his ear, his voice grew a little louder. He was beginning to look cornered; perhaps Ferguson was going to work on some scar tissue.

Ferguson brought up the matter of the press conference on 14 December, just 15 days after he was shot, where Warren had announced he was back, fit and ready to return to business. The barrister asked if Warren knew a flower girl in Romford. At the press conference, Warren had been asked the same question. This was not a press conference, this was court. Warren hesitated for a moment. He was under oath, nothing would be worse than finding the defence or the press had got hold of her. The married father of four tried to duck. 'I've come here today as a victim of a shooting, and now I am getting a character assassination . . . the purpose of the defence is to throw as much mud as possible, hoping some will stick. It has no relevance to the case whatsoever.'

Perhaps Warren hoped a bell would ring, and he would be nursed in to his corner. But Mr Justice Fennell merely warned him that he was being asked questions by a senior member of the bar and must answer.

Ferguson continued: 'I do not propose to mention the girl's name unless you compel me to, but it is a fact that you did know a girl in Romford involved in running a flower business.'

Warren: 'That is true.'

Ferguson seemed to be enjoying himself. He had wound Warren up like a real pro and was now in control. Cuts and bruises had appeared.

'Not to put too fine a point on it, you have been conducting an affair with that girl.'

Before Warren could answer, the judge stepped in and sent out the jury. But the damage had been done. Ferguson, in trying to prove there were people other than Marsh who might have had a motive to kill Warren, had exposed one of the country's highest profile businessmen as having lied at a press conference, and insinuated he was an adulterer too. The trial had temporarily switched from being the Crown against Terry Marsh to the World against Frank Warren. Whatever the justifications, the result had been close to legal anarchy. Had it been a fight, the referee would have stopped it earlier.

In the absence of the jury, the admissibility of Ferguson's line of questioning was debated. A compromise was reached, with Ferguson continuing his questions into Warren's past but referring to certain people in a roundabout way, with a legal nudge and a wink, though it was perfectly clear who they were.

Ferguson: 'Did the person [the flower girl] about whom we were speaking have a relationship with another man?'

Warren: 'I believe so.'

The tabloids soon unearthed the flower girl. She was Nicola Tarrant, 28, a pretty blonde former model – like Frank's wife – who ran a flower stall with her sister Mandy outside the church in the main square in Romford. She used to parade in the ring with the round numbers at Warren's promotions. She had a child by another man who, Ferguson suggested, might not have had a very high opinion of Frank. Later the prosecution pointed out the man, Andrew Holt, had been in custody at the time of the shooting. Later he was convicted for dealing the drug Ecstasy. The flower girl questions did not turn out to be relevant to the case, but they were great copy.

Ferguson wasn't finished with Warren. He opened a new offensive which within moments had the promoter on the run: 'I was shot at and it is not a very nice experience sitting here having your life taken apart,' defended Warren. Ferguson was unmoved, launching into the lifestyle and business contacts of a man he claimed frequently mixed with 'men of violence or potential violence'. Or was related to them. Hadn't Frank's brother Robert been charged with assault recently? 'Yes, but he was cleared last week,' replied Frank, exasperated. What about Uncle Bob Warren, who in the 1950s was sentenced to seven years' imprisonment for grievous bodily harm, after the gangland stabbing of Jack 'The Spot' Comer? Warren pointed out the offence was 35 years ago. 'I was only about three then – and I do choose him to be a relative.'

Warren closed his mauling by Ferguson: 'Believe me, some of the questions which have been asked today leave me a lot of explaining to do to the banks.' Not to mention the missus.

The thought for the day in the next morning's edition of the *Sun* was: 'Frank incensed'. The headline was simple: FRANK AND THE FLOWER GIRL in screaming 92-point. The *Daily Mirror* had: I LIED ABOUT THE FLOWER GIRL! The tabloids had helped build up Warren as an anti-establishment champion, one of us who had made it against unfavourable odds and was now a millionaire living in the Hertfordshire stockbroker belt. More than once these papers have had to cough up to Frank Warren and print apologies. A little revenge didn't go amiss. There isn't much better copy than a fallen idol. The Ferguson-Warren clash was the best fight in London for ages.

John Botros, Warren's business partner, gave a collected performance in the witness box. On the night of the shooting he was in the back of the Bentley with Warren. As he got out, he noticed a strange masked figure standing a few feet away, holding a gun. After hearing two shots, he saw Warren turn and run alongside the Bentley in an attempt to escape another shot.

'It seemed the gunman was intent on shooting him again. I moved to intercept the gunman between two cars, which is where I made contact. I didn't look up. I hadn't done this sort of thing before and I guess I was frightened of being shot. I simply put my head down and ran at the gunman. I was not trying to identify anybody. I was trying to stop the gunman killing Frank Warren,' he told the court. For a fleeting moment the two men were locked together before the would-be assassin broke free.

'I pushed the gunman against the Jaguar [the car behind the Bentley]. He then pushed me off and ran away. I particularly remember him running away because he ran very fast and very athletically. I looked across at Frank who was shouting at the driver, "Harry, you should telephone for an ambulance." I could see blood spreading over his waistcoat, and then a crowd gathered round.'

The chauffeur, Harry Whiting, attempted to chase after the gunman, but he was too slow to keep up. He escaped across the green. So, while the victim, his partner and driver all got a look at the gunman, he was by virtue of his disguise and speed impossible to identify.

Through a combination of bad luck and the East End cheek of a few kids, the gunman was not left entirely alone as he waited for Warren to arrive. A group of youngsters had noticed the solitary figure with a dark green jacket, dark trousers and trainers, with a scarf covering his face, standing near the Barge Aground pub. He was alone, the youngsters were in a group. He became a figure of fun. One of the boys, Bradley Parsons, was dared by two girls to go and speak to the stranger. He told the court how he had gone up and asked the man the time. 'He said something I didn't hear, because of the scarf. I couldn't understand it, he was mumbling. He pulled his right hand out of his pocket and showed me his watch. It was ten to eight. He was wearing black gloves, and there was clingfilm visible underneath. He was a white man.'

The youngsters went into Tesco, Parsons having proved his

manhood by speaking to this weird figure. When they came out, he was still there. Parsons and his younger friend John Richardson, approached him. Parsons asked him what he was waiting for. He answered, 'My mate. We're going down the club.' Parsons admitted to the court that he was being sarcastic with him. 'I said, "See you later mate" and stuck my thumb up to him and walked away.' By the time the youngsters had emerged again from the supermarket, the man who had called himself Paul had gone, and the police were looking for a gunman.

Ann Curnow asked Richardson if the person he'd seen reminded him of somebody.

'He did. Terry Marsh.' He had the same sort of build and height, and the same sort of local-sounding accent. Richardson explained how he had met Marsh at the Dagenham Swimming Club two months before when Marsh had been training for a swimming exam necessary for his Equity card. He had chatted to the former world champion. But in his first statement to police, the 14-year-old had not mentioned Marsh's name. Only after Marsh was arrested, and Richardson's mother asked whether the man in the green jacket had looked anything like Terry Marsh, did he name the former boxer.

For all the important, powerful people connected with the trial, the case might have rested on the evidence of these two kids who had spoken to someone for a dare. Inadvertently, they came very close to getting a clear sight of the gunman; had they persisted a little longer, they might have identified him more precisely. As it was, the only identification witness who caused the defendant any visible anxiety was a woman who had seen a man running past her car, minutes after Warren was shot.

Margaret Brett told the court that as she sat in traffic, she saw a man hurdle into the road over a four-foot high barrier. He put a hand out to warn her against moving off as he ran past. 'His hood was not up as he came in front of the car. He had short, tight curly hair, a longish face, a prominent nose, and a V-shaped face with a square jaw. I noticed he was carrying something white in his hand. He was of medium build but extremely athletic, otherwise he might have fallen over the barrier. But he didn't even stop, he carried on running.'

At this point Marsh called over his solicitor Henri Brandman and gave him a note which was passed on to Ferguson, the judge and Mrs Brett. Days later, during his summing up, Mr Justice Fennell said Mrs Brett's evidence, 'given in a rather appealing Geordie accent, had clearly caused a flutter amongst the defence'. The note asked Mrs Brett if she could convince the judge of her identity, and the professions of her husband and son. The answers were written down. Justice Fennell told the jury that neither Mrs Brett nor her family were connected with Warren or the police. Mrs Brett was never asked by the police if she could identify the man she saw beyond her given description.

As the trial entered its second week it was clear that although around 20 people had seen the gunman, none could make a positive identification. The gunman was fortunate Warren arrived late, so the number of potential witnesses was smaller than it might have been. But there was one man who remained standing outside the entrance to the theatre, waiting for a friend to show.

William Hawes, aged 69, from Poplar in East London, has been a fight fan for years, and this relatively small, untelevised show at Barking Theatre was just the type of event where only real boxing fans turn up. Hawes said he heard two loud bangs and thought they were fireworks. Then he saw what, it later transpired, was the scuffle between John Botros and the gunman. Hawes told the court: 'This man [the gunman] came running towards me. He stopped two or three feet in front of me and he held his hands up, moving them from side to side excitedly . . . He was in front of me for three or four seconds . . . before he ran off.'

In his first statement to police, Hawes could not identify the man. Later, he said the figure enacting the strange dance 'bore a similar resemblance [sic] to Terry Marsh', but stressed he could not say it was definitely Marsh. The defence was quick to pick up that Hawes had taken a while to come up with Marsh's full name. Under cross-examination, he became confused, more by the method than the subject of the questions.

Ferguson said: 'Now, Mr Hawes I put it to you, that on December 3rd . . .'

'Now look,' Hawes shouted, interrupting, 'you've got the dates in front of you, don't give me dates, I can't remember those . . .' Hassled and muddled, he gulped water. It was revealed that when police visited his house to take a further statement on 3 January, he had given the gunman's name as not Terry, but Rodney, Marsh – a flamboyant, blond football star from the seventies. Though the mistake was in the name, not the identity, as the prosecution was keen to make clear. Hawes in fact said the gunman was the 'spitting image of Rodney Marsh, the world champion,' before going on to describe in fair detail the career of Terry Marsh, whom he had seen box. He realised his mistake but was unable to remember the first name he was looking for until the next day when the police returned. Hawes said the man resembled Marsh, and at some point said, 'If I name him I won't be able to show my face on the boxing scene again.'

It was beginning to sound quite damaging, until Ferguson asked if a detective sergeant who had interviewed him, Michael Carroll, had given Hawes three £25 tickets for a Frank Warren boxing promotion. Yes, he had. Ferguson then suggested Hawes had told a friend he could 'make a few quid' out of giving evidence. This friend, Jimmy Walker, was sitting in court next to the defence solicitors. Hawes exploded: 'That man is a lying bastard, he is evil. I never said anything of the kind.' Waving his finger and shaking with anger, he screamed at Walker: 'You should be ashamed of yourself, Jimmy.' It transpired that they knew each other through Alcoholics Anonymous. The rules of anonymity and friendship had been breached. Walker had suddenly assumed the role of a grass.

William Hawes was given time to compose himself by Mr Justice Fennell. Then Ferguson brought up a conviction in the 1940s for larceny, now known as theft, that even Hawes's wife and children did not know of. The defence was fighting rough. A lot of effort had again been put in to discredit a prosecution witness. Only, on this occasion, it was not a millionaire boxing promoter, but a pensioner who liked to see a fight and who, from his point of view, happened to have been standing in the wrong place at the wrong time when Warren was shot.

Marsh appeared concerned at the state Hawes was in after the unexpected introduction of Walker. From the security of the press box, it had initially seemed a comical sight, as if an Alf Garnett type figure had been invited along to amuse everyone after the intense events of the previous days. But the increasing anger of Hawes, as unflattering parts of his private life were brought up, coupled with the confusion and distress he clearly suffered as he was thrust into the hostile atmosphere of a major court case, was sobering. On a day that was expected to be relatively uneventful, the trial had thrown up comedy, personal pain and the spectre of police malpractice. Court two had not seen anything like it for some time.

Detective Sergeant Carroll was called. He explained, somewhat awkwardly, that he had acquired three complimentary tickets from Burt McCarthy for Mr Hawes because he had become friendly with the elderly man, and had felt sorry for him as he could not afford to go to big fights. Hawes had not known the tickets were being got for him.

'Have you done this before for anyone else?' asked Ferguson, raising his intonation at the end of the sentence in expectation of the answer.

'No.'

'So, there are no other boxing fans who are pensioners for whom you have done this?'

'No,' replied a rather embarrassed policeman.

The case, as they say, continued, with Marsh well ahead on points.

Case number T900715 resumed in court two on Tuesday, 30 October. It was the day the prosecution produced its most important witness, the day it was claimed that Marsh had talked about the 'night he shot Frank Warren', a day when the trial reached a higher dramatic pitch.

Marsh was arrested on 16 January 1990 at Gatwick, and taken to Hackney police station to be interviewed. He was a difficult, unco-operative, wise-cracking prisoner, who began his interrogation by spoiling a form asking if or when he would like a solicitor to be contacted. An officer then noticed a key on the floor. Marsh said the police would find it opened a locker at King's Cross station.

'That's where you'll find the gun,' he said.

The officer asked, 'Is that the truth?'

Marsh replied: 'You find it, you're the fucking copper, and by the way, don't hit me again.'

No one had struck Marsh, but the interview had to be stopped for him to be asked if he was making an official complaint of assault. He wasn't.

What kind of gun was in the locker?

'Well there's an Uzi, an Ingram, 500 rounds, and oh, by the way, a phosphorus flare gun.'

Officers were despatched to King's Cross, where they checked the locker and ransacked a few others before realising perhaps Marsh had been winding them up.

WP Sergeant Susan Toublic told the court that as Marsh was led away to a cell, she noticed he was carrying his wrist watch. It had been taken from him at Gatwick and put in a police envelope, which had later been opened on the table in the interview room. Marsh had already been told it would possibly be of evidential value, she said.

On 20 January, Marsh had appeared at a magistrates' court charged with the attempted murder of Frank Warren, and was remanded in custody at Wormwood Scrubs prison. There he allegedly met the man whose evidence was potentially the most damaging heard against the defendant during the trial, Peter Harris.

In fact Peter Harris was an alias used, he said, to avoid detection by the police, though judging by his list of convictions, not with a great deal of success. He was often known in prison as Peter. And Bob. A small time Mr X. His real name wasn't revealed in court.

Harris entered the courtroom wearing sunglasses and an anorak with the hood up, like a boxer approaching the ring.

Once in the witness box, he removed both, revealing a strong, wide-jawed face, neat black hair and moustache. He wore trainers, jeans, and a checked shirt and tie. Speaking in a slow, sonorous London voice he completed the witness oath. Ann Curnow led him through his testimony.

Following his own arrest on 13 January 1990 on charges of fraud and deception Harris was remanded in custody. Marsh's presence was a talking point in prison; Harris had been face to face with him on four to five occasions before they actually spoke; Marsh had shared a cell with a friend of Harris, referred to as Dennis. Harris asked Marsh to write a message to his wife Jackie for her birthday, which he did: 'You're a cracker, Jack,' though only on condition Marsh could get extra food from the hot plate where Harris was working.

One afternoon as the prisoners were let out to exercise, Harris was walking on his own, and then was joined by Dennis and Marsh. The three chatted briefly, and shortly Dennis went off.

Harris said Marsh revealed what had happened to him 'the night he shot Frank Warren'.

Curnow paused, for the first time in control of the stage. She recounted: 'He told you what happened, "the night he shot Frank Warren"?' The words hung round the courtroom like the spirit of an executioner; Marsh stretched his neck once again.

Harris continued: 'I told him to be very careful of what he said in prison. He said, "you seem a sensible fellow" and just carried on talking.'

Harris said Marsh had been worried because the trainers he had worn the night of the shooting were the same as those he wore when arrested, and that a footprint had been found at the scene of the crime that would match up. (No such footprint was ever found or indeed mentioned elsewhere in the trial.)

'I told him he was crazy as one of the first rules of major crime is that whatever you use, you take off, put in the bin, and burn.

'He told me the gun that he used on Frank Warren was the same as that used in an attempted robbery,' the idea being if the gun was found after another crime, then it could not be connected with the shooting of Warren.

Harris said Marsh told him he had two 9mm guns – one illegal, one legal – a firearms certificate, and 2 boxes of ammunition, only one of which the police had found.

Marsh sat still, staring.

'He said he thought he had killed him because of the blood and mess that was there after the shot was fired. He thought he had actually killed him.

'The impression I got from Terry Marsh regarding Frank Warren was that he hated him very badly, a very personal, deep dislike. He said that Frank Warren tied people up in legal documents then stuffed them. He said he would make a comeback and show the world what he was capable of.'

Harris said this information had only come to light when he had mentioned to the officer in charge of his own case that he had met Marsh. 'There was no particular reason, it was just talk. He spoke to me a little further and it progressed from there.'

Harris later pleaded guilty at Crown Court and was sentenced to two and a half years. The judge had been aware Harris had helped the police, but knew no specifics, an occurrence described by Detective Superintendent Jeff Rees, the officer in charge of the investigation, as infrequent but not uncommon.

The prosecution had finished with its witness. But barely had Miss Curnow's rear reached her seat than Ferguson was on his feet: 'Did you expect to get two and a half years?'

Ferguson's demeanour was often that of the generous fireside raconteur, spinning tales between sips of Black Bush whiskey. But when the need arose, he was brutally direct. Peter Harris was used to tough interrogation, but can rarely have heard it so elegantly and authoritatively delivered. The main prosecution witness had a criminal conviction for every one of his 36 years. And Ferguson went through them one by one, casting aside with sarcastic benevolence, 'your convictions as a juvenile . . .'

When Peter Harris appeared in court earlier in 1990 charged with fraud and deception, 74 items were considered, including the following 61, read out by Ferguson: 20 credit cards, three cheque books, seven driving licences, 17 bank cash cards, three vehicle registration documents, two birth certificates, one insurance certificate, one driving certificate, two P45s, three club memberships, one AA membership, one British visitor's passport.

There were a few suppressed, embarrassed giggles in court at the length of the list. Ferguson paused while it sank in with the jury. 'All these items you were not entitled to. You intended to deprive members of the public of their money.'

Harris: 'I was looking after them for someone else.'

Ferguson: 'Out of the kindness of your heart?'

The giggles became less suppressed.

Harris's previous convictions were read out. They filled six sheets of paper and took over half an hour to go through.

His offences varied from the minor like obtaining petrol by deception, to the more serious like malicious wounding, punching a police officer – when on crutches – to the bizarre like stealing fish. The image of a man flogging stale fish from inside his raincoat hardly helped Harris's credibility.

When Ferguson had finished the roll-call of crimes, he rounded on Harris: 'You used Terry Marsh as a means of ingratiating yourself with the authorities and thereby reducing the sentence. I would suggest there is not a word of truth in what you said Terry Marsh said to you. You are a man, as demonstrated by your record, who is an inveterate, habitual liar.'

Harris replied: 'Criminal yes, liar no.'

For the prosecution, it was vital to prove that far from gaining by the revelations, Harris would suffer. Under re-examination, Curnow asked what life would be like now back in prison, after he'd grassed on another prisoner. The answer: 'Hell'.

Harris put on his sunglasses, raised his hood, and left the court which was now buzzing with inquisitiveness. As he passed Marsh, the two exchanged glances and a slight smile.

A succession of young police officers, well versed in the duty of giving evidence, described their roles in the searches of Marsh's various abodes on 17 January. A three-hour search of his parents' house in Basildon uncovered a green woollen hat, black peaked schoolboy's cap (it was never quite clear why this was worth producing), and green woollen gloves. In the loft a locker was discovered with ammunition boxes and a green hooded jacket wrapped up in a bag. From Marsh's flat at 11 Bridewell Place, Wapping, police seized bundles of correspondence.

At Marsh's marital home, Gaynesford in Basildon, police found a pair of Hi-Tec blue-green running shoes, with red decoration, white-grey toes and white laces. The prosecution claimed they matched the description given by one of the young witnesses. Also found were two cans of WD40 lubricant, magazines and books about guns: *Complete Small Gun, 1300 to the present, Modern Small Arms* and *World Encyclopaedia of Modern Guns*. Marsh was into guns, it seemed.

The jury had to sit still, quiet as ever, as the police plodded through their evidence. At the end of the trial, the judge praised the jury for their conduct, for bearing up under considerable pressure created by the media interest in the case. For two and a half weeks they were powerless to speak though ultimately potent. Normal people suddenly cast in an extraordinary role, this jury of seven men and five women on appearances was a fair cross-section of the British public. What were they all thinking? They were hearing so many contradictory things, having to concentrate on so much material, with adversaries craftily pulling for the loyalty of their opinion. It was hard not to keep wondering what they were making of all this. After one day of the trial, one of us happened to sit next to a member of the jury on the tube home for four stops. It was a struggle not to turn round and ask, 'So which way do you think it's going to go?'

Following the young officers' evidence, Curnow took part in an unlikely double act with Detective Inspector Peter Wiggins. The police officer – tall, good-looking in a conventional way, with a neatly groomed beard – read himself, and Miss Curnow read Marsh, from the edited transcripts of the officer's interview with the prisoner, her textbook accent providing a bizarre antithesis to the bluntness of the script, some of which couldn't have been bettered in fiction.

Wiggins asked Marsh about his boxing career. He replied: 'I could have been a contender, Charlie,' the familiar line from *On the Waterfront* delivered by Marlon Brando to Rod Steiger during a car journey that ends in Steiger's murder. More stifled laughs in the court.

Wiggins asked how Marsh had reacted to the diagnosis of epilepsy. 'I nearly had a fit,' was the ex-boxer's reply. More laughs. Marsh smiled slightly in recognition.

Wiggins: 'Can you give the date you married your wife Jacqueline?'

Marsh: 'No regrets.'

Wiggins: 'You're laughing, Mr Marsh, is there something you find funny?'

Marsh: 'The whole thing is a charade, but carry on.'

Wiggins: 'Have you finished Mr Mask. Can I now ask you a question?'

Marsh: 'That's Mr Marsh, not Mr Mask. Marsh with a M.A.R.S.H.'

Wiggins: 'Very funny, Mr Marsh, very amusing . . . Mr Marsh is now staring at me making no comment.'

Marsh: 'No, you're staring at me.'

Wiggins: 'Facial expression does not register on the tape. You are now sticking your tongue out at me.'

Marsh: 'He's just twitched his nose. It works both ways.'

Wiggins: 'Don't interrupt.'

Marsh: 'Bullshit.'

Wiggins: 'Pardon?'

Marsh: 'Identical to the previous one.'

Wiggins: 'Mr Marsh has just shouted bullshit . . . Now if you will give me your name just for the tape, please Mr Marsh.'

Marsh: 'Er, it's me again.'

Throughout the inquisition Marsh never admitted a thing, a point Ferguson was later to emphasise. He could have added that Marsh ran rings round Wiggins.

Did Marsh have an alibi for the night of 30 November? Wiggins had to work hard to eke out details.

Marsh said he dropped in at the Opposite Corner, the gym on Metropolitan Wharf run by Ambrose Mendy, at about 7.15pm. From there he went to the flat he owned but seldom used in Bridewell Place, Wapping, as someone was coming round with a

view to buying some furniture. He stayed longer than anticipated as the waste disposal blocked; the visitor never arrived. He
left Bridewell about 7.45, and went to see his Aunt Winnie in
Stepney Green.

There Marsh said he drank tea and talked about family
matters, mainly with his cousin Maria in the living room. He
picked up clothes for his 'littl'un' that had been given by a third
party to Winnie.

His transport that evening was a hire car borrowed from his
brother John, which he had picked up at about 6pm from his
parents' home. From his aunt's he drove to Strings, a bar in
Basildon where he stayed until closing time with John, and two
friends, Steve and Mark Darts.

Officers were sent swiftly to check Marsh's story with his aunt
and cousin. The next morning, 18 January, Marsh was interviewed again.

Wiggins: 'Your aunt said she never saw you at that address on
30 November.'

Marsh: 'Bullshit. You are bullshitting.'

Wiggins: 'Your cousin said she thinks you went there, but
can't be sure, she burst out crying. Her father asked her to be
truthful, she could not confirm the time you gave.' The officer
accused Marsh of lying.

Marsh: 'No.'

The accusation and the denial were repeated, pantomime-
style. In a sense it seemed as if Marsh's alibi had been blown: his
aunt said she hadn't seen him. But the response of his cousin
Maria, who *thought* Marsh had been there, was sufficiently
positive to mean the alibi meant little to the prosecution. On that
vital count, Marsh was safe.

Thursday, 1 November, day nine, the final day of evidence.
Assistant prosecutor Nigel Sweeney, who had joined Miss
Curnow over the last few days, informed the jury that the round
figure of Marsh's debts, assessed from documents seized from
his home was £124,348.81. Of that, £62,521.96 were debts of his
various companies, and £61,826.85 private. The prosecution

could now argue that financial desperation, possibly to be exacerbated by the libel trial, played a large part in Marsh's motivation.

That was the last blow struck by the prosecution. A series of its witnesses then did probably more to help Marsh than harm him.

The statement of Jonathan Rendall, a sports journalist, was read out. He thought the 'suspicious figure standing still' was 'a black guy'. Colin McMillan, Warren's boxer topping the bill that night at Barking, 'noticed a coloured man standing there'. Their descriptions of the 'figure's' height and build were similar to those of other witnesses.

Kevin O'Callaghan, a forensic scientist with the Metropolitan Police, explained how three cartridge cases of the Geco brand were found at the scene, two fired, one unfired. Judging by the marks on the cases, the weapon used was very probably a 9mm Luger. 'Like the one I have here,' he said, producing a gun, cradling it gently. O'Callaghan's deep, gruff voice was a middleaged white version of Frank Bruno's; big and broad with a crooked nose, the police scientist could have passed for a former heavyweight himself. As in all good crime stories, even the minor characters in this plot were colourful.

The gun O'Callaghan showed the court was not that used on the night. That has never been found. The demonstration gun was passed round the jury, as part of a complex explanation of why the gunman might have expelled a cartridge by accident. Ferguson argued the handling of the gun during the shooting had been amateurish, showing none of the coolness that would be expected from someone who, for instance, had served in the heat of action in Northern Ireland. Anyone can make a mistake under pressure, said O'Callaghan. But crucially, the markings on the spent cartridges found at Marsh's parents' house were more consistent with a Browning pistol such as Marsh owned, than those on the cartridges found at the scene of the crime.

In came Robin Keely, a scientist with the Met, an expert in firearms discharge residue. Diminutive, wearing thin-framed glasses, he had the air of an Open University lecturer, speaking in measured sentences to the court, his classroom, which had to pay full attention to his difficult subject matter. A blackboard might have helped. Eventually the salient points were clear: the hooded jacket allegedly worn by the gunman contained none of the fibres on the overcoat of John Botros, who had grappled with him. Any bullet fired expels a residue which settles on the clothing of the user of a gun. Keely concluded from his analysis: 'It is my opinion that particles found on the glove and smock [jacket] are more similar to the residues on the cartridges found in the house, than the Geco cartridges found at the crime scene.'

The forensic evidence, of dubious value to the Crown, ended there, and the case for the prosecution was then closed, shortly after lunch on the ninth day.

Richard Ferguson later said, 'The prosecution barely laid a glove on the defendant.' And now he tried to get the case stopped.

The prosecution case boiled down to Harris, claimed Ferguson. 'Is the court justified in allowing this case to proceed on evidence which emanates primarily from such a tainted source as Mr Harris?' he asked.

'I would ask you, m'lud, don't prolong the agony. There are very few cases where one can make a submission like this with confidence.' Mr Justice Fennell turned down the application.

Ferguson thought Marsh should not give evidence, and drew his man into a fifteen-minute huddle with Henri Brandman in the dock. In keen whispers they discussed their next move. 'But if we do that . . .' one would say. 'By saying nothing . . .' Brandman whispered almost too loudly. Did Marsh want to have his say from the witness stand, after remaining the silent star for so long? Did he want his chance to take centre stage? Terry Marsh had always been a big talker.

Journalists rushed off to file copy, others shuffled around muttering, contributing to the general hum of the courtroom. Curnow and Sweeney looked a little subdued, talking quietly from time to time. The police officers looked drained and disappointed – so many months' hard work could very well be coming to nothing; the court staff busied themselves with tidying papers, moving to and fro. After ten minutes Ferguson and Brandman broke from the huddle, nodding with confidence at their new game plan. The jury were led back in by their usher.

Ferguson addressed the judge: 'On behalf of the defendant I undertake no evidence.'

Not since 1979 when the former Liberal party leader Jeremy Thorpe, represented by George Carman QC, declined to give evidence had this been done in such a high publicity case, though it happens fairly frequently in run-of-the-mill cases. Thorpe was seen but not heart in court; and found not guilty.

The next day, Friday, was made a day off in order to allow counsels to prepare their final submissions. For them, the judge, court staff and jury, it had been nine punishing days.

The court rose, and Mr Justice Fennell left. Marsh gave his familiar wave and wink to the public gallery before descending into the cells. Ferguson strolled out elegantly, his juniors by his side. Curnow lit a cigarette in the corridor, as she did hurriedly after every session, as Henri Brandman brushed past. He'd been keen every day to exchange opinions with observers on how the trial was progressing. 'I'm quite pleased after today. And at least I'll be able to have a normal day in the office tomorrow. I've hardly had time to go in since this started,' he said scuttling off, his heavy briefcase, over-stuffed with papers, tucked awkwardly under his arm. Outside Marsh's family were waiting to talk to him about how things were going, and off they went for a cup of tea in the café over the road.

The queues for the public gallery were as long as ever on the morning of Monday, 5 November. Every day Marsh's loyal band were there before opening time: mother Maisie, brother John, Glenn Murphy and several friends, all of whom had travelled west from Basildon, Rainham or similar parts. Terry's father most often stayed at home, getting the tea ready. The spectators followed the case carefully and knew all its ins and outs. One morning John Marsh said: 'As an independent, what do you think? I think he'll get off. The evidence just isn't strong enough.' Earlier Maisie had said: 'All I want is to get my Terry home. They've got nothing on him.' The family group would take lunch in a café across the road from court, Maisie often with a couple of friends, no nonsense matriarchal East Enders. They were just an ordinary English family who happened to have a famous son dominating the national news. One day they were leaving the cafe and the owner, a brusque Italian lady, thought they hadn't paid, when one of the group who had already left had done so for them. 'No, we paid,' said Maisie sternly, sounding both offended and utterly unwilling to continue the conversation. 'OK,' said the Italian, backing down. Maisie and her friends would sit and chat in low voices over tea and sandwiches, return to the courtroom, always for the whole afternoon, then travel home. This odd routine wasn't to last much longer.

Marsh had maintained his level of alertness throughout the trial, listening carefully to witnesses, passing notes to Brandman, leaning forward to look at items of evidence as they were drawn from police envelopes and bags. By now he had developed a firm relationship with his shaven-headed prison officer he shared the dock with each day. They would share knowing looks, smile simultaneously at Ferguson's *bons mots*, and look bored together. When evidence possibly troublesome to Marsh was brought up, the officer looked concerned. From now on, he'd be able to say, 'I knew Terry Marsh the champion once.'

As Ann Curnow began her two-hour final submission, there was little to amuse themselves with.

'Let's consider the scene on 30 November 1989, outside the theatre in Barking.' The last act was beginning.

The shooting of Frank Warren was a 'planned assassination attempt . . . The Crown's case is that Terry Marsh had a powerful motive to wish to dispose of Frank Warren,' Curnow said forcefully, pausing for dramatic effect and moving her gaze along the line of jury members.

She reminded the jury how Harris had recalled Marsh's words, that Warren 'tied up people in legal documents and stuffed them'. She said Marsh had a 'festering dislike' of Warren, whom he saw as 'standing alone in the way of his re-establishment. That is a very, very powerful motive.'

Marsh's swift and severe decline had left him a desperate man, she claimed. The public announcement through the *Sun* of his epilepsy had ended his boxing career and employment as a fireman. Marsh blamed Warren for his removal as a commentator from *Seconds Out*.

In 1988, said Curnow, Marsh took out a manager's licence 'and didn't make a very good job of it'. He was losing money. In January 1989 Warren and Marsh had a meeting at the former's office in Tavistock Place which Warren described as 'civilised if rather cool'. Marsh asked for their manager-boxer contract to be rescinded. Warren refused.

Then on 25 January 1989 Marsh uttered the remarks on Thames TV's *Midweek Sports Special* that prompted Warren's libel action against him. Warren sued on 3 February. On 21 February the British Boxing Board of Control turned down Marsh's application to box again, thus cutting off another source of income. Curnow was building an image of scaling resentment and hatred.

In August 1989 Marsh applied to de-register his promotions business from Value Added Tax, meaning it was earning below £25,000. The libel case was looming, with the possibility of a large settlement and costs to pay. 'By the end of November he was owing £124,000. He has got a huge mortgage on his house, his business has done so badly that it is to be de-registered. He had lost his commentary job, lost his fireman's job and he was facing, if he lost the libel action, both costs and damages.'

'Marsh is sufficiently badly off to have had to dispense with his own counsel and solicitor as he can't pay them,' Curnow continued. 'He can't settle the action as that would mean an apology, it would mean having to admit that what he said on television had been a dreadful lie about Frank Warren.

'If the plaintiff in libel dies, then the action dies with him. There is no evidence Marsh knew this but anyone would know that if a plaintiff was dead he couldn't give evidence. Warren's death would effectively have finished the libel action. Only Frank Warren stood between Marsh and personal vindication.'

This was the comparatively easy part for Curnow. As for

identification, she had to settle for saying there was a consensus description among witnesses of the gunman. And, all the youngsters noted gloves, jeans and trainers, and a cream or white scarf or face garment. The description of the trainers fitted the pair found in Gaynesford. Marsh wears his watch on his right hand as they had said.

As for Hawes, he saw the gunman as the mask slipped and hood was down. His reticence to come forward and his statement that he didn't get a good look at the gunman was because 'he didn't want to get involved'. But in the end he said the gunman looked like Marsh. There was nothing wrong with Hawes being given tickets by the policeman. 'Do you think that's a really heinous crime? If you think that man has come to court and to have his private life stripped bare, all for three complimentary boxing tickets, it's a matter for you.'

Curnow was deliberate, speaking in the foreboding tone of one who had sent many a person away before. Ferguson took notes ceaselessly. The prosecution counsel gathered momentum. Did the description given by Mrs Brett of the man she saw running in front of her car closely resemble Marsh? Short curly tight hair, quite a long face, prominent nose, V-shaped face squared by a thin chin, and a white scarf flapping to the left-hand side. The man who vaulted the barrier athletically. During her evidence 'there was a disturbance' as Marsh talked to Brandman. Mrs Brett had rattled the defence.

Curnow moved on to Peter Harris. 'He is a man who has got what we describe colloquially as form, as long as your arm, or both arms . . . You know mostly he has pleaded guilty. His crimes range from fighting to theft, burglary, forgery and drugs . . . A man who has recently seen more of the inside of prison than the outside.'

She claimed there was definitely contact between Marsh and Harris, as the birthday card written by Marsh to Harris's wife proved. Curnow said certain things told to Harris could only have come directly from Marsh: his owning a firearms certificate, that the gun was never found and would be used by some confederates in an attempted robbery, that Marsh thought he had killed Warren because of the blood and mess, that the ammunition in the loft was 9mm.

'If he is telling the truth it tallies with several other bits of evidence in this case. If at the end of the day . . . the jigsaw is complete, you will be able to put your hand on your heart and say this case is proved.'

A jigsaw? That was it. Would this case be enough to convict the defendant? Ferguson did his best to ensure not.

Richard Ferguson has not quite reached the eminence of George Carman QC, who was once addressed by a judge as 'your Honour', but it can only be a matter of time. A bundle of junior barristers arrived and sat in the back of the court during his final submission to hear one of the masters at work. Speaking deliberately, to make sure the jury, judge and press, did not miss a word, with his thin glasses resting on the bridge of his nose, he leant on to the lectern, clasped his hands, and began: 'There are times I have to pinch myself in this case, because I have just listened to Miss Curnow for two hours make a brilliant speech about nothing, stringing together idea after idea, sprinkled here and there with evidence which relates to the charge which you have to deal with, and ending by creating the impression there is some sort of case against Terry Marsh. The fact of the matter is that when you steady yourself and think about it, there is no evidence against this man, with the exception of the testimony of Peter Harris.'

Ferguson's approach was not to hammer away at the jury, but caress them into accepting his point of view. He adopted a little layman's wisdom: 'Times have changed for all of us between now and November 1989, and they have changed for Terry Marsh even more in the last three years or so. On 4 March 1987 Terry Marsh stood proudly as light-welterweight champion of the world, a courageous but fair boxer, a respected master of his own destiny . . . you will be the masters of his destiny and make the decision that will have the greatest possible influence on his life.

'What is there? There is the evidence of a man who can't even stand before you in his own name . . . There is the evidence of a man who comes into this court dressed like a fugitive, there is the evidence of a man whose criminal list of convictions fills six pages. You may think it is an insult to your intelligence, and a travesty of justice to ask you to convict anyone on the testimony of Peter Harris.

'Harris told you Marsh told him that the gun was being used in a robbery or attempted robbery – that hasn't happened. He said Marsh thought he had killed him because of the blood and mess, when there is no way the gunman could have seen the blood and mess, because there wasn't any while the gunman was at the scene.'

The consensus description of the gunman was meaningless, and could apply to virtually anybody in his late 20s or early 30s. There was no identity parade, because the police did not have the courage of their convictions.

He paused, lest the importance of his next points be missed: the defendant is presumed innocent, and has to be proved guilty beyond all reasonable doubt.

Marsh was a man of good character, who had defended his country in live action; he was experienced with guns. 'Do the actions [of the gunman] as described to you fit someone who has seen service in the Royal Marines, who has been fired at and returned fire and shown his skill, courage and nerve in the boxing ring?' Would an experienced gunman have wasted a cartridge? Marines are trained to shoot twice to body and then once at their prostrate victim.

'But there would have been no mess up, no fumbling . . . if a trained marine had done this shooting. This shooting has the hallmarks of someone who bungled it and panicked.'

Ferguson's oration reached a climax. 'No one condones the shooting of Frank Warren, and hopefully one day the real culprit will be brought to justice. But justice also demands you should put a decisive end to the prosecution against this defendant. At the end of the day we say Terry Marsh is innocent, you will have the right and privilege in due course of proclaiming that to the world, and we hope you will do it.'

A director would have cued applause. Marsh grinned in recognition of a great performance.

The next day and a few minutes of the one after were taken up with Mr Justice Fennell's summing up. Delivered in his measured voice – strongly reminiscent of a Radio 4 continuity announcer – his greatest emphasis was on the evidence of Harris. It was admissible in law but needed to be treated with very great caution. 'It is wise to look for independent support, because he has 36 previous convictions . . . you wouldn't hang a dog on the evidence of Peter Harris,' said the judge, showing his own gift for a common turn of phrase. At 10.07am on Wednesday, 7 November, he asked the jury to try and reach a unanimous verdict. 'You will be given plenty of time.'

Almost four hours later, Terry Marsh looked up at the public gallery with his broad, crinkly grin.

'Exciting, innit?'

And so it was. The members of the jury were now returning, presumably with a verdict. Before lunch, the jury had re-entered the court only to ask for further direction on the evidence of Peter Harris. That had been a surprise. A fairly quick jury decision had been expected. Henri Brandman shuffled nervously in his seat, his normally glistening pate now burning red with anxiety. Even Richard Ferguson struggled to hide his perturbation. And now, will they or won't they? Is he or isn't he? But no, the jury wanted to inform the judge they were unable to reach a unanimous verdict, as he had expressly asked them to. Mr Justice Fennell frowned at length. This was most unsatisfactory, but there was little option but for him to accept, or order a retrial. 'Very well, I will allow a majority of 10–2,' said Fennell. The jury, looking a little chastised, filed out into their hidden debating room.

A sweepstake on the length of the jury's deliberation was running among the journalists, the winner being whoever guessed the time to the closest minute. A pot of £54 was eventually won by a BBC Radio reporter.

Outside, members of the public, mainly old women, had been

gathering since the morning, presuming they were going to see their hero Marsh emerge a free man. As everyone filed out of the Old Bailey for lunch, a cabbie slowed down and shouted out of the window, 'Any verdict yet?' He looked disappointed at the negative reply, and drove off. London was waiting for the jurors' decision. It was Wednesday, 7 November, two and a half weeks after the trial began.

At 3.54pm the jury re-entered for the third time. The clerk of the court turned to the foreman. 'Have you, at least ten of you, reached a verdict?'

The foreman, a friendly-looking man in his thirties with red hair and beard, rose from his place: 'Yes.'

'What is that, guilty or not guilty?'

'Not guilty.'

The foreman smiled, a little timidly, at Marsh, as if to say 'sorry you had to go through all this, you know we were always going to let you off'. Marsh broke into a huge smile which quickly vanished, as nerves appeared to overcome him. The prison officer who had kept Marsh company in the dock and developed a strong rapport, punched the air in victory and blew the tension out of his cheeks. Wild, animal cheers went up in the public gallery which was soon hushed as Mr Justice Fennell indicated he wished to speak. The second, minor indictment, for illegal possession of ammunition had to be dealt with, but in the circumstances could wait until tomorrow. 'Mr Marsh, you are free to go, but must return to court at ten o'clock tomorrow morning,' said the judge, before gathering up his papers and leaving.

Three cheers for the jury were voted from the public gallery, led by Ned Rawlings, the Navy's former heavyweight champion and friend of Marsh's, to a scornful look from Miss Curnow. Ferguson jauntily tapped the dock on his way out. 'Terry, I'll see you tomorrow.'

'Yeah,' said Marsh quietly, before turning down the steps to the custody area for the last time.

Journalists ran out of the court room, some to file copy, others to get in position for the ex-boxer's departure. No one was too sure what was happening, but surely he would say something outside. He didn't.

A flustered Henri Brandman emerged outside the court house with a brief statement. Reporters herded him to and fro in a scurrying scrum, goaded by photographers shouting 'Baa! Baa!', as they all tried to catch the words of the solicitor. 'Having been through ten months . . .'

'Say it again! Speak up!'

'Having been through ten months of hell, Terry wishes in the first . . .'

'Louder mate, can't 'ear ya!'

Brandman was told to move by a police officer, so the scrum heaved up the street, where another officer told it to move back to where it had been; back and forth it went. Looking on the verge of a heart attack, Brandman battled through the end of the statement.

'. . . Terry wishes in the first instance to be reunited with his family and there will be no further comment at this stage.'

The crowd had swelled by now to several hundred and a couple of fire engines, there to salute Marsh the former fire-fighter, added to the chaos and congestion. Richard Ferguson, now in civvies, smiled serenely, watching the bizarre scene from the pavement. Another day's work was over.

Marsh meanwhile was already on his way, having been bundled out of a side door and into a van with a leather jacket slung over his head. He had disappeared like a thief in the night.

Reporters and photographers set off in haste for a restaurant in east London. Apparently a press conference would be held there.

CHAPTER TWELVE

The Buy-Up

'Bleedin' liberty takers,' said Peter, the doorman at the Phoenix Apollo restaurant. He pushed his tortoiseshell glasses up to their proper resting place on the bridge of his nose, straightened the lapels of his jacket and stretched his neck forward, motions exclusive to those skilled in the prevention of admission to others.

'We stopped at some traffic lights and one of them tried to open the door of the van. I was holding on to the handle inside and almost fell out. A couple of flashes went off, then I managed to shut the door again. Who do they think they are? Bleedin' liberty takers.'

The 'liberty takers' in question were mobile, motorcycling press photographers, which had followed the van from the Old Bailey to east London. In it were Marsh, John Marsh, Mendy, a few friends, and Peter. These snappers-on-wheels make motorbike couriers look like grannies on push-bikes. Near the end of the journey they surrounded the white van, preventing it from moving, until police broke up the blockade, and guided the van safely into dock, near the back of the Phoenix Apollo, Stratford Broadway.

Out of the van rushed Marsh and Mendy. Marsh, a free man for the first time in ten months, used skills picked up in the marines and the fire brigade to clamber over a brick wall leading to the restaurant. The leather jacket was still over his head, a practice normally reserved for suspects or defendants wishing to prevent recognition. There was a logic to this. Mendy, along with Marsh's solicitor Henri Brandman, already knew they would sell Marsh's story exclusively to one of the newspapers. Earlier that morning Brandman had been talking to journalists along those lines in the canteen of the Old Bailey while the jury was out considering its verdict. A key part of the exclusive would be the pictures. Images across every front page of Marsh emerging victorious and undefeated from the court, arms aloft with a huge smile of vindication, could have cost the subject several thousand pounds, which he could ill afford to lose. As it was, most of the papers ran pictures of Marsh with jacket over head, or of anxious faces seen through the open door of the van.

But Marsh says his actions were born out of anger as well as financial gain. 'I wanted to make the press pay for everything they'd said, and had planned to say, 'cos I knew in the final week of the trial, they had their headlines made out already – they would have slaughtered me if I'd been found guilty. I would have been a "man possessed, whose mistake on the perfect crime was that he told an inmate" – something along those lines.'

By 4.30pm most of the reporters and cameramen had made their way from the Old Bailey and were gathered outside the door of the Phoenix Apollo, waiting to be asked in for a press conference. Passers-by looked bemused. Why today all of a sudden should 40 journalists and four camera queues be outside this place?

A few minutes passed. Marsh's contingent pushed their way through. It soon became clear no one was going in without Peter's permission. 'I'm very sorry ladies and gentlemen, we hope we won't keep you waiting too long,' he said in a polite voice.

Reporters milled around the door, like hopeful punters at an elite nightclub. Soon it was apparent there was only one way in. 'Mr Higgins and Mr Wallis, are you there?' resounded Peter. 'Come through.' Two gentlemen of the press representing the *Sun* entered the restaurant. The first bid of the auction for Terry Marsh's story was about to be made.

Higgins, small and plump, was so much of a gentleman, so polite, that *Sun* readers had a few years ago been invited to direct abuse at him over the phone – 'Ring Higgy the Human Sponge,

He'll Soak It Up'. The paper's editor Kelvin MacKenzie had taken exception to his reporter's habit of smiling through any adversity or insult and amused himself by publishing this innovative reader service. But now Higgins was deputy news editor and working on the big stories. Once inside Marsh recognised his partner, Neil Wallis, the 'Wolfman', the author of the epilepsy exclusive three years ago that had been the beginning of Marsh's troubles. Since then the reporter's stories had been the subject of a number of complaints and libel writs dubbed 'the Wallis Collection' by colleagues. This rather comic-looking pair came out fifteen minutes later, and jumped into a Mercedes parked outside and telephoned their office in Wapping with a progress report.

Soon Peter shouted out, '*Daily Express*!' 'Yes,' came the reply from a reporter, his self-esteem rising as he pushed through the anxious crowd of journalists who were fast realising this stage of events would leave their notebooks empty of comments from Marsh. The only journalist who seemed to get in for nothing, so to speak, was a girl from the *News of the World*, who evidently knew Peter, and told him how nice his hair looked straightened.

Stratford Broadway isn't one of London's prettiest spots. A busy road leading out of London, it is littered with drab, cheaply-built post-war buildings. The shops are the poorer high street chains and even less well off local businesses. Among this dross is the glitter of the Phoenix Apollo restaurant, not exactly a gem, more a piece of costume jewellery. It gives the impression that five different designers were allowed free rein over a part each, and told to imitate their favourite style. The exterior is American ranch, the low sofas quasi-Japanese, the bar English, and the soft lighting French. It has a cosy garishness. The interior walls are half-timbered and mock-Tudor, decorated by scenic prints and items of Victoriana. The food is 'continental', a breathtaking blend of European cuisines, with a slight bias to the Greek. The owners, brothers Pani and Gil Panayiotou, originally came from Cyprus.

The restaurant is used to celebrities. Pictures of famous visitors fill an entire wall. For the past couple of years Ambrose

Mendy had used the Phoenix Apollo as an unofficial HQ, and Marsh had been one of a coterie of celebrities who frequently visited, along with Nigel Benn, an assortment of Page Three girls, footballers and actors. There are cocktails for star guests: Henri Brandman, Floater (no spirit) £1.50; Nigel Benn (Caribbean knock-out, three rums mixed) £5.50; Terry Marsh (Gaelic) £2.60; George Michael (Greek Coffee); Roberto Duran (tequila). Only Benn had his own dish, the Brontosaurus Ribs at £15. After the media had gone, Marsh stayed the night up above, where the Panayiotou brothers live. Without opening its doors for business, the restaurant received priceless publicity.

'We couldn't have paid a million pounds for the coverage in the press and on national television,' said Gil Panayiotou. 'You could see the restaurant on the six o'clock news, it was amazing. We had no idea it was going to be that big.

'There was no party as such. The atmosphere was really quite subdued, which is the way Henri wanted it. And Terry just had an orange juice.' Though Mendy had told reporters Marsh was washing down his meal with Perrier Jouet Belle Epoque champagne.

'Terry had his favourite meal, a mixed grill. Off a china plate. He seemed very relaxed, just upset about being inside for ten months, though obviously it's very hard to say what was going on inside his head. Terry's not a very emotional person – I couldn't imagine him crying for instance.'

Gil Panayiotou is an affable, hospitable restaurateur. Short and tanned, chatty and smart, with a speciality in the unexpected one-liner, Gil works 24 hours a day but still looks for other challenges beyond the restaurant. These days he is a would-be revolutionary song-writer, politician and football director. His ambition is to have the actor Anthony Quinn, star of *Zorba the Greek*, eating at his restaurant.

He and his brother run a highly successful business. The food is good, though eccentrically garnished: a helping of roast duck arrived with two miniature cocktail umbrellas stuck in it. Welcome guests are generously offered a drink. 'Gentlemen, have a Gilly Willy on the house. It's our special cocktail.'

A less likely solicitor to the celebrities it would be hard to imagine than Henri Brandman. Stocky, balding, bespectacled, Brandman doesn't give the impression of someone who works with Page Three girls, star footballers, actors and the like. But a strong sense of humour, a prescient mind and keenness for legal battle have served him very well. Henri Brandman's family, one of the last Jewish families to quit the East End, lived above what is now the Phoenix Apollo in Stratford, and had a shop downstairs. They sold out to the Cypriot Panayiotou family who opened a restaurant and nightclub. When the father died, his sons took over.

Then disaster struck. The place was gutted by fire. 'Actually it turned out to be a bit of a blessing in disguise,' says Gil. 'And as the place was being reborn we decided to call it the Phoenix Apollo – we thought it was a blinding idea.'

When it reopened as an enlarged restaurant in 1985, the Panayiotou brothers hit upon the idea of asking Page Three girl *par excellence*, Sam Fox, along to its renaissance party. It so happened that Brandman represented Fox, and couldn't pass up the chance of seeing the brothers for the first time in years. Soon Henri was solicitor, close friend and conduit of several celebrity guests – chiefly footballers from his beloved West Ham. Somewhere along the line Terry Marsh's mate, the actor Glenn Murphy, whose cousin Jason Wright was going out with Maria Whitaker, came along. One night Suzanne Mizzi was in and said to Gil Panayiotou why don't you come boxing tomorrow? So off they went to the York Hall to watch Gary Stretch (in his Warren days) and the next day Terry Marsh turned up at the restaurant and said could he hold a press conference and before you knew it the World Sports Corporation was publicising one of its first promotions at Gil's place. Gil introduced Ambrose to Paul Ince, and to Henri, whose boxing connections thus far had been limited to dating one of the daughters of Board doctor Adrian Whiteson, and soon the Phoenix Apollo, Stratford, was the vortex of high society. 'Henri was instigational,' says Gil. 'It's nice, a real network of friends and celebrities has built up.'

Ambrose brings his friends and associates, Gil and Pani give them the best service; Gil went to the States to do the food for Nigel's fight against Doug de Witt; Ambrose makes sure the place gets in the papers. Business is good, and got even better after Terry Marsh was freed from the Old Bailey.

The journalists hanging around outside his restaurant in the cold would have been grateful for any sort of cocktail, even a Gilly Willy. Particularly those not participating in the auction, which was gathering momentum. Representatives of different news-papers scribbled offers which were passed via Peter and a member of the restaurant staff to Brandman. Negotiations continued past 5.30. The press crowd decided to cheer itself up. Joke offers were made. A round zero from the *Guardian*, a pint and a packet of crisps from the *Observer*, £10 to a charity of Mr Marsh's choice from the *Daily Telegraph*, but still nothing to write about or anybody to quote. Then Ambrose Mendy came out.

Never shy of a camera or notebook, Mendy acted as Marsh's spokesman. Surrounded by a heaving scrum of journalists, he delivered the compensation to all the losers and non-participants in the auction. It was a collected performance, which said a lot more about him than Marsh, though Mendy was a little ruffled when a BBC TV reporter asked: 'Sorry, what was your name?'

Mendy addressed his audience: 'Obviously he [Terry] is in good health and in good hands. He has said nothing about his ordeal. He looks fit. I am a fairly composed person normally but I am delighted. I have protested his innocence for ten months and I feel vindicated. Me and Terry are not blood relatives but obviously we have a great affinity. It has been a big day, it's fantastic.'

'What were his first words?' called out someone.

'They are not repeatable. Terry Marsh is a great guy and I can but smile. He has always been a man of the public and at the end of the day it was Joe Bloggs on the jury who set him free. Listen, Frank Warren was best man when I got married, but I am still delighted for Terry. It wasn't Terry Marsh that did it, and that's all I care about. I am a great believer in street credibility, but I am a great believer in role models and giving people hope . . .' A few pens paused, struck by his temerity, but accepted Mendy's regret for Marsh's non-appearance.

'I can only apologise he didn't come through the front door, since he is a man of the people. If it's good enough for the Guildford Four it's good enough for our man. But I am sure you understand, his loss of earnings over the last ten months is horrendous. You are journalists, you know how it works and appreciate the financial situation. At the first proper press conference we hope we will get you all drunk.'

Mendy continued his peroration. 'Terry just wants to go back to being Joe Bloggs. He stood up to everything and at some point in his mind the cracks might begin to show. Terry has had some really good friends through this and that is what he deserves, he had some magnificent people around him. I am training with Nigel Benn, we even broke the training camp, but what a cause. It's your support that has helped Terry keep up his confidence to keep going through this,' he concluded. A few journalists looked at each other in puzzlement, unable to recall any such support, but then it is always nice to be appreciated.

While this was happening, one of the *Sun* men gave a V-sign from an upper window to the press throng below. His paper, along with the *News of the World*, had won the auction. Going, going, gone for £140,000, one of the biggest buy-ups since cheque book journalism took off. The figure neatly matched Marsh's debts.

The next day, Thursday, 9 November, he returned to the Old Bailey, surrounded by minders. The charges for the illegal possession of ammunition, at the request of the prosecution, were laid on file, meaning they were effectively dropped. If the ex-boxer had been found guilty, any sentence given would have been likely to be less than the ten months Marsh had already served in custody. But it seemed Marsh's troubles weren't over. Frank Warren announced he was going to press ahead with the libel action. The Crown Prosecution Service considered bringing fraud charges against Marsh, concerning a £37,000 mortgage application on the family home. The charges were never brought because, according to a police source, they were 'to a large extent

dependent on his wife's evidence', which was no longer forth-
coming.

That hadn't been the only time Jacqui Marsh had failed to give
evidence. Shortly before Marsh's arrest for the attempted
murder, she made eight statements to the police, without which
it is doubtful Marsh would ever have been charged. Upon his
arrest at Gatwick Marsh said to police officers: 'Who put you up
to this? My wife?'

Jacqui had claimed Marsh had bragged about going to
Warren's home 'to do a recce'. She had accused her husband of
the shooting during a blazing row in front of police at Marsh's
parents' home. Detective Superintendent Jeff Rees, the officer in
charge of the case, was naturally keen for Jacqui to give
evidence. But in law, a wife does not, if summoned, have to give
evidence against her husband. Common law used to hold that a
wife, or husband, could not give evidence against their spouse,
even if they wanted to; the thinking being that the bond of
marriage effectively made two people as one. The 1984 Police
and Criminal Evidence Act allowed a wife or husband the choice
of giving evidence in most cases.

Jacqui Marsh was summoned as a prosecution witness.
Accompanied by a lawyer, she arrived at the Old Bailey and got
as far as the door of court number two before turning around.
Either she decided at the last minute not to give evidence, or, as
her husband says, she was prepared to go into the witness box
but her testimony would not have satisfied the police, who
decided not to call her.

Jacqui soon revealed she had 'shopped my Terry' in fury. After
eight turbulent years of marriage they had split by the time
Warren was gunned down. She told the *News of the World*: 'I
was supposed to give evidence against him – but I decided not to.
I was in such a state I didn't know what I was doing. It was a
crazy situation.

'I wanted to hurt him for all the suffering he'd put me through.
I never wanted him to go down. I only meant him to have a few
sleepless nights of worry.'

Terry Marsh believes the police tried to lean on Jacqui

following her own problems. Suggestions were made about custody, if I came out, and they supplied her with a shoulder to cry on. They bought Kelly a birthday present . . .'

Shortly after the trial, Frank Warren said on TV-am's *Frost Show*: 'It's a bit of a way to get back at your husband. And obviously a hell of a waste of tax-payers' money and that I would believe is a vindication of the prosecution case that they had. Obviously they were depending on those statements, and for her to give evidence in court which she was not prepared to do. I think the police were resting their case on a number of statements I think his [Marsh's] wife made . . . in each of those she actually said he was planning to kill me and she said that he had made the attack on my life according to the statements, and that he had been planning to do that for quite a while.'

'We were a bit frustrated,' said the police officer later. 'We would love to say, *that* was the case presented to the Crown Prosecution Service and that we wanted to present to the court. The case is not something that has been satisfactory for us.'

Henri Brandman made threats of legal action against the police after stories about Jacqui's statements were published, but they came to nothing. Scotland Yard might have relished a further challenge which would have been seen as an opportunity to vindicate the decision to prosecute. The police were heavily criticised in many quarters for continuing with a case which after a few days seemed unlikely to end in a conviction. 'What we want is for Marsh to take an action for wrongful arrest, so all the evidence could come out,' said the officer. 'If he [Marsh] admitted it [the attempted murder] now there is nothing we could do about it,' he added, pointing out that law prevents anyone being tried twice for the same offence.

The CPS stuck by its decision. A spokesman told the *Daily Mail*: 'As far as we are concerned there was sufficient to prosecute. There was strong circumstantial evidence added to other things which I cannot discuss.' *The Times* was told: 'We considered it was a properly brought prosecution. It was committed for trial by a magistrate. There was an application by the defence ... for the charge to be withdrawn but this was rejected by the trial judge.'

The fact that Richard Ferguson had tried to have the trial stopped indicated how sure the defence was of its case. Despite the majority verdict, barely a glove was laid on the defendant, as the eminent counsel put it. The defence's thoroughly researched fight plan compiled evidence of its own against nearly all the prosecution witnesses, a file of reputation-damaging material which either humiliated or made a laughing stock of the witness. About 15 other items of such material were kept under the counter, judged too sensitive to use. Some of the information came from the defendant and his friends, some by good luck. The news that the pensioner William Hawes had been in Alcoholics Anonymous arrived fortuitously in Henri Brandman's office, for instance. The information that Frank Warren was friends with the flower girl, Nicola Tarrant, which led to Richard Ferguson asking Warren if he had had an affair with her, was not a great secret to those in the know, as the question at the promoter's first press conference after the shooting showed. According to Warren's uncle, Jimmy, Marsh had seen the promoter in the company of Nicola Tarrant on social occasions. 'Frank and Marsh used to go out. Marsh met her, Frank's friend, so he told his brief what happened. It was a rotten thing to do really. Frank wasn't there to give evidence against him.'

One of the only witnesses the defence could not taint was Margaret Hilda Brett, whose description of the features of the man she had seen running in front of her car was uncomfortably close to that of the ex-boxer. Terry Marsh himself is still bothered by her evidence and wonders why her original deposition did not contain such a detailed description. 'If I was in prison now, on the say-so of that woman, I'd be tearing my hair out, saying someone get out there and check her out.'

Other aspects of the evidence against him make him even more bitter at spending ten months in jail over nothing. He thinks the green jacket taken from his parents' house was brand new. 'And I don't know if it was mine or my brother's 'cos we've got so much stuff from when we was in the services.'

The evidence of Peter Harris, despite his list of convictions, probably did most harm to Marsh, who thinks Harris has turned on fellow prisoners before. 'He weren't even a grass, a grass tells the truth albeit in an immoral way, to save his own skin,' says Marsh. 'What happened is that I've gone in to the jail, and they [other prisoners] said to me, "did you do it?", and I've said, "of course I didn't". And they've all said but they found bullets on you, and I said "I had a firearms certificate" and they said "why are you wearing prison clothes", and I said "'cos the police have taken all my gear". It's a joke, they've got a pair of trainers, but those trainers I never had until six weeks after the incident – brand new trainers, which I was wearing off the plane. So one's talked to another, and another, and Harris 'as turned round and said, "and the police have even got a footprint from trainers that he left behind and what he was wearing at the airport". But I'd actually said to people how ridiculous that was because they showed me these trainers and I naturally assumed they had a footprint [at the scene of the crime]. But I said they were talking about shoes I hadn't had at the time.' It turned out there was no footprint at the scene of the crime.

'But you know, Chinese whispers, Harris has got it a little bit wrong, and added a bit and added a bit, put it all together. It's 70 per cent truth and 30 per cent lies. He never got the full story.' Marsh is convinced that without the evidence of Harris he would never have been committed for trial. He also has doubts about William Hawes, the pensioner kindly given three tickets for a Frank Warren promotion by a police officer. It bothers Marsh that in his first statement Hawes said he could not put a name to the gunman, and that someone supposedly too poor to afford boxing tickets was seen a few weeks after the trial by Henri Brandman at a testimonial dinner for the West Ham footballer Alan Devonshire. Tickets cost £60 each.

The aftermath of the trial brought even more intensive press coverage than the event itself. Added to the drama at the Old Bailey, there was a repentant wife, the boxing tycoon's friend the flower girl, and Marsh's prison revelations. Wearing a T-shirt reading 'Who Framed Terry Marsh?' – taking off '*Who Framed*

Roger Rabbit?' – Marsh grinned broadly for the *Sun*'s cameras, and voiced his jubilation at being released and bitterness at having ten months of his life taken away for nothing. He gave a grim description of the conditions inside Wormwood Scrubs, and appeared happily reunited with Jacqui. Marsh, ever resourceful, had taught himself a bit of Italian and written parts of an autobiography while inside. Ever stubborn, he wound up the screws endlessly, at one point smearing himself in baby oil so he was impossible to grapple with – a successful device which got him in solitary confinement, away from the other prisoners.

Once outside, he instantly had a practical joke up his sleeve. On the first day out and about with the *Sun*, the deputy editor rang him from the newsdesk to find out how their expensive purchase was performing. 'Ah, well, bit of a problem,' said Terry. 'This guy came up and put a gun in my hand and then he took a picture of me.'

'Oh Christ,' said the voice down the phone, 'did he say who he was?'

'He said he was from the *Daily Mirror*!'

Friends criticised the police for going ahead with the trial, and offered overwhelming support for Terry, whom they had said all along was innocent. One told the *Daily Mirror* that Terry had told him: 'I didn't shoot him. If it had been me, I sure as hell wouldn't have missed.'

Some of the 'Jail Diaries of Prisoner 0100' wasn't the most riveting material, but the *Sun* was content. It had always seen Terry Marsh as one of 'theirs', a celebrity who belonged to Wapping. Once again, albeit at a heavy price, a series of Marsh personas was being presented through the pages of the *Sun*. His image had gone from the fighting fireman to world champion, to the tragic victim of epilepsy, and upon his release to a victim of a miscarriage of justice. A few days later, he appeared in a new incarnation: The Comeback. Marsh swore he would box again, if not here then in the States, three and a half years since last pulling on a glove in anger. America was warned to prepare itself for The Return of Fighting Fireman. Barely unnoticed during all this was the collapse of Terry Marsh Promotions, wound up with debts of £34,860, a reminder of the problems Marsh faced in his freedom.

The Marsh family meanwhile was recovering from the trauma of the trial. Maisie had British Telecom intercept all calls, and refused to talk to any press, even the local paper which she trusted and was grateful to for its support for Terry. Having kept a firm hand on the family tiller, she wasn't going to let slip now.

Warren said his personal security would be relaxed, though he would make sure there was security on hand for his wife and children 24 hours a day. When he saw Marsh at the libel trial, the promoter would look him in the eye, and say nothing. 'I am not interested in talking to Terry Marsh. It's cost me a lot of money.'

'Contrary to popular belief,' says Terry Marsh,' I did not shoot Frank Warren.' If he didn't shoot Frank Warren, who did? There have been suggestions someone he owed money to was responsible for it. Richard Ferguson said in court that Nicola Tarrant's boyfriend, 'might not have had a very high opinion' of the promoter, though Holt himself was in custody at the time of the shooting, on remand for supplying drugs. Coincidentally Terry Marsh met him in prison. Nothing seems to have come of the police's original, day-after theory that a professional assassin was responsible for the shooting.

For Marsh the bitterness over what he sees as wrongful imprisonment will never go. 'I know the mentality of the police, I recognise it from the Army. They are like little dogs, they love to be rewarded, to be patted on the head and told they've been good boys. It's like when I was a kid if I was given a maths problem or a physics problem and I couldn't get them right and the homework had to be in the next day. To save face so as not to be told off for not doing my homework, I would put an answer down — any answer — and that's what the police have done. I would suggest, from a victim's point of view, to use the prosecution's words, that "an angry or bitter ex-fighter" is a lot more comfortable to live with than a vendetta or big city business hitmen. Lo and behold, I was arrested. Because of the public profile they needed a body. Now they can close their file and get on with the next case ... I don't know whether I'm famous or infamous!'

A few days after Marsh's acquittal the police did indeed close their file.

CHAPTER THIRTEEN

The Punch-Up

Ten days after his release Marsh made his first public appearance, at an evening which in many ways sums up the decline of Warren – the fight between Nigel Benn against Chris Eubank for the World Boxing Organisation middleweight championship. The WBO is a new commission, which has yet to earn the full respect of the boxing world. As the fourth major commission offering world titles, it had multiplied the number of champions without improving the quality. If its titles aren't *worthless* in pure boxing terms, they aren't necessarily worth a great deal, but when it is a good, domestic showdown, such detail is cast aside.

The hyping of the fight, based on a supposedly profound hatred between the two combatants, was unpalatable to boxing purists. Mendy, managing Benn, said his man would receive £1 million, the highest purse ever for a boxer in Britain; Eubank managed by Barry Hearn would get £600,000. (In the end the real figures were £400,000 and £120,000 respectively.)

But even those irritated by the pre-fight nonsense recognised it was the fight of the year, which reflected the changing power structure of British boxing. It was also one of the best post-war contests fought in the country. Rarely have two men given so much of themselves in a boxing ring.

Benn, 'The Dark Destroyer', is also the only current British boxer with a strong following. He delivers bludgeoning punches with a speed and aggression customary in fighters from across the Atlantic. An unabashed brutality excites crowds to a fever pitch. He fights in the way some people fantasise they would respond if their best friend was attacked, with superior, unremitting power, and if nothing else he has managed to change the connotation of the name Nigel from the banal to the belligerent.

Benn's defensive inefficiencies and tendency to brawl rather than box have made him vulnerable, and his contests against good opponents compelling. A bad loss often effectively ends a boxing career, but even after losing to Michael Watson in May 1989, Mendy and Benn were able to resurrect the boxer's career in America, in one of the most adroit management feats in boxing. Mendy realised that Benn's popularity would survive one defeat, but knew he needed to get away from home and to a fresh start. Nigel went to Florida on holiday and met a trainer, Vic Andretti, a Londoner now based in Miami. It was decided to drop Benn's old trainer, Brian Lynch, and work with Andretti.

Lynch, aged 51, was an untried trainer with a jewellery business in Upminster. One day he was training his son at a gym in West Ham and a young fighter came up and asked him for some help. Lynch's dream of training a champion had walked through the door – The Dark Destroyer.

'He wasn't the fighter he was until he came with me. He was just a swinger who'd put his head down. His legs used to be wrong. But you can see something that someone's got, and I went for it.' Lynch's big idea was that Benn should spar the absolute bare minimum so as not to leave too much power in the gym. Even as a concept for established champions that was dubious, but for a boxer who had started late and was short of finesse it was never going to work. Benn relied on power alone as he plundered through 21 opponents before Watson found him out.

Lynch maintains his approach was the right one and only Nigel's lack of discipline brought defeat. 'I told Nigel how to beat Watson. I told him exactly how Watson would fight. Nigel didn't listen to a word. The preparation was all wrong. I wanted him to go to the weigh-in and then drive back home quick, sleep a few hours in the back room with the blinds down and then have a nice meal, spaghetti or something. Instead he was driving up Ilford High Road with the top down in the sun and getting his hair done. If you can't trust someone to go home at the age of 25, when can you?'

Benn's life has been hard. His parents struggled to control the wildest son in their large family in West Ham. 'I was a layabout but I wanted to be somebody,' Benn has said. In danger of being a nobody, he joined the Army. 'People thought I'd be out of the Army in two or three days but I stuck it for four years, 256 days. The Army made me. If I hadn't joined up I'd have been inside. I love my brother John so much that I followed him into the Army. I come from a very close family. Mum used to keep things away from my dad because he is a very strict man. He used to say he'd burn my fingers if I didn't stop nicking things.'

Benn, the hungry fighter, has, thanks largely to his four-fight American campaign, been able to satisfy simple material voracity. He has a Bentley, two BMWs, and a Porsche with a £6,000 stereo. He likes gold jewellery and his wardrobe is flooded with designer suits. Nowadays his home is a palatial house in Chigwell, Essex.

Benn's extravagance in and out of the ring made him big box office, but Eubank, unknown outside boxing circles, had talked his way into the fight, ranging a series of insults at his opponent: who was alternately a 'mere street brawler', 'coward', and 'dimwit'. Benn, with Mendy pulling strings, exchanged the malice. And ticket sales soared. Eubank, arrogant about his ability, and dismissive of his sport as 'a mug's game', predicted his own victory, as boxers always do, but with inflammatory self-confidence.

It was quite an evening. For the first time in a long while a big arena was full for boxing. The National Exhibition Centre in Birmingham, a vast barn, was stuffed with 10,000 spectators. ITV networked the fight live, at a cost of £200,000, one of the highest fees ever paid for a domestic fight. Screensport broadcast it all over Europe. The show was promoted by Barry Hearn who was reaching a new peak in his three-year-old career in boxing promotion.

It was exactly the sort of event that Frank Warren should have been staging. Benn, the only boxer apart from Bruno capable of drawing such a crowd, had set himself free from Warren's control two years ago, joining Mendy. Earlier he and Ernie Fossey had passed up the chance to manage Eubank. Beating Benn would have been sweet revenge. Watching it all on television must have been hard for Warren, especially as he had more or less singlehandedly opened up independent television coverage of boxing. So many people he had been involved with and so much he had achieved, culminated in the most dramatic boxing night for years. Warren would not have wished to attend, being set against so many people involved: Marsh in a libel trial, Benn and Mendy in an action for loss of earnings. He would not have seen Terry Marsh on television being received as a returning hero by the crowd. Shortly before the main event, the besuited ex-boxer vaulted over the ropes of the ring – a trademark from his fighting days – and waved to the crowd, his face beaming at the public's applause. The man accused of shooting Warren was back in the boxing society that adored him.

Even the style of the show owed a lot to razzmatazz modernisations that Warren had first introduced. Before each support bout the house lights were dimmed and the boxers and their cornermen spotlit on their route to the ring, accompanied by loud dance music, in this case Nigel Benn's new record, 'Stand And Fight'.

A boxing crowd is older and tougher than a typical football crowd. There are very few teenagers, for it is an expensive night out, and the audience is packed with 200 pound men in £400 suits, all of whom look as if they could handle themselves in the ring if it came to it. People drift around restlessly during the supporting fights. Some have come to see a specific boxer, others spend more time at the bar, checking their betting slips, and waiting impatiently for the main event of the evening.

If boxing is a hard man's world, it is also a man's world pure and simple. Boxers often emphasise the importance of their own family, probably because such a lonely and committed pursuit requires great patience on behalf of a wife.

But the female place in boxing tends to consist of a variety of support roles: the loyal wife who can't bear to watch her husband fight, the mother at ringside who makes more noise supporting her boy than half of the rest of the crowd put together, the dolly-bird card girls, the Page Three girls in the celebrity lounges. Every boxing crowd is dotted with ordinary women usually following fighting friends, but among the real cognoscenti there are very few. It is not just the fact that chauvinism pervades boxing which limits women to the margins of the sport. It is a world where one man's strength is pitted against another's, where masculinity is worshipped by man. Men enjoy fighting more, and enjoy watching it more. Women's relatively rare curiosity about boxing is inspired by its utter indifference to their own femininity and a wonder at men's fascination with it. It is comparable to many males' attitudes to childbirth. Women's traditional distaste for boxing is nothing to do with female squeamishness or faint hearts. It is more like commonsense.

Minutes before the main attraction the MC read out a list of celebrity names who took it in turns to stand up and take a rather embarrassed bow. There was, as they say, a galaxy of stars present. Footballers Paul Ince (Benn's cousin), Vinny Jones, Bryan Robson, Paul Gascoigne, Gary Lineker, John Fashanu and Cyrille Regis; rugby league stars Martin Offiah, Ellery Hanley and Sean Edwards; singers Aswad, Mica Paris, and Sinitta; athlete Linford Christie and two dozen big boxing names – the biggest cheer in this category honouring Bruno. Big fights have always attracted big names. Celebrities have always been fascinated by the prospect of a human conflict, though unlike the public, they are readily given free entrance by organisers who are keen to lend a glamour to their events which will reflect on themselves. But this collection of celebrities was exceptional. Nigel Benn was a big attraction.

The boxers in the main event had arrived in their dressing rooms four hours beforehand, about 6.30pm. Eubank, in a later interview with the *Independent on Sunday*'s Jonathan Rendall, said: 'I made sure everything was in place, massaged my feet and then laced up my boots. Ronnie Davies my trainer was with me – at all times! – because I like his company. Ronnie usually sings to me, old Irish rebel songs, songs which are good luck to me.' Later, 'the referee Richard Steele came into the dressing room. He said: "You're fighting for the championship of the world. This can make you or break you, but it will not be no dirty fight. You understand? I am the man in this ring. You do as you are told. When I say break, you break. You are not going to win this fight by cheating, and I am telling Nigel Benn the same things." I was proud to be spoken to like that.'

After the celebrity roll call, Land of Hope and Glory was blasted from the PA, everyone of the audience on its feet. A slight delay, and then Eubank emerged to Tina Turner's song, 'Simply the Best', his pre-fight slogan. But the music stopped as he was only a few yards out of the entrance of the auditorium.

'It was a case of sabotage,' Eubank told the *Independent on Sunday*. 'Someone had taken the tape out of the machine, snapped it and put it back in. Barry Hearn lost his mind over it. He spun me round and we went back to the dressing room. Then Barry came up to me and said: "We've been messed about enough. We don't need no robe and no music. Let's just go out there and take this guy. Can you do that?" I said: "Yeah, sure. Just be cool Barry." ' So Eubank re-entered without soundtrack, and flipped into the ring, wearing a white cloth cape. He stood impassively for several minutes, shifting his erect stance only every now and then, waiting for the Benn contingent to arrive. 'I stood in the ring and sucked in all the hate from the Benn supporters. I redirected it towards Nigel Benn; it was like a prism, channelling energies back to him.'

The champion's entrance, delayed to try and wind up Eubank, was presaged by a band of drummers from Benn's former regiment, the Royal Fusiliers. When a fighter comes out to a huge reception it is spine-tingling, gladiatorial stuff. The audience feels the fear of what their hero can do, and also, what may happen to him. Surrounded by half a dozen bigger men, the boxer appears as both the most powerful being and conversely, the most fragile. Unease overlayed by excitement spreads throughout the crowd.

Then Benn made his grand arrival, the flag of St George borne in front, his gloved hands resting on Mendy's shoulders, his seconds glancing anxiously around. First boomed Phil Collins' 'In the Air Tonight', then a storming reggae number.

Benn climbed through the ropes in black sequin shorts and bomber jacket, looking sensational. The two fighters preened themselves in front of each other in their different ways, Benn flashing punches into the air, Eubank maintaining his rather laughable quasi-aristocratic stance. 'This is showbiz,' said a boxing fan nearby, 'but it's bloody good.'

Eubank said he had called Benn 'Benjamin' in the lead-up to the fight, because to call him by name would have made it impossible not to think about him and his awesome punching power. 'Before that night, I never looked at him. I always said, "I'll face the man on the night in the ring, but not before." In the ring I looked at him and saw a relentless savage. But I also saw a man with a slight doubt on his mind. I saw that when he looked into my eyes he needed reassurance. I thought: "It's too late for that, mate. You're mine." ' Referee Steele brought the two now de-robed fighters together for the mandatory words on conduct and brought their gloves together. 'Benn smashed his fist down really hard,' Eubank said. 'That was a mistake. Beforehand I'd been wondering, does Benn really hit as hard as they say? When he hit my glove I knew. I could feel the power. I didn't need to test one of his punches like I usually do.'

Steele touched the boxers lightly on the back of the neck in that gesture that says, 'behave yourselves, boys'. The bell rang for round one. Fighters do not savour a big occasion. They are not like tennis players at a Wimbledon final. They are in the ring to make as much money in as short a time as possible. It is too dangerous to hang around. 'When it's all over I feel a sense of relief that my pride is no longer on the line,' says Eubank. Only Nigel Benn was never going to allow him to win quickly.

Benn had been accused of lacking 'heart' when Michael

Watson had beaten him – the worst criticism that can be levelled at a boxer. His performance against Eubank dispelled that. The first encounters went to Eubank, who strode around the ring at the end of the first round for a full 15 seconds as if to prove he was not scared of the champion. However, Benn's punches then began to get through, including one in the third round which made Eubank bite his tongue. He was in considerable pain for the rest of the fight. The most captivating aspect of it all was that both men appeared vulnerable and on the point of losing at different times. In round five Benn's left eye began to close up. He knew, as his vision began to slip away, that he had to finish the fight, and waged an even more vicious assault than before. Benn is a fighter who expresses himself more clearly between the ropes than any other British boxer, his rage, but also his hurt. When he is hit, hurt is etched all over his face; it might as well be written on his forehead. His style grows more ragged, which gives his opponent encouragement.

Benn was hurt now, but knocked Eubank down in round eight. It looked as if the eccentric challenger was finally losing his will. But Eubank too, was desperate to survive, and though he may not please the boxing purist, is immensely strong. And then in round nine, the gigantic effort Benn had put in suddenly seemed to rip him apart, as Eubank powered in to him with a two-handed attack, sending the man who had come out to the sound of drums wobbling around the ring. Richard Steele separated the two men to protect Benn from further punishment. 'Oh no, Nigel, Nigel, Nigel,' cried a man sitting behind, his head in his hands.

It was over, abruptly, like a car screeching to a halt just before it smashes in to a wall. Eubank slumped to his knees and screamed in ecstasy. Seconds later, a champion, he proposed to his girlfriend Karron in front of millions of television viewers.

The couple have since married.

Barry Hearn expected Eubank to win. It was about time he had a world champion. After all, he had been promoting boxing for three years, a long time in Barry Hearn's life.

Hearn's operation is run from a two-storey, grey stucco Edwardian house in Romford, Essex, opposite a shopping centre and just down the road from a multi-storey car park, an unlikely place to find one of the most successful men of the last decade. The smart but unostentatious entrance appears like some sort of secondary office for Hearn's Matchroom headquarters, not the real thing. Perhaps behind a secret door there is a magic snooker table that would carry you off to another place, where the sun always shines, and King Barry of Essex would be sitting on a throne of £50 notes? But Barry likes things simple. Home is just down the road in Brentwood, and why bother to struggle with getting into London every day?

This modest residence is the seat of Hearn's empire. On the first floor, the voice of Essex boomed out. 'Alex, Harry? In 'ere boys. Sorry to have 'eld you up.' Hearn sat behind his desk, smiling broadly. At the other end of the rectangular room, decorated in simple grey, there is a state of the art television and video, sofas, and a bookcase crammed with over a hundred boxing and snooker videos. On every wall, photos and cartoons of his sportsmen mirror Hearn's achievements. And three stuffed frogs play miniature billiards. Hearn, wearing tracksuit bottoms and a T-shirt bearing the name of the Boca Raton Resort Club, is a tall, broad, bright-faced, better than average-looking 43-year-old, determined to stay as young as possible for at least a few more years. Incipient middle-age spread is his greatest fear.

'I was at a party last night in Preston after the Davis-Hendry final. What a match. Sixteen-fifteen their man on the final frame, what a night,' he grinned even more expansively. 'Thanks for hanging around, how can I help you?'

Barry Hearn communicates. The man who was responsible for taking snooker away from its working men's club image (and derisory prize money), and in to millions of homes, wants to take over British boxing.

'I'd like to carry on doing what I'm doing now for another ten years. Ten world champions in ten years, then that will be enough. I will monopolise boxing. That's not an ambition, that's automatic.'

But is what is good for Barry good for boxing? 'I'm a benevolent dictator,' he said, fixing his gaze. 'I find it works better like that. If I let other people do it, they fuck it up.'

Some see Hearn as archetypal Essex Man. A wheeler and a dealer who made big money fast and who, in the 1980s, the decade of the salesman and the marketing strategist, found a new market for an old product, using heaps of charm, arm-twisting and plain old hard work as he swept to a fortune. But others say he is more complex – that there is self-parody and charm which make him a bit different. But this may not be enough to fulfil his latest dream. Boxing, as Barry has already discovered, is rather different from snooker.

He was born in Dagenham in 1948, the son of a bus driver. After leaving grammar school with a couple of 'A' Levels he joined a firm of accountants, Bristow Burrel, in 1966. One of his favourite stories is of the day he went to take his chartered accountancy exams and saw the man in front of him faint. 'My first reaction was: they pass 50 per cent – I'll have his spot.' He joined a larger firm, Thompson McLintock in 1970, but it was made clear that from his background, and without a degree, progress would not be speedy. Not one to take snobbery lying down, Hearn began to diversify, handling his own clients on the side. Hard work and persuasion got him the sort of job he craved. One of Thompson's biggest clients was Deryck Healey International, a fashion consultancy. In 1973 Hearn convinced Healey he needed a full-time financial director. 'It was a time of my life that was really exciting. It was a blinding time. Deryck taught me how to sell. We took America by storm.' He adopts a mid-American sales voice: 'We re-designed the American way of life, we invented: DOUBLE KNIT.'

One of Hearn's tasks was to look at possible acquisitions. He had always loved sport, knew how to sell, and got a buzz out of it. He saw sport's potential as a product, more than just a game. He persuaded Healey to buy the Lucania chain of snooker halls for £500,000, also putting in some of his own money. When the chain was sold in 1982 for £2.5 million, Hearn owned a third, most of which was invested in property and forestry in Scotland.

He had already left Healey to start Matchroom – a snooker club above his offices in Romford, and kept up his fruit machine and pool table business in the East End.

'Even as late as the mid-1970s, the public associated snooker with no-goods and no-hopers,' wrote Gordon Burn in *Pocket Money*. 'They associated it with the sort of semi-criminal underworld where fly-by-night promoters disappeared with the takings (this happened in the 1976 world championship and the gentleman in question was last seen driving a taxi in Canada) and, even worse, when most people thought of billiard halls, they thought of somewhere like the Regal in Eric Street in the East End, the notorious hall owned throughout the 1950s by Ronald and Reginald Kray.'

Hearn re-invented snooker for television. In 1978, 35 hours of snooker were broadcast. By the mid-1980s, many people watched that amount in a single week of a big tournament. The world championship at Sheffield was now allocated 130 hours of air time. Snooker had become the most popular sport on television. Design and organisation of major tournaments, promotion, player management, overseas markets, it was a new ball game. And it was all Hearn's game. 'It would have been more of an achievement to fail,' he says, grinning.

He dominated the sport through his business acumen and the best snooker player the world had ever seen. One of Frank Warren's problems in boxing has been the lack of a long-lasting champion. By the time Warren was bulldozing his way into the boxing scene, Hearn had already discovered the man who has been his closest friend for 15 years, his greatest investment and product of all. Steve Davis, six times world champion, millionaire, the respectable face of snooker, literally walked off the streets and in to one of Hearn's Romford snooker halls.

Like Warren, who had Wallace, Gumbs and Bugner fighting at the crucial weights, and who were all crowd pullers in their different ways, Hearn carefully selected his players for the Matchroom stable: Terry Griffiths was the housewives' favourite; Tony Meo was the free spirit, and Steve Davis was simply the best. After he was beaten by Dennis Taylor in the

1985 world championship on the final shot Hearn appeared understandably shaken, but did not sulk for long. He signed up Taylor, who fitted in as the easy-going entertainer, the chirpy Irishman in victory or defeat.

Unlike Warren, Hearn did not have to battle against an Astaire-Duff-Lawless type of group. Snooker had no equivalent. By the late 1980s, the real challenge was gone; it was time for something else for the restless Hearn. Now snooker is less of a concern, the machine runs smoothly, and Barry's batteries are directed towards boxing, of which he says he has always been a fan.

Hearn pays tribute to Warren for busting the monopoly of the cartel. 'Without him I wouldn't be in boxing. I don't owe him anything for it, he did it for himself, for selfish reasons. But if it had been left to me I might have said, I can't handle the aggravation.'

The move from an environment of immaculately dressed sportsmen-cum-dinner guests, sipping drinks in between fathoming precise angles to pot small spheres, to a world of bare-chested gladiators spitting water in between trying to thump each other into submission, has not been as easy as he hoped.

'I've lost a million pounds, something like that,' he confesses. Shortly afterwards, he had to lose a few staff as well. No matter. Barry sticks to his philosophy: 'I'm a sports promoter and having done snooker, the rules of promotion are much the same in any sport – to give people what they want to see, televise it, syndicate it, sponsor it, wrap it up and sell it. That's what we've been doing here for nearly 20 years.'

The difficulty is that Hearn is endeavouring to control a business that often resembles a great champion who has been cut and is trying desperately to finish off his opponent. It is violent, macho, impatient, angry, amoral and proud, and doesn't take advice from outsiders kindly. Boxing is not corporate, it is not clean, primetime 7pm viewing.

Hearn started at the top, co-promoting Bugner v Bruno at White Hart Lane in 1987. Then came the reality of boxing: half-empty halls, the struggle to get television, and, worst of all, a shortage of first-rate fighters. Some bad mismatches took place —partly as they are unavoidable to an extent, but partly because of Hearn's eagerness to give his fighters a chance for glory. Jess Harding was destroyed by Gary Mason in just over a round. Jim McDonnell lasted longer but was completely out of his depth against Azumah Nelson, and then hurt so badly by Jimmy Weiss he had to retire. People started to say Hearn should stick to what he knew. The refrain from older members of boxing's cognoscenti was: 'Barry 'Earn? What the fuck does 'e know about the fight game? He's not part of our family, 'e's just bought his way in.'

Hearn kept going, working 18 hours a day and reckoning a lot of promoters who had come in on the back of the Warren revolution would not be able to compete. He offered his fights to ITV for less money, and paid undercard fighters more, just as Warren had done. He signed fighter after fighter, building a stable of around 35, and promoting about 70 shows in 1990.

Finding television at home or in the States was hard. But then along came Screensport, a satellite channel that broadcasts all over Europe. 'The one stroke of luck I've had in boxing is Screensport. I wish I had been that clever to have known what it was going to be – now of course I can tell some people that I was that clever. When I came in to boxing everyone said I'd just get the crumbs from TV. I just sort of learnt for a year, which was a drag, and then I put on a fight for ITV, so obviously that upset Warren.' In 1989, out of 50 shows, 35 lost money. Fortunately for Hearn, he had the financial stamina to mend badly burning pockets. 'I went to Screensport and everyone was saying, you should be with BSB like Jarvis Astaire, or Sky. The truth of it is, I wasn't with them because I couldn't get with them.'

But Screensport offered to buy 20 shows, which allowed him to go out and sell the events. Suddenly Hearn had a voice.

'The boxing is now profitable, thank God. The Screensport contract alone is worth over a million pounds. We've created our own little monster here,' he says, not entirely unhappy with his creation. Boxing bosses, however, need champions. Although Chris Eubank is not managed by Hearn, he fights only on his

promotions, and is identified with him. In his first defence of his
WBO title, Eubank disgraced himself by butting his opponent
Dan Sherry. Lucky not to be disqualified, he was later fined
£10,000 by the Board of Control. Not exactly a glittering jewel
in Barry's crown. There was never any worry that Steve Davis
was going to smash Stephen Hendry over the head with a cue.
Alex Higgins might have, but Barry would never have had him as
one of his boys. But in boxing unpredictable things happen. The
violence that sustains the public's interest in it ensures that.
Disorder is part of boxing's appeal. Gameplans only work up to
a point, as Hearn discovered when Herol Graham was knocked
unconscious on his feet by Julian Jackson when close to stopping
his man and winning the WBC middleweight title. Until that
devastating punch, considerable shock waves must have been
passing through even Hearn's substantial wallet as thoughts of
rematches, title unifications and American networks abounded.

Most boxing people like doing business with Hearn. The
word is that he is straight. 'The secret is to negotiate until a
common ground is found. And I obey Rockefeller's rule: always
leave a dollar behind for someone else. If you are good to people,
pay them what you said, on time, they'll come back for more.
People don't understand that I deal straight, that I stick to what I
say. For them it's like a game of poker with a new player and they
don't know his game.

'When I negotiated Bugner-Bruno I gave Joe's manager Bill
Mordy the 12.5 percentage we'd agreed. I couldn't understand
his amazement. I didn't realise a lot of others stitched up
everyone else.'

Hearn is better educated than his competitors. He did not
grow up as fast as Warren or Mendy. Frank and Ambrose
married young and by the time of turning 20 were running
families and businesses. Their lives have been helter-skelters.
Hearn learned more from a salesman than he did from the street.
He didn't hustle, he passed a few exams, put on a white collar
and tie and went to the office. And he appreciated that he had a
lot to learn initially, avoiding flirtation with the ambitious
financial projects. In those days, he would never have had either

the contacts or the guts to promote boxing shows in the way the young Warren had done. But he was always listening and always learning.

His negotiating technique has more than a dash of barrow-boy banter but is based more on the flattery of the salesman. Sometimes he is so slick he sounds scripted. Hearn was born to negotiate.

The telephone rings. 'Your man's in a different class to mine, but I have got to have the options on his first three defences. Fax me through a draft contract and we'll talk again. I'll be in New York, staying at the Plaza, have you got their number? I'm there on Wednesday, Thursday, Friday. Speak to ya later.' The phone goes down. 'He's the most slippery Mexican bastard I've ever talked to, everything's "always in the post". Still, we'll get there in the end.'

Hearn wants to clean up the image of boxing in the way he did for snooker. He wants better matchmaking, better facilities, better security staff, more women in the audience – 'common-sense stuff'. But boxing and commonsense have never been good friends, a source of constant irritation to someone who is first and foremost a businessman. The spectre of Hearn storming up through the middle of the pack, withstanding massive losses and still going strong, irritates smaller, under-capitalised promoters and infuriates Britain's most established boxing promoter, Mickey Duff. He criticises Hearn for going in to boxing as a sop to his ego, and once sent him a letter accusing him of being a 'Johnny-Come-Lately trying to run the sport after five minutes'. Suddenly the veteran Duff does not dislike Frank Warren quite so much. 'Sure he's got problems, but at least he's in boxing because he wants to make a profit.'

'Duff understands his boxing obviously. But he's 61 and he's going to feel 70 soon,' says Hearn. 'I would not criticise him as an operator in terms of his boxing knowledge, but I don't like him. He shouts and hollers and I haven't got time for people like that. He's a bully. He still interests me in his own way because he's been there a long time, but he's got to change. My fighters work for *anybody*. If Duff wants one of mine, it's only a phone call away. I'll ring him and say, there's a great fight on, that's what people want to see. But he comes back – "we want this we want that" – Jesus, he's got a bad attitude.'

Frank Warren is now barely seen as a rival. 'I would have thought he's going to go out of business now. He won't agree with that, but the man's struggling. We all struggle from time to time, and I hope he gets through it, because as a person I actually enjoy his company. The organisation behind him is probably not as strong as it should be. People see me as Matchroom but there's a team, I've got very good support.'

Hearn's secretary Michelle comes in with some letters to sign. 'Can we get in early tomorrow?' She squirms a little, as if to say 'Ooh, Barry, you are awful.' But she agrees.

'Thanks babe, sweet.'

Usually Barry gets in early on his own. If he doesn't have the success he expects in boxing, it won't be for lack of trying.

As the marketing of a sports star has become more sophisticated and increasingly lucrative, so the competition to be the force behind a boxer has grown more intense. Matchroom is not the only new contender. In 1989 the Levitt Group won the race to sign up the Seoul Olympics super-heavyweight gold medallist, Lennox Lewis. The Group was founded by a flamboyant insurance salesman, Roger Levitt, a self-made man and, incidentally, friend of Barry Hearn. At one time his company was one of Britain's biggest brokerages, selling insurance and pension-linked invest-ments to up to 5,000 clients and companies, which also had a sports management and consultancy wing.

The boxing manager Frank Maloney had met Roger Levitt at some of Nigel Benn's fights, and was advised by a boxing writer to put the idea of Lennox Lewis to Levitt. Lewis is quite a prospect. Born and brought up in the East End, when he was 12 he moved to Toronto, Canada, which he represented at Seoul. However, a British world heavyweight contender always creates an extra interest in America, his nationality automatically setting him apart from almost all the others. If he can win the British and European titles, comparatively easy tasks, then he can be propelled into close contention for a shot at the big one. American managers and promoters are always happy to negotiate for what they predict will be a 'horizontal' heavyweight opponent from the old country, which, they have to keep reminding themselves is the founder of modern boxing.

Cooper, Bugner and Bruno all had two chances each to win the world title, which no British boxer has held since Bob Fitzsimmons in 1897. Levitt appreciated that if Lewis won any of the world titles, his company could make commission on one of the richest athletes in the world. The competition for Lewis was stiff. Someone rang Lennox Lewis's solicitor and told him Maloney was a gangster funded by drugs money. 'I've got a fair idea who did it, but I won't say in case of libel,' says Maloney.

But Levitt and Maloney got their man, thanks to an offer of £200,000 for three years, which amounts to a salary, something unheard of in boxing, plus a country training retreat, housekeeper, chauffeur, bodyguard when needed, and a house in Kent. So much for fighting out of hunger to pay the rent and food bills. This is boxing in the 1990s, pre-packaged with the best possible deal for the fighter; Lewis is the first boxer to have had a paid-for pension scheme at the age of 24. If it served him well, it was a major coup for Maloney. 'People used to see me as a bit of a joke, but not any more. It's gone the other way, there are so many jealous people.' He added with some pride, 'I even get hate mail now.'

Maloney initially perceived his biggest problem to be if Lewis didn't match his promise. Before his man fought Gary Mason on 6 March 1991 for the British and European titles, he said: 'I stand to become a hero or an absolute fool.'

He need not have worried about Lewis, who won comfortably; it was the Levitt Group that collapsed. A routine check by Fimbra, the investment advisers' regulator, allegedly discovered the firm was propped up by money that shouldn't have been there. Roger Levitt was arrested and charged with stealing £650,000. 'I should have stuck with the crooks I knew in the East End,' joked Maloney shortly afterwards. The boxer's Levitt contract was passed on to liquidators at Peat Marwick McLintock, though Levitt himself hopes to return as Lewis's commercial manager.

Maloney remains Lewis's manager, and after the victory over Mason, a Mickey Duff fighter, entertained friends at Cauthen's, a theme pub in Aldgate which serves as his social HQ. With a large wad of notes sticking out of his top pocket, sipping champagne and with a smile as broad as Lewis's shoulders, Maloney asked anyone who had watched the fight on TV what Duff's defeated face looked like. Victory over the old guard was particularly gratifying.

Maloney is convinced the type of arrangement he had with the Levitt Group is the way forward: an alliance between a boxing man and a money man. East End and West End join forces. He is not the only one involved in such a tie-up – Harry Holland, who co-promoted with Warren in his early days, is a manager-promoter with financial backing from Winners Worldwide, a partnership that manages a number of bands including Level 42 and Dire Straits. Unlike Levitt, however, since forming in mid-1989 they have built the scale of promotions slowly, peaking with Nigel Benn's victorious comeback against Steve Simms at the National Exhibition Centre in April.

It has never been tougher at the top. For the first time since the war, no single force dominates British boxing. Mickey Duff soldiers on, driven perhaps most by a desire not to be beaten; but his company National Promotions, run with Astaire and others, peaked with Bruno's fight with Tyson in 1989. The decline of Lloyd Honeyghan, once a great world champion, has left them struggling to find decent prospects. Appalled by the new levels of hype and infuriated by the inflationary practices of Warren then Hearn, they have struggled financially too. Colin Hart of the *Sun* estimates the company lost £750,000 in 1990, though with the BBC still loyal, and a new deal worth £500,000 from Sportscast, a British Aerospace company, to provide 48 tournaments a year for live television into pubs and clubs, they won't lose too much sleep.

Frank Warren opened the door for all the new players when he swung a demolition-ball into the cartel, which then swung back in at him, as new competition thundered in. But Hearn's rise, Maloney's hold over Lewis, and the threat of smaller competitors like Winners Worldwide is unlikely to annoy him as much as the prominence at times achieved by the World Sports Corporation, run by his old employee.

'Shoot,' said Ambrose Mendy, flicking off the huge video screen in his office with the remote control. 'What d'you wanna know?'

Whatever you do want to know, Mendy has an answer. Strong opinions are not a problem, especially on the British Boxing Board of Control, which has refused to license him. 'The Board are racist. I didn't just come over on a banana boat. . .'

To Mendy, the Board is a crusty institution run by prejudiced duffers out to protect their own narrow-minded interests. It might deal with hundreds of black boxers, but it wants black faces to stay within the ring, and not get involved outside. To the Board, Mendy is at best a maverick it could do without, and at worst an undesirable sort the likes of which it abhors. His unsanctioned activity in boxing has undermined its authority as Frank Warren did, but rather than say 'if we can't beat him, he'd better join us', it has decided to keep Mendy at a minimum of an arm's length.

Since 1988 Mendy has tried and failed to get either a promoter's or a second's licence from the Board. Though, with unfortunate inconsistency, the Board did grant him one-off permission to be in Nigel Benn's corner when he fought Chris Eubank, after a special request by the World Boxing Organisation.

'As for why we haven't given him a licence, that's for Mr Mendy to say,' said John Morris, the Board's general secretary, several months before Mendy faced fraud charges in April 1991. 'We pass no comment, we don't have to give reasons why we don't license people. If you know any reasons, you keep them to yourself, and I'll keep mine to myself. Mr Mendy, and the Board might not like me saying this, is in many ways quite a remarkable guy. And he has a certain amount to offer. He's come a long way, and we'll see where he's going.'

Though the Board is hardly a nest of radical thinkers, it is unlikely Mendy's rejection has anything to do with his colour. Boxing's racial attitudes have moved with the rest of the country's, if anything a bit quicker. There was a time when black boxers were thought of simply as opponents, and when barely a black face was to be seen in the crowds, even when Maurice Hope and John Conteh fought to glory in the early 1970s. In the early 1980s followers of the National Front or British Movement thought boxing was a good medium for expression of their ideals, but that thankfully died down. These days, especially in London, the black community comes out more and more to support its boys, and plenty of boxers have followers of mixed race. But equally there will be a few in a boxing audience who can only respect a black man in the ring.

About 350 of the 1,000 licensed boxers are black; Mendy has been the only black person prominent in the management side of the sport, and even he is peripheral to the establishment.

The Ghanaian-born boxer Tee Jay who has lived here since he was a toddler, feels racism has inhibited the managerial career of his father, Isola Akay, who managed Tee Jay before passing him over to Frank Warren.

'It's not fair that black managers are kept in the background. People don't seem to want a black person in control. That's why Ambrose has done very well. He has done very well for Nigel but he still gets criticised.

'But that's the way it is in England, we're still not like America where there's black managers, black promoters. I think it will be like that for a long time.

'But I suppose through boxing I meet all sorts of people and because I am a boxer I get accepted by people who might not usually look at a black person without thinking they're a thief or a mugger. But boxing has made them accept you're an athlete and they respect that.

'Black people never support their own. It's terrible. Before you used to see black fighters but never black people in the crowd, but now they are supporting their own fighters. They used to sit at home and criticise another black person doing well, as if you're doing well, you're sold out, you're not one of us any more. Now they have started going to boxing and to football to watch the black players and they are changing with the times. In the days of Maurice Hope no one used to watch, except for cricket when they could go in abundance.'

Mendy started bringing a smart crowd of mainly black faces to ringside, plus a host of celebrities, again mainly black. He labelled his boxing outfit the Pack, and soon it and Mendy's network of clients and friends was dubbed as the Black Pack, fast-living, high-achievers, like the best known rugby league player, Ellery Hanley, footballers Paul Ince and John Fashanu, and Linford Christie, the athlete, all of whom Mendy has acted as agent for. Proud of black people getting on, Mendy resents the accusation of inverted racism. 'Is Terry Marsh black, is my friend Kathy Lloyd black? My mother was a Jewess, my ex-wife is white, I have staff who are white. I don't mind white people,' he paused, while a favourite old joke came to mind. 'I even let my children play with them.'

John Morris is right that Mendy has come a long way. The son of an immigrant from the tiny West African state of Guinea Bissau and a half-Russian, half-Brazilian Jewess from Bridgwater in Somerset, Mendy was brought up in a family of eleven children in the East End. It was not an easy childhood, and Mendy was in trouble with the law in his teens. 'I was brought up among gangsters and have never denied I got into trouble,' he once said. Throughout the seventies there were a string of mostly minor sentences for theft, handling stolen property and burglary. In 1981 he was jailed for six years for trying to obtain £70,000 by deception. Upon his release in 1983 he became the trade commissioner for Guinea Bissau, and worked in Frank Warren's office as a publicity agent. After Warren sacked him, Mendy formed his sports management agency, the World Sports Corporation – its slogan: entertainment with style – and before long was the Armani-suited, Mercedes-driving agent of Nigel Benn and others, living in a substantial house in Wanstead, not to mention being one of the most controversial figures in boxing.

Mendy is an issue that divides boxing devotees. His detractors call him an inverted racist, a bullshit artist and exponent of the doctrine that nothing succeeds like excess which is damaging boxing's image. His backers admire his charm, energy, verbal talents, the deals he swings, the buzz he has put back into boxing and they have supported his case for a Board licence.

Mendy is cherished by his friends and close associates as the best friend anyone could have. Jon Robinson says: 'If there was a problem and I had to call on certain people to help, Ambrose would be top of the list. People can talk about all sorts of things but he is a one-off. Now if you said to me, put your hand on your heart and swear Ambrose has never done anything wrong, I couldn't do that. But go to boxing in the Albert Hall one night and say, "all those with a criminal background please leave the hall, and all those who never got caught join them", and there would be nobody there. So who are we trying to kid? There is a resentment to Mendy because he has brought a different atmosphere to boxing.'

Everyone admires his public relations skills. 'My business is hype, and hype moves at a pace – yesterday's news is yesterday's blues,' says Mendy. He gets Nigel Benn more publicity than a royal wedding. Colin Hart of the *Sun* says, 'Mendy is one of the best PR people I have ever come across in Britain. He knows exactly how to manipulate the tabloids. The papers know it's bullshit but we go for it. As long as someone has actually said something, they'll take it. As someone from the old school of journalism I find this sort of thing very hard to take – that we give licence to these characters, and go along with a story for the sake of a good headline. Like Benn's million pounds for the Eubank fight. Total bullshit.'

Robinson helped Mendy on his way when late in 1987 he called a meeting at his office above the flower shop in Hackney Road with Frank Maloney and Terry Marsh. The three teamed up into a promotional unit, with Mendy as commercial and publicity manager. Not long afterwards Maloney and Mendy fell out when the former went to manage Lennox Lewis. Now they are friends again.

'I met Ambrose and he gave me all this wonderful sales chat about how we could change boxing, and it appealed to me,' says Maloney. 'Working with Ambrose was a buzz. Ambrose lived on hype, his adrenalin made you go with him. He could hype a tea bag into a superstar. He taught me that so much in boxing is just front. You could see him sitting there and something would come into his head, and you could see his eyes – he'd had a flash. I can remember he said Benn-Watson was sold out when we didn't even have the tickets on the road.'

In order to get their faces known, Maloney and Mendy went to Miami for the IBF conference. They wanted to get Roberto Duran to fight in London. Ambrose found his address and doorstepped him. Duran agreed. 'He was a character, all he wanted to do was meet people and drink champagne,' says Maloney. They managed to get Duran in the ring for a couple of exhibition bouts lasting three rounds.

After the heated negotiations with Mickey Duff for a fight between Nigel Benn and Michael Watson, it went ahead in a 'supertent' in Finsbury Park in May 1989. The whole experience had been a helter-skelter, and Maloney was relieved to go to Levitt, and Marsh's interest in promotion had already faded.

Mendy meanwhile, was fixing up a deal with American TV to screen Benn's comeback fights which culminated in the challenge for the WBO middleweight title against Davy de Witt.

Mendy says the champion's camp pulled one of the oldest tricks in the book, making noise all night to keep the contender awake. 'You would have thought an earthquake was going off in the hotel, but we had Nigel in a room a couple of floors down, away from our suite of rooms, where they thought he was staying.' The night-time successfully passed, Benn duly won the fight. Mendy's game plan was working – Benn's big-punch appeal continued his exposure on American TV, and the purses were much bigger than at home.

Mendy had made Benn, but Benn also had made Mendy. It was an ideal manager-boxer relationship; with Mendy confessing to his man he was in to take as much money for the both of them as possible, and mutually discussing which fights to take. Benn understands the need for hype and willingly participates. It was a modern boxing partnership, unfettered by a contract, though a little old-fashioned discipline would not have gone amiss in Benn's preparations for his fight against Eubank, when he struggled to make the weight.

In March 1991, Mendy was resident at his WSC headquarters near Tower Bridge, overlooking the River Thames. He sat swivelling on a black leather chair behind his large, crescent desk, good looking, well-groomed and comfortable in his rather elegant, spacious attic office. Downstairs the reception area walls are adorned with photographs of Mendy and friends, Nigel and the other sportsmen he advises.

'My plan now is to take Nigel Benn back to the middleweight championship of the world, and to maximise his role as a model for the kids who are coming up in the game. He's very much part of what I want to say to the kids, which is when you're an amateur, you should understand that you are the person who calls the shots, and not the manager.'

All his friends-cum-clients are considered to be role models. 'I have no problems with boxing, from a medical point of view it is the most protected of sports, with immediate medical facilities. In football the referee will be somewhere else and a player might be lying there concussed. But anyway, we are bereft of real quality role models. If you want to extrapolate, stimulate and correlate boxing, you look at the likes of Howard Winston, John H. Stracey, Alan Minter, John Conteh, Ken Buchanan, Charlie Magri . . . all great names, all in dire financial positions. What an indictment of boxing.'

The brass plaque outside the door of Bissau House announces: 'the Trade Development Counsellor for Guinea Bissau'. The WSC sign fell off. Mendy says his biggest weakness is his sweet tooth, with creme de menthe and lemonade (mixed) and M&Ms being particular weaknesses. These pearls of information and everything else you want to know about Ambrose Mendy but wouldn't have time to ask are contained in a thick leatherbound file given to all visitors to Bissau House.

Seven 'O' Levels, three 'A' Levels, RSA exams, apprentice footballer with West Ham, former accountant, Patron of the Sickle Cell Society, founder of the Black British Profession and Business Council – Mendy, born in August 1954, has had a busy life. He has five children, two from his first marriage made at the tender age of seventeen, and three by his second wife, Jennifer.

His great gifts, he says, are communication and being able to mix with high and low, or as he once said, 'I'm as Cockney as jellied eels and as African as groundnuts. The cosmopolitan make-up allows me to relate to situations.'

Some interviewers have found Mendy's hyperbole a little hard to swallow, and when he says things like, 'Thousands of years on, I want someone to pick up a grain of sand in the desert and say: "That might have been Ambrose Mendy," ' you half expect him to stand up, spread his arms and break into a rendition of 'My Way'.

Mendy admits a tendency to exaggerate. 'When you go with the truth, you build bullshit on top of the truth. That's OK. It's like a cake, as long as the sponge is OK it doesn't matter if the icing messes up as long as it's sweet.'

He considers himself a businessman, a seller of products, which in his case are sportsmen. Like all good salesmen, he has a product criterion and a sales pitch.

'My criteria of operation is that something must be naturally charismatic and it must have credibility, otherwise forget it, I wouldn't even bother; they are the two essential ingredients and I think boxing is a charismatic sport because it is with us every day.'

His products must be well-packaged, in the case of 'The Pack' in uniform shiny black and white tracksuits. It's all part of product identification. You wouldn't catch Mickey Duff dead in one. Boxing has always been driven by hype, but Mendy has taken it into new frontiers. To Warren's mould-breaking Mendy added the accessories of the 1980s – the tracksuits, marketing-speak, vodaphones and PR girls. Mendy's job as an agent is a relatively new phenomenon, he has never been a promoter in the old sense, but a one-man service industry, thriving on being a social animal.

Despite all the innovations he introduced, Warren in his heyday as a promoter was returning to old values of presenting good knock-about boxing nights for a working-class audience.

For part of that heyday, Mendy was in his team. Now they hate each other. Warren claims to have barely known him, that a friendship has been invented because Mendy asked him to be his best man for his second marriage in 1985, and Warren agreed, albeit a little reluctantly. After that, Warren has claimed, he had to ask Mendy to stop telling people they were business partners.

'We were a formidable team,' says Mendy, who sees it differently. 'And you know, the crazy thing is, one on one I had some of the funniest times of my life with Frank Warren. I was the best friend he'll ever have. If we had stayed working together there is no limit to what could have been done. He is one of the big disappointments of my life. The best thing I can say to you about him is that he's a good dad to his kids, and his kids love him.'

Warren and Mendy both love football. 'I'd been at West Ham as a youth team player, and I knew a lot of footballers, and I suggested we start representing them, in those days it was guys like Paul Walsh, Pat Nevin and Mark Walters. He just vetoed it.

'I recognise the fact that boxing is a sport that is dying simply because of the lack of commercial interest. Today there is golf, snooker, pool, darts and everything. We've got to compete with everything. But it will never die because there will always be people such as myself who recognise the potential of making an even match, who believe in *laissez-faire*, in giving the public what they really want, not what you think they want. Boxing has an almost fraudulent aspect about it in the sense that the public feel they are being deceived. You look in one corner and you know who's going to win, but you've got to give them what they want. It's all about bums on seats.'

Mendy had learnt that much from his time with Frank Warren, and how to think big, like starting a basically one-man company. His life has been full of surprises, bumps and bruises. 'You gotta keep going if you feel you're on the right road. One of my sayings is, "It ain't over 'til the fat lady starts singing," and I don't hear any music.'

However, soon the volume was turned up, as Mendy found himself on charges of attempting to defraud various companies to the tune of £650,000.

The trial at Wood Green Crown Court in April 1991 was a complex one and lasted two weeks. The prosecution said Mendy was at the heart of attempts to defraud companies by falsely obtaining authorisation signatures so that money could be withdrawn from their bank accounts. A bogus bank official rang a company and explained that a signature of authorisation had been lost in a computer failure, and a new one was needed. After collecting a signature from the company, a person pretending to be from the company called a bank representative to authorise the transfer of large sums of cash. The scheme did not work and no money was ever obtained this way.

Police made an early morning raid on Mendy's home, which they secretly recorded. A police expert said handwriting on a letter to his wife resembled the writing on notes which made up a 'fraudsters index' found at the World Sports Corporation. The index detailed companies that had been targeted for the attempted fraud. Mendy said the letter to his wife, Jennifer was forged: it began 'Jen', which he said he never called her. However, on the tape-recording of the police raid he could be heard addressing her by that name. The police did not ask for further written evidence. In court Mendy said the documents found in a ceiling void at his offices had been planted, and he implicated Frank Warren. Papers stolen in two burglaries were later used by Warren's lawyers in a High Court battle concerning the right to manage Nigel Benn. 'It was stated in court that a private investigator found the documents in a dustbin, which was not possible,' said Mendy.

The public gallery was packed with Mendy's family and friends. The footballers and the models turned out in force – Fashanu, Ian Wright, Chris Hughton, Kathy Lloyd, Suzanne Mizzi – prompting one bemused policeman to sigh, 'It's like bloody *Dallas* in here'. The court was bursting for the final day; Ambrose always puts bums on seats. The jury took five and a half hours to return a guilty verdict. It was not a unanimous decision. Jennifer Mendy broke down in tears, and screamed at them 'You corrupt bastards, he's not even guilty, how dare you.' Nigel Benn had to lead her out of the court room.

There were shades of scenes from Tom Wolfe's *Bonfire of The Vanities*, as Mendy, who remained composed, asked rhetorically why there had been no black people on the jury.

Before the sentence, Nigel Benn gave an emotional plea for the judge to be lenient, saying that he had lost a brother when he was young, and found another in Ambrose. Letters were read out as evidence of Mendy's charitable work. He was sentenced to two and a half years. His brothers claimed a fit-up on the television news that night.

However, not everyone was unhappy with the verdict. Warren denied the allegations Mendy made in court. 'If he'd said those things outside court I'd have sued the arse off him. Mendy is a joke, a fraudster and a proven liar.'

John Morris had said he 'wanted to see where Ambrose was going'. It is now unlikely he will receive a promoter's licence for some time, and re-establishment after such a high profile case will take a lot of work. But a loyal staff, and lot of high profile friends, will do everything to help. Though angry, Mendy did not seem too perturbed by it all. He announced he would be working from prison, and that the World Sports Corporation would carry on, business as usual. A Nigel Benn fight, in which he will 'do it for Ambrose' is a reasonable bet, and Mendy, who is appealing against the verdict, is almost certain to be released in 1992.

'I am uncrushable,' he vowed. 'I can survive anything however bad. After this I'm coming back – Ambrose Mendy Mark II.'

CHAPTER FOURTEEN

Any Way Back?

A dim, miserable day in the Docklands, April 1991. In the empty car park of the London Arena, a couple stand arguing. The woman drops the bags of shopping she is carrying and bursts into tears; the man walks away. They are the only people in sight. The hall of the Arena is deserted – a huge, ghostly shell. A couple of guys are working out in the fitness centre recently built in a corner of the complex. The restaurant above the foyer of the auditorium, Pizzarena, is closed.

On mid-week days the plan was for the Arena to be buzzing with training athletes, five-a-side football teams, and local kids playing tennis. That didn't happen, and the big event bookings were few and far between. A highlight of April 1991 was an angling exhibition. In the offices adjoining the hall, Frank Warren, John Botros and their staff were working to save it; a few weeks later, they had moved out. Warren's grand vision of becoming a sports and entertainments magnate had foundered for the time being.

The final blow which ended Warren's Docklands dream was a petition issued by a cleaning company owed £60,000 by Arena Developments (Europe) Ltd, Warren's company which ended up running the London Arena. There were 23 other unsecured creditors owed £900,000, including the Inland Revenue (£467,516), and an architects practice owed £150,000. The banks had also run out of patience, with Security Pacific owed £22.5 million and Landhurst Leasing and Midland Bank owed £1 million each.

The Arena was put into administrative receivership, and was run by two partners at Price Waterhouse, the receivers.

The future of the Arena is uncertain. The receivers want to sell it, possibly to Occidental Finance Holdings, and try to refund some of the creditors, though the value of the building remains in dispute, and a sale would be unlikely to provide sufficient funds to repay the creditors. As Warren's company is insolvent, he can't repay the debts. If sold, the Arena could remain as an entertainment venue, or be converted into an office block. Warren may just return as manager in the future.

The trouble started in February 1991 when Loxway, which had indirectly owned the Arena, was wound up in unusual circumstances. A West End law firm, Davenport Lyons, which used to represent Warren, issued a petition, and claimed it was owed £42,000 by Loxway. It also claimed it was owed £11,000 by Frank Warren Promotions, which had been dormant for a couple of years. In March 1991, proceedings began at the High Court to put the company into administration. An action by the promoter Mike Barrett, who claimed Warren owed him £25,000, was put on file. Earlier, Arena Management Limited had been wound up and Botros survived a personal bankruptcy action. The wolves were at the door, though at the time Warren and Botros were still confident the Arena could be saved.

Larry Gillick, the Scottish businessman behind a consortium that tried to save Tottenham Hotspur football club before Amstrad's Alan Sugar came along, was behind the Occidental deal. Gillick is as much of a mystery as are his reasons for trying to save two stricken business empires. Once a property dealer in Scotland, he is known to have connections in the Middle East and Arab oil money may be his main source of funds. With the support of the Tottenham manager Terry Venables, whom Warren introduced to Gillick, he was also trying to find £20 million to save Tottenham. One day at his Harley Street offices Warren was deal-making in one room while the Tottenham consortium was discussing its future in another.

Rex Williams Leisure's troubles have continued, with the managing director installed by Botros and Warren, Jeff Williams, trying to make RWL the first company in receivership to be refloated on the Stock Exchange. 'It was a perfect example of how businesses fail, and there is a parallel with Spurs,' says Jeff Randall of the *Sunday Times*. 'It would have been easy to see why Spurs should buy into Sportswear, but without the right management any business will fail. Rex Williams didn't have any management in place. Frank bought a publishing company and didn't know anything about it, and didn't have the right people to run things. It was doomed to failure, and I think now he would admit that.'

If the decline of Rex Williams Leisure was caused by poor acquisitions and inadequate management, the whole concept of the Arena may just be five or ten years too early. Even according to its most optimistic publicists, Docklands may not now be the place it was meant to be in 1991 until 2001. Building the Arena was a brave venture but it may take a decade for it to become healthily profitable. The Arena could pass through several owners and guises before someone gets a bargain and makes some big money. Like Eddie Shah, who broke journalism's print unions but failed to capitalise as fully as others on his own revolution, Warren may prove to be a pioneer who paved the way for others to find a greater fortune, such as Barry Hearn, now enjoying the fruits of Warren breaking the mould of boxing.

Hearn can't really understand why Frank ever bothered to build the Arena. 'Would I want my own arena? Nah, I can go and rent one for nothing . . . No one would want a full sale. He'd get hardly anything for it, and why is anyone going to buy something that is going to lose money? I mean, do you need losses that bad that you are prepared to purchase them? That's basic, innit? With Thatcherism we had an entrepreneurial, yuppy world that encouraged you to go for it. We have all done it in one way or another. Frank went for it. If he'd found oil in the London Arena, everyone would have said he's a clever sod. That's life,' says Hearn, with a philosophical sigh.

If Frank Warren hoped his name would feature less in the press after the *brouhaha* that followed Terry Marsh's trial, he was mistaken. In January 1991 he was cleared of a drink-drive charge, although he admitted driving his Bentley over the legal limit. The magistrate, setting something of a legal precedent, decided the wording of the Metropolitan Police's regulations did not give Warren a choice of providing either a blood or urine sample. After a positive roadside breath test, when Warren was tested at Vine Street police station but the intoximeter was broken, he was told he would have to have a blood test.

Between this incident and the date of its coming to court the Bentley had in fact been stolen on 30 November 1990, a year to the day of the shooting, while Warren was throwing a party to thank friends for their support throughout his ordeal. John Botros had left the car parked for four days on a yellow line near Euston station while he went to visit his daughter. The wreckage of a Bentley was later found at Alpha Autos scrap yard in Park Royal, run by David Carrol, Bob Warren's son-in-law. The number of the engine, found under tarpaulins in the back of a broken down British Telecom van, showed it was indeed the Bentley registered under Frank John Warren's name.

David Carrol, who has known Warren since his teens, insists the remains of the Bentley were placed at his yard by someone who then contacted the *Sun*. 'Somebody dumped the bits here. The *Sun*'s trying to get back at Frank as usual. It was dumped by the back gate on open land. Something funny is going down.'

Alongside car trouble, came boxing problems. The Board of Control suspended Warren's licences because he allegedly failed to pay £10,000 owed to Tom Collins, the European light-heavy-weight champion. Warren, ever the legal gunslinger, threatened a High Court action for restraint of trade, but paid up and duly had his licences restored. He said he would be seeking 'substantial' damages from the Board for a stain on his reputation, said he had not admitted indebtedness, but needed his licences to go ahead with a major promotion, the visit of Julio Cesar Chavez, the Mexican light-welterweight world champion and one of the world's top three fighters. In the end the promotion had to be cancelled at the insistence of the American promoter Don King.

The appearance of George Foreman, the gigantic, 42-year-old, wise-cracking, former world heavyweight champion on a comeback trail, was the highlight in a quiet boxing calendar at the Arena. Early in 1991, Warren apologised publicly to his boxers for their underemployment in the year following the shooting. They appreciated the difficulties he had been through, but earlier several had found themselves at the office at the same time, asking when more fights were going to start coming their way. Tee Jay remembers: 'There were about six other guys there, it was the first time I'd seen all the boxers together since the press conference after the shooting. Everybody is worried, but it's not his fault, he means well for us. It's not his fault.'

The boxing operation has showed small signs of an upward turn. In an age when marketing is more important than ever, Warren has some highly sellable young boxers under his wing: Nicky Piper, the 'Great Bright Hope', Mensa member and nice guy; Tony 'Wild Boy' Collins, WBC light-middleweight international champion and a stills photographer's dream; and Colin 'Sweet C' McMillan, an outstanding prospect, who turned down a university career for boxing. He became the British featherweight champion in style and could well take a world title one day, but is self-managed and has no obligation to Warren, who has so far promoted most of McMillan's shows.

More and more young men box now because they want to do it, not because they have to. There are simply fewer hungry fighters, fewer kids going into the gyms, and other channels for aggression are being found, such as martial arts.

'There's more chances for kids now,' says Tee Jay, 'especially black kids. They can get better jobs and they are accepted more now. The ghettoes aren't as bad as they were. Before there was all the riots, hard times. Parents don't like their kids to box, because of the dangers of boxing. A lot of parents grew up with Muhammad Ali, he was everybody's hero. What happened to him put a lot of people off. I think boxing is on the way out now in this country.'

Talented young black kids who are getting into sport may hear of Nigel Benn earning lots of money but when they get to the gym and find out how hard it is they forget Benn and think may be it would be easier being John Barnes or Linford Christie. Frank Warren himself has given the sport a prognosis of 30 years. Only time will tell. Could boxing go the way of cock-fighting, and deteriorate into an illicit backroom activity? Or will the urge for one man to fight another and for both to realise the sense of getting paid for it, prevail?

If many more people like Chris Eubank keep on saying boxing is a mug's game, then younger generations will listen, and not put up with the unbalanced relationship that currently exists between manager and fighter. Unless it is modernised, boxing could lose its ability to draw in talented young fighters. Eubank's denigration of his sport has ironically won him as much attention as his success in the ring. Controversy is part of the game's charisma, a charisma that still has immense potential. Why else did 10,000 people go to watch him fight Nigel Benn, and then Gary Stretch? Barry Hearn wants to clean up boxing's image, but seediness, brutality with a dash of garish glamour, is the core of its appeal.

The story of Frank Warren and Terry Marsh did nothing to make boxing more wholesome, but this in itself will not have discouraged supporters. The image of boxing will never be clean. How can it be, when stripped down of its ever-growing number of trimmings, it is a matter of primitive conflict, of human struggle, of men facing up to their inadequacies.

After his acquittal Terry Marsh embarked on trying to make a comeback, that classic element of boxing's lore. Another challenge, another mountain to climb. In May 1991, after extensive tests, he was granted a boxing licence by Nevada state athletic commission, the first stage in a quest for another world title. It has to be America, because the Board of Control will not give him his licence back. However, it appears unable to stop him fighting under the World Boxing Organisation in London, a boxing commission with whom the Board has no official links, although it does sanction their fights. General secretary John Morris accepted the situation, albeit reluctantly. 'We don't believe Marsh should fight again, in his own interests, but this isn't a war,' he said.

'They're playing the numbers game,' said Terry, 'saying I'm more likely to have a seizure than someone who has never had one. But a knockout is a complex form of a seizure, and I've never had one of those, so who's to say I am more vulnerable than the next boxer?'

Providing loyal support is his brother, John, six years younger than Terry. He often hangs around with his elder brother, particularly when Terry is preparing for a fight. One of his closest friends, John is a former amateur boxer and one-time soldier. The comparisons with Terry are obvious though he has a more relaxed, laid-back character.

The initial plans were for a comeback fight in the summer of 1991, followed by a WBO World welterweight fight against the American champion Manning Galloway in London, with The World Sports Corporation assisting with the promotion. Ultimately, he still hopes to fight Hector 'Macho' Camacho, for his light-welterweight title, before retiring once again, this time as the only boxer to have been an undefeated champion at two weights. Will Terry Marsh be able to unearth his old talent? Certainly the desire is there. From January he trained daily, in Basildon and at the Henry Cooper in the Old Kent Road. Weights, skipping, sparring, putting himself through the rigours again. Why? Because that is the way Marsh has always led his life, and because, for the moment, at the age of 33, he cannot think of anything else to do for money but box. It is an old trap. Few returning champions are ever as good as they were. Barry McGuigan, cut to shreds by the intrinsically inferior Jim McDonnell, and Lloyd Honeyghan, in need of money but without his old power and arrogance, must come to Marsh's mind. But former champions always believe they will be different, that their pride and courage that once took them to the top, will again carry them through. Marsh is no exception. He is a fighter.

'My spirit and my will have not been broken. They say they never come back. But what they should say is, "they never come back from defeat." And I've never experienced that.

'I've got a quiet life now. I do my own thing. I'm not answerable to anybody. I don't put myself up for things. The rest of it is a charade.' He doesn't want to finish up as a second-rate celebrity, appearing on afternoon game shows, and opening supermarkets in the middle of nowhere. Though boxing is his immediate aim, he cannot see what he will be doing in ten years' time. He will allow his son Carl to box, but only with the proper medical tests. Perhaps Terry Marsh will make a comeback as a trainer?

'I don't know. I'd just like to be out of the country, living in a proper democracy,' he says, the bitterness of his imprisonment still evident.

What will become of Frank Warren? No one suggests he will end up in Islington selling shirts in Chapel Street market, but his immediate future is ill-defined. After quitting the Arena he moved back with his staff to the old office in Tavistock Place. The plan was to carry on promoting. As his lawyer, Steven Heffer, said: 'The way he sees life is "let's get on and do some business". That is why he will continue to make do. He won't get bogged down.'

In ten years Warren could yet be a millionaire impresario, with a well-oiled business that would allow him to spend at least a couple of months a year in the south of France with his family. One dream has died, but he will do his utmost to fulfil another. He would like to disappear from the newspapers, save for mentions in the financial pages of ever-increasing profits, and become something of a Gatsby figure – a wealthy, enigmatic, shy friend of the famous.

If Frank Warren had enjoyed greater social advantages, he would probably now be a successful operator in the City, or a lawyer living in Mill Hill. Terry Marsh would be an officer in the Marines. As it is, both have had to battle through life. They are survivors. Both in their different ways are formidable personalities. Both rose from modest backgrounds to exceed all expectations. Of the four Marsh brothers, Terry is the one who has made a name for himself. Of Warren's immediate family, Christine is a medical assistant, Robert is a scaffolder, and Mark is in and out of work. For a time it seemed almost as if Marsh and Warren brought each other luck and fortune, then things fell apart. In the end it was a dispute prompted by the greatest divider – money – and embellished by bizarre circumstances. They will never exchange another word. If the libel trial ever happens, they will be pitted against one another yet again, but whatever the result, neither will ever give ground. Marsh says Warren knew his fighter had epilepsy; Warren maintains he did not, and Marsh recognises that on this matter neither man will give way: 'I'm not talking as Terry Marsh now, I'm talking as a third person: there are two people who will go to their graves arguing over that fundamental point.'

Since their first meeting in 1981, both at times have experienced more in a year than others do in a lifetime. Everyone in boxing has a story.

Bibliography

Burn, Gordon, *Pocket Money*, (Heinemann, 1986)

Campbell, Duncan, *That was Business, This is Personal*, (Secker & Warburg, 1990)

Fletcher, Geoffrey, *The London Nobody Knows*, (Hutchinson, 1989)

Hauser, Thomas, *The Black Lights*, (Pan Books, 1988)

Hugman, Barry (ed.) *British Boxing Year Books*, 1985–1991, (Valiant Sporting Books)

Kray, Reg & Kray, Ron, with Fred Dineage, *Our Story*, (Pan Books, 1989)

McGhee, Frank, *England's Boxing Heroes*, (Bloomsbury, 1988)

McIlvanney, Hugh, *McIlvanney on Boxing*, (Stanley Paul, 1990)

Mullan, Harry (ed.) *The Book of Boxing Quotations*, (Stanley Paul, 1988)

Oates, Joyce Carol, *On Boxing*, (Bloomsbury, 1987)

Oates & Halpern (eds.) *Reading the Fights*, (Prentice Hall Press, 1988)

Pearson, John, *The Profession of Violence*, (Granada, 1984)

Plimpton, George, *Shadow Box*, (Sports Pages/Simon Schuster, 1989)

Samuel, Raphael, *EastEnd Underworld*, (Routledge & Kegan Paul, 1981)

Taub, Michael, *Jack Doyle: Fighting For Love*, (Stanley Paul, 1990)

Index

ABA *see* Amateur Boxing Association
Adams, Tony 88
Ahumada, Jorgo 95
Akay, Isola 252
Albert Hall (Royal Albert Hall) 64,
    124, 137–8
  'cartel' 76–8, 79, 81, 99, 105, 106,
    108, 110
Alexandra Palace 102, 112, 161
Ali, Muhummad *see* Muhammad Ali
Allen, Winston 103
Alma pub 40
Amateur Boxing Association (ABA) 48
Amoru Sandu, Abdul 162
Andretti, Vio, 234
Andries, Dennis 113, 127, 134
Anglo-American Sporting Club 69
Arena Developments (Europe) Ltd 261
Arena Management Ltd 262
Arum, Bob 82, 109, 181
Ashleigh Centre 137
Astaire, Esther (mother of Jarvis
    Astaire) 72
Astaire, Jarvis ('Godfather') ('Mr X')
    42–3, 65, 66–8, 70, 72–83, 116,
    250
  Bruno 59
  BSB 245
  Duff-Watson case 164
  Warren 42–3, 98–100
Astaire, Nadine (náa Hyman) (2nd wife
    of Jarvis Astaire) 75
Astaire, Phyllis (née Oppenheim) (1st
    wife of Jarvis Astaire) 73, 74, 75

Baker, Stanley, 25, 31
Barber, Lynn 31, 168, 171–2, 192

Barking, Broadway Theatre 174–6,
    192, 208, 211
Barrett, Mike 43, 48, 74, 76–82, 116
  McGuigan 130
  Stretch 164
  Warren 98–100, 262
Basildon, Festival Hall 131
Basildon, sports centre 137
Basildon Evening Echo 149, 155
Bass, Benny 8
Batten, Jimmy 159
BBC (British Broadcasting
    Corporation) *see under* television
Beffel, Jacqui *see* Marsh, Jacqui
Benn, Nigel ('Dark Destroyer') 11, 59,
    124, 134, 162, 181, 222, 224,
    225, 233–5
  comeback 255
  Eubank 233, 235–6, 237–40, 251,
    254, 256, 266
  Mendy 123, 163–4, 252, 253, 254,
    255, 255–6, 259, 260
  Simms 250
  Watson 71, 255
Berg, Jack ('Kid') ('Whitechapel
    Whirlwind') 8, 9, 65, 66
Berner Boys' Club 11
Birmingham, National Exhibition
    Centre 115, 235, 250
Bissau House 256
Blanchard, Alex 123
Block, Simon 155
Bloom, Joe 77
Bloomsbury Crest Hotel 84, 91, 98,
    102, 105
  PW's headquarters 103, 117, 123
Bloomsbury Hotel 44
Bluehouse Amatuer Boxing Club 13

Board/Board of Control *see* British
    Boxing Board of Control
Botros, John 167, 169–75, 178, 182–5,
    195–6, 198, 209, 261, 262
boxing 5–10
    blacks 251–3, 265
    boxers' earnings 54
    boxers' lifestyle 94–7
    and chess 17
    crime 58–62, 177, 182
    early 5–7
    ethics 62
    finance 100
    future of 265–6
    heroes 85–90, 132
    house-fighters 80–81
    'hungry' boxers 9, 130, 249, 265
    international organisation 49–50
    Jews 6, 8
    managers 46–7, 51–3, 119–21, 130,
        152, 163–4, 186, 266; *see below*
        promoters *below*
    matchmakers 46
    promoters 45–58, 63–83, 164, 240–
        60
    promoters' 'cartel' broken 98–127
    purse bids 141
    regulation of 5–8, 36–7, 48–51
    relationships 119–21
    role models 256
    unlicensed 34, 36–44
    weight-divisions 49
    women 236–7, 247
Boxing News 16, 51, 151, 152
Boyson, Rhodes, MP 21
Brandman, Henri 71, 119, 163
    TM trial 198, 209–10, 211, 213, 216,
        218–20, 223–4, 227, 228
Braton, David 65
Breland, Mark 124
Brett, Margaret 197–8, 213, 228
Britannia Leisure Centre, Shoreditch
    91–2
British Boxing Board of Control 7–8,
    36–7, 42–4, 48–9, 50
    Astaire 72–3
    betting 156
    block-booking 108
    Bruno 87–8
    contracts, fighter-manager 163–4
    Duff 82

eliminators 86
Eubank 246
fourteen-day rule 98, 104
indemnity system 101
Marsh 155–6, 157–8, 212, 266–7
medical procedures 143, 145, 146,
    162–3
Mendy 251–2, 354
Solomons 65–7
television 105–6
Warren 98–9, 101, 103–6, 162–3,
    264
Warren shooting 176
British Medical Association 136
Broughton, Jack 5
Brown, Philip 79
Bruno, Frank 86–90, 112, 114, 135,
    168, 237, 249
    Brown 79
    Bugner 167, 244, 245
    Gardner 77
    Tyson 110, 250
    Witherspoon 129–30, 156
BSB (British Satellite Broadcasting) 245
Buchanan, Ken 134, 256
Bugner, Joe ('Big Bad Joe') 102–3, 106,
    167, 180, 244, 246, 249
Bugner, Marlene (wife of Joe Bugner)
    103
Bumphus, Johnny 91
Burgess, Harry 51–3, 74
Burkeman, Sally, MP 73
Burn, Gordon 243
Burns, Sam 52, 65, 66–7
Burrows, Bob 103, 105, 112, 140

Café Royal, National Sporting Club 8,
    63
Caledonian Road Baths 53
Camacho, Hector ('Macho') 140, 145,
    267
Cambridge Rooms club 58
Campbell, Duncan 58–9
Cancer Research Council (CRC) 41, 42
Cardiff, National Sports Centre 151
Carlsbert company 123
Carman, George, QC 210, 314
Carpenter, Harry 86, 89, 105
Carroll, David (son-in-law of PW) 264
Carroll, Det-Sgt Michael 199, 200
Central Television *see under* television
Chavez, Julio Cesar 264

Chitilada, Sot 118–19
Christie, Errol 111, 112, 124–5
Christie, Linford 237, 253
Christie, Lloyd 84, 93
Cirelli, Nico 101
Clark, Jimmy 61
Clarke, Ray 43–4, 65, 67, 70, 79, 101, 104, 105, 106, 110–11
Clay, Cassius *see* Muhammad Ali
Clennell, Lindsay 38
Clore, Charles 73
Cobb, Tex 180
Cohen, Izzy 64
Collins, Phil 239
Collins, Tom 122, 264
Collins, Tony ('Wild Boy') 120, 166–7, 265
Colson, Roger 53
Comer, Jack ('Spot') 26–7, 28, 195
    King of the Underworld 26
Comer, Rita 26–7
Connery, Jason 159
Conteh, John 95–6, 134, 159, 252, 256
Cook, Jimmy 121
Cooper, Henry ('Our 'Enery') 7, 25, 58, 90, 102, 109, 249
    Muhammad Ali 1, 64, 67, 75
    pub/gymnasium 1–3, 124, 267
Corbett, Jim ('Gentleman Jim') 7
Cox, Susan *see* Warren, Susan
CRC (Cancer Research Council) 41, 42
Crown Prosecution Service (CPS), TM trial 227–8
Cruz, Steve 130
Curnow, Ann, QC (Mrs Dennison) 188–91, 197, 202–5, 207, 209-14, 217
Curry, Don 115, 118, 130, 167

Daily Express 321
Daily Mail 227
Daily Mirror 179–80, 195, 230
Daily Telegraph 324
Dalton Watson company 171
Darts, Mark and Steve 207
Davenport Lyons 262
David Frost Show (television series) 227
Davies, Ronnie 238
Davis, Steve 243, 246
Day, Bobby 56
Decker, Jeff 56

De Costa, Andrew 84
Dennis (at Wormwood Sorubs) 202
Deryck Healey International 242–3
Dimes, Albert ('Italian Albert') 26–8
Double R Club 58
Douglas, Rod 11
Doust, Dudley 74
Dove, Ted 171
Downes, Terry 38, 52, 66–7, 73, 75
Doyle, Jack 86, 94
Droy, Horace 22
Droy, Mickey 22–4, 25
Duff, Lily (wife of Mickey Duff) 70
Duff, Mickey (Morris) (Monok Pragor) 53, 57, 65–83, 116, 250
    Bruno 87–8
    Conteh 95
    PW shooting 177
    Hearn 247–8, 250
    McGuigan 130
    McKenzie 91, 93
    Maloney 18
    Mendy 255
    Solomons 63
    Warren 29, 42–3, 98–100, 119, 247
    Watson 164
Duran, Roberto ('Hands of Stone') 59, 255
Duran Duran (pop group) 183

Earls Court arena 64, 95
Eastwood, Barney 130, 161
Edmonton, Pickett's Lock 162
Edwards, Cornelius Boza 134
Edwards, Jeff 108–9
Empire Pool *see* Wembley Arena
Empress Hall 65
Ernie *see* Possey, Ernie 133
Eubank, Chris 50, 124, 134, 245–6, 266
    Benn 233, 235, 237–40, 251, 254, 256
Eubank, Karron (wife of Chris Eubank) 340
Eubank, Peter 128
Eubank company 123
European Boxing Union 101
Ezra, Ronnie 65

Farrell, Ray 22
Fashanu, John 237, 253, 259

Fennell, Judge Desmond 188, 198, 199, 209, 210, 216, 217
Fenwick, Doctor 157, 158
Ferguson, Richard, QC 189–90, 192–5, 198, 203–4, 206, 208–11, 213-18, 228, 231
Field, Cliff 39
Figg, James 5
Fight Night (television series) 111
Pindley, Dr Leslie 145, 147, 157
Finsbury Park 255
Fitzsimmons, Bob 7, 249
'flower girl' see Tarrant, Nicola
Forbes, Pepe 50, 122, 131, 133
Foreman, George 354–5
Fossey, Ernie 45, 102, 113, 114, 117, 153, 174
    Eubank 166–7, 236
    FW shooting 178
    Marsh 92, 133, 136, 141–2
Fox, Samantha 223
Frank Warren Promotions 169, 185, 193, 262
Fraser, Francis ('Mad Frankie') 27–8
Frazier, Joe 102
Frost, Joey 16
FW see Warren, Frank

Galloway, Manning 267
Gardner, Chuck 77
Gardner, John L. 105
Gardner, Mike 79
Geldof, Bob 161
George, Charlie 23–4
Giant Promotions 166
Gilbody, George 14
Giller, Norman 86
Gillick, Larry 262
Giovanni, John 22
Glanville, Brian 65
Goldsmith, Harvey 173
Gordon, Otis 44
Goult, Mark 174
Graham, Herol 124, 163, 246
Green, Dave ('Boy') 55
Griffiths, Terry 243
Guardian 75, 224
Gumbs, Roy 106, 122, 124, 130
Gutteridge, Reg 93

Hagler, Marvic 43
Hanley, Ellery 237, 253

Harding, Jess 245
Harlequin Video 171
'Harris, Peter' 201–4, 209, 211, 213–15, 216, 229
Hart, Alan 78
Hart, Colin 62, 69–70, 149, 250, 254
Hatcher, Gene 131
Hauser, Thomas 51
Hawes, William 198–200, 213, 228, 229
Healey, Deryck 242–3
Hearn, Barry 50, 116, 124, 167, 184–5, 240–48, 266
    Eubank 233, 235, 238, 240
    Marsh 134, 138, 147, 153
    Warren 167, 171, 244, 245, 251, 263
Hearns, Thomas ('Hit Man') 14, 59, 114–15, 124
Heenan, John C. 5
Heffer, Steven 179, 180, 268
Hendry, Stephen 241, 246
Henry Cooper pub/gymnasium 1–3, 124, 267
Higgins, Alex 246
Higgins, (Higgy) 220–21
Highbury (Arsenal) stadium 57, 75
Hill, Billy 26
Hippodrome Theatre, Popular 9
Hoffman, Stan 133
Holland, Harry 120–21, 250
Hollister, Alby 40
Holt, Andrew 195, 231
Honeyghan, Lloyd 120, 130, 134, 250, 267
Hope, Maurice 76, 109, 134, 252, 253
Hopkin, Sir David 48
Hopper, Christopher 78
Hornsey Town Hall 101
Horrie, Chris 147–8
Horsecraft, Kenneth 35
Hoxton Baths 53
Hyman, Nadine see Astaire, Nadine

IBF see International Boxing Federation
Illustrated Sporting News 6
Ince, Paul 223, 237, 253
Independent on Sunday 192, 238
International Boxing Federation (IBF) 3, 50, 131, 132, 156, 162, 255
'In the Air Tonight' (song) 339
Isle of Dogs, Mudchute Farm 162

It'll Be All Right on the Night (television series) 147
ITV (Independent Television) *see* television: independent

Jackson, Julian 246
Jameson, Derek 38–9
Jenden, Kevin 22
John Paul II, Pope 180
Johnson, Stevie 114
Jolly Jack *see* Solomons, Jack
Jones, Colin 112, 115, 118, 123, 127, 167
Jones, Ken 89, 116, 153, 168
Judaean club 9

Kameda, Akio 137–8, 141, 151, 152, 153
Kaylor, Mark 112, 126
Keely, Robin 208–9
King, Don 1, 45, 264
King of the Underworld (Comer) 26
Kowalski, Didier 84–5
Kray, Reginald *see* Ronald 25, 27–8, 58, 69, 100–101, 243
Kronk gymnasium, Detroit 89, 124

Lacey, Alan 166
Lamb, Alan ('Lancaster Lion') 55–6
La Motta, Jake 96, 166
La Motta, Stephanie (daughter of Jake La Motta) 96
Lawless, Terry 60, 75–7, 80–83, 87–9, 98–100, 117, 119
Lee, Jean (aunt of Susan Warren) 117
Lee, Robert 50
Leonard, Sugar Ray 65
Levene, Harry ('Bald Eagle') ('Harry the Hoarse') 63, 65–7, 73, 76, 78, 104, 105
Levine, Joseph 70
Levitt, Roger/Levitt Group 248–50
Lewis, Lennox 248–51, 254
Lewis, Ted ('Kid') 9, 58, 65
Lewisham Concert Hall 54
Lewisham Theatre 47
Lilley, Bert 14
Liston, Sonny 58
Lloyd, Kathy 353, 259
London, Jack 64
London Arena 172–4, 178, 182–5, 261–3, 265, 268

London Ex-Boxers Association 96
London Prize Ring Rules 6
London's Burning (television series) 188
Loxway company 169, 172, 183, 185, 262
Loxway Travel company 172
Lustig, Lawrence 118–19, 153, 181
Luton, football club 162
Lynch, 'Brian' 71, 158–9, 234–5

McAree, George 3
McAuley, Dave 134
McCallum, Mike 124
McCarthy, Burt 34–7, 42, 44, 75, 99, 101, 102
  Bob Warren 27, 29
  Bruno 87–90
  Christie 111, 124–6
  Marsh 13–14
  TM trial 200
McCarthy, Leslie 34–7, 44, 117
McCarthy, Sammy ('Smiling Sammy') 59, 73
McConachie, David 118, 119–20, 165, 173
McCrory, Glen 134
McDonnell, Jim 166, 245, 267
McGirt, Buddy 155
McGuigan, Barry ('Clones-Cyclone') 90, 130, 134, 150, 161–2, 166, 168, 190, 267
McIlvanney, Hugh 90
McKenzie, Clinton 55–6, 90–93, 138, 151
MacKenzie, Kelvin 221
McKenzie, Leon (son of Clinton McKenzie) 93
McLean, Lenny (cousin of FW) 33–4, 39, 42
McLintock, Frank 102
McMillan, Colin ('Sweet C') 174, 176, 208, 265
McVicar, John 58
Mad Frankie *see* Fraser, Francis
Magri, Charlie 76, 109–10, 113, 114, 118–19, 123, 134, 256
Mail on Sunday 179
Maloney, Frank 62, 83, 122, 248–51
  Duff 70–71, 80
  Marsh 18–19, 138, 152–3, 156
  Mendy 254–5

Manley, Joe Louis 17, 131–4, 140, 141, 155
Marks, Councillor Dave 137
Marsh, Carl (son of TM) 159, 268
March, Jacque (*nee* Beffel) (wife of TM) 18, 94, 139, 142–3
  marriage break-up 159
  TM trial 226–7, 230
Marsh, James (Jimmy) (brother of TM) 10, 135
Marsh, Jim (Jimmy) (father of TM) 10, 13, 150, 210
Marsh, John (brother of TM) 13, 160, 187, 208, 210–11, 219, 267
Marsh, Kelly (daughter of TM) 94, 132, 143, 227
Marsh, Maisie (mother of TM) 10, 149–50, 187, 210–11, 231
Marsh, Terry (TM) 2–4
  ABA lightweight champion 15
  actor 157, 159, 197
  arrested 181, 200–201
  athletics 136, 137
  'aunt Winnie' 207
  Benn–Eubank 233, 236
  boxing style, 130–31, 133, 134–5, 138
  British light-welterweight champion 90–93
  career develops 16–19, 84–5, 90–7, 128–38
  comeback 266–9
  Commonwealth Games 15–16
  'cousin Maria' 207
  early life 10–17
  epilepsy 142, 157, 179, 191–2, 212, 269
  Essex Fire Brigade 17, 92, 94, 96–7, 131, 134, 137, 145, 148–50, 218
  European light-welterweight champion 128–9
  finance 207–8, 212
  FW signs 18–19
  'hypoglycaemia' 157–8
  image 94
  on managers 151
  marine 15–16, 132, 208, 215
  marriage 17
  marriage break-up 159
  personality 129, 132, 135–7, 148, 152, 155
  press after trial 219–28

promoter/manager 156, 159, 254–5
purses 141, 144, 151–2
retirement 140, 142, 147–60, 165, 212
RSPCA medal 137
Sun story 139–45, 148–9, 151, 154, 155
television 93, 112, 139–40, 150–51, 159, 212
trial 187–232
world light-welterweight champion 131–3, 214
Martin, Jerry ('Bull') 44
Martin, Jonathan 79
Mason, Gary 86, 245, 249–50
Matchroom club 241, 243, 248
Mathan, Sid 93
Mendoza, Daniel 6
Mendy, Ambrose 18, 156, 188, 223–5, 246, 251–60
  Benn 71, 163, 164, 181, 233–6, 239
  'cartel' document 108
  fraud trial 259–60
  FW shooting 206
  leaves FW 132, 153
  TM trial 187, 219–20, 232
  Warren vii, 29, 33, 36, 117, 258
Mendy, Jennifer (wife of Ambrose Mendy) 257, 259, 260
Mec, Tony 243
Midweek Sports Special (television series) 112, 159, 191, 212
Mile End Arena 53, 69
Miller, Mike 114, 117, 136–7
Miller, Reggie 124
Milligan, Mike 65
Mills, Freddie 58
Minter, Alan 43, 256
Miranda, Julio 162
Mohammad, Darren 12–13
Moisha Blue Boy 26
Mooney, Tommy 14
Mordy, Bill 246
Morris, John 48–9, 72–3, 110, 111, 251, 253, 260, 366
Mosley, Sir Oswald 10–11
Moynihan, Colin, MP 82
Muhammad, Matthew Saad 95
Muhammad Ali (Cassius Clay) ('Louisville Lip') 1, 64, 67, 75, 102, 265
Mullan, Harry 99, 101, 116, 151

Murphy, Glenn 165, 187–8, 210–11, 223
Murphy, Kieran 18–19
Murray, 'Kid' 84
Muswell Hill hall 131

Napoles, Jose 2
National Boxing Council (NBC) 37–44, 100
National Promotions 73, 77, 110, 250
National Sporting Club (Café Royal) 8, 63
Nawrat, Chris 108
NBC, *see* National Boxing Council
Nelson, Azumah 245
Neumann, Randy 133
Newbon, Gary 111
News of the World 107, 108, 221, 225, 226
Newton, Tommy 15
Nickels, Brian 80
Nkalankote, Tusikoleta 131

Oates, Joyce Carol 17, 94
O'Callaghan, Kevin 208
Occidental Finance Holdings 262
Oliva, Patrizio 128, 131
On the Waterfront (film) 305–6
Oppenheim, Phyllis *see* Astaire, Phyllis
Oppenheim family 73–4
Osuji, Sylvester 174, 176
Our 'Enery *see* Cooper, Henry
Owen, Johnny 79

Panayiotou, Pani *and* Gil 321–4
Parsons, Bradley 196–7
Pastrano, Willie 75
Patterson, Floyd 74
'Paul' (gunman at FW shooting) 175, 177, 196–7, 208, 213, 215
Pavarotti, Luciano 183
Peludo, Art 156
Perez, Nicky 161
Peter (at Phoenix Apollo) 219, 220, 221, 224
Phillips, Al 75–6
Phoenix Apollo Restaurant 219–25
Pini, Signor 101
Piper, Nicky ('Great Bright Hope') 265
Pirate Promotions 19
Pitsea Roadrunners Club 137
Pitt, Nick 43, 106, 108

Plimpton, George 17
Pocket Money (Burn) 243
Police and Criminal Evidence Act 1984 226
Porter, Ricky 79
Powell, Jack 29
Powell, Mary 25, 29, 36, 117
Premierland 9
Price, Jimmy 114, 124, 130
Privilege company 171

Quarless, Noel 105
Queensberry Rules 7

Raging Bull (film) 96, 166
Rainbow, Finsbury Park 33, 37
Rainey, Howard 126
Randell, Jeff 168, 182, 185, 263
Rawlings, Ned 317
Rees, Det-Supt Jeff 177, 203, 226
Rendall, Jonathan 208, 238
Restrictive Practices Act (1988) 104
Rex Williams Leisure Ltd (RWL) 169–73, 182–5, 193, 262–3
Richards, Steve ('Colombo') 39
Richardson, Charles (Charlie) and Eddie 28, 35
Richardson, John 197
Roberts, Les 63, 77, 79, 86
Robinson, Jon ('Tiny') 3
   International Boxing Federation 50
   London Arena 173
   Mendy 123, 156, 254
   on promotion 46
   Warren 28, 39, 41, 42, 101–2, 117, 122, 152–3, 155, 180
   WSC 156
Robinson, Sugar Ray 64, 69, 95
Rosanbloom, Maxie 8
Royal, Tottenham 37
Royal Albert Hall *see* Albert Hall
Royal Fusiliers 238
Royal Oak gymnasium 60, 119
RWL *see* Rex Williams Leisure Ltd
Ryde, Dr David 157

Sacco, Ubaldo 131
St George's Amateur Boxing Club 10–15
St Helens club 114
St Pancras Amateur Boxing Club 141
Sanigar, Chris 84–5

Savold, Lee 64
Sawyers, Tom 6, 7
Scapecci, Alessandro 128–9, 151
Scott, Mr Justice 164
Screensport (satellite TV channel) 235,
    245
Sculley, Alfie 22
Seconds Out (television series) 111,
    139, 150, 191, 212
Sellers, Nat 65
Selsdon, Lord 172
Seys, Jose 124–6
Shah, Eddie 263
Sherry, Dan 246
Shorvon, Dr Simon 146
Sibson, Tony 101, 113, 162–3
Silvertape Ltd 171, 193
Simmons, Henry 107–8
Simms, Steve 250
'Simply the Best' (song) 238
Sinatra, Frank 183
Singer, Al 8
Sky Television (satellite TV channel)
    345
Smith, Andrew (child) 145
Smith, 'Bonecrusher' 86
snooker 241–4
Solomons, Jack ('Jolly Jack') 63–7, 78,
    83, 111
Sonny the Yank 26
southpaw 55
'Spurs Adventure 3000' 171
Spinks, Michael 89
Spinks, Terry 58, 73
Sportscast company 250
Sports Network (UK) 154, 169, 185
Sportsnight (television series) 105
Spot see Comer, Jack
Spurs see Tottenham Hotspur
'Stand and Fight' (song) 236
Stayton, Albert 35
Steele, Richard 238, 239, 240
Stevens, Harry ('Aitchie') 2, 38
Steward, Emanuel 124
Stracey, John H. 2, 11, 76, 109, 110,
    134, 256
Stretch, Gary 61, 164–6, 223, 266
Stretch, Roni 165
Sulaiman, Jose 49
Sullivan, John L. 7
Sun 139, 139–45, 151, 154, 155, 212
    Bugner fight 180

FW car 264
FW shooting 177, 179
    TM trial 195, 220–21, 225, 230
Sunday Express 144, 179
Sunday Times 106–7, 108, 109–10,
    119, 130
Sweeney, Nigel 207, 209

Tank Malling (film) 158
Tarrant, Nicola ('flower girl') 178–9,
    193–4, 228, 231
Tate, Frank 162–3
Taylor, Dennis 243–4
Ted (of Henry Cooper gymnasium) 1
Tee Jay 119, 154–5, 186, 252, 265
television 45, 47, 50, 52, 53–4
    Astaire 75
    BBC, 'agreement' 78–9, 99, 105–6,
        108, 112, 250
    BBC, TM trial 224
    Benn–Eubank 235
    boxing finance 99, 100
    Hearn 244, 245
    house-fighters 80–82
    independent (ITV) 78, 81
    Marsh 139–40, 159
    'most popular sport' 113, 114
    snooker 243
    TM trial 227
    US 255
    see also under Warren, Frank:
        Marsh, Terry: and individual
        programmes
Terry Marsh Promotions 160, 330–31
Thames Television see under television
    independent
Thomas, Eddie 79
Thomas à Becket pub 1
Thompson, Billy 73
Thorpe, Rt Hon Jeremy 187, 210
Thurston, Dr John 37
Tibbs, Jimmy 59–61, 89, 186
Tijuana Tumblers 81
Times, The 179, 227–8
Tindall, James 171
TM see Marsh, Terry
Torres, Jose 120
Tottenham Hotspur Football Club
    (Spurs) 262–3
    see also White Hart Lane
Toublic, Sgt Susan 201
Turner, Tina 238

Turpin, Randolph 40, 64, 95
Tyson, Mike 86, 89, 110, 250

United Guarantee Corporation (UGC)
    167, 169

Variety Club of Great Britain 75
Venables, Terry 262
Vickers, Morris 75–6
Viewsport company 73–4, 75

Walker, Billy 58
Walker, Jimmy 199–200
Wallace, Keith 106, 112, 113–14, 124,
    130
Wallis, Neil ('Wolfman') 139, 145,
    220–21
Wardle, John 170
Warren, Barbara (1st wife of FW) 31–
    2, 115
Warren, Bob (uncle of FW) 25–9, 34,
    35, 44, 99, 177–8, 195
Warren, Christine (sister of FW) 20,
    268
Warren, Francis (son of FW) 116
Warren, Frank (father of FW) 20, 25,
    30, 116
Warren, Frankie (US boxer) 140, 141,
    155
Warren, Frank John (FW) 3–4, 246
    Benn 236, 259
    career succes 128–38
    'Coe–Ovett race' 41–2
    drink-drive charge 263–4
    and Duff 67, 82–3, 248
    early life 20–33
    finance 41–2, 100–102, 153–4, 163,
        166, 169–72, 179, 182–6, 193,
        251–4
    future 268–9
    Hearn 248
    interview attempt vii-viii
    licensed 43–4, 82–3
    lifestyle 115–19, 170, 173–4
    litigation 179–80, 192, 264
    McGuigan 161–2
    manager 33–44, 57
    marriage, first 31–3
    marriage, second 115–16
    Mendy 350–51, 253, 258, 259, 260
    NBC 37–44
    post-TM 186

press 116, 118
promoter 98–127, 236, 243, 244,
    258, 264
rape acquittal 31–2
shot 3–4, 174–80, 264; see also
    'Paul'
sponsorships 123
staff 117–20, 122–3, 131, 153,
    173–4, 178, 253
Sun story 141, 144
Tee Jay 252
television 103, 105–6, 111–15, 122,
    123, 139–40, 150–51, 169, 174,
    186, 191–2, 212, 227
TM's epilepsy 269
TM's career 181–9, 128–41
TM's manager 93
TM's retirement 149, 150–51, 153,
    159
TM's trial 187, 191–5, 224, 225, 231
Warren, George (uncle of FW) 25
Warren, Iris (mother of FW) 20, 116
Warren, Jamie (son of FW) 31–2
Warren, Jimmy (uncle of FW) 25, 34,
    178, 228
Warren, Mark (brother of FW) 20, 268
Warren, Robert (brother of FW) 20,
    118, 176, 178, 186, 195, 268
Warren, Susan (Sue) (3rd wife of FW)
    115–16, 177, 178
Warren Promotions Ltd 154
Warren Sports Promotions 38
Waterman, Peter 73
Watkins, Alan 168
Watson, Michael 71, 124, 163, 164,
    234, 240, 255
Watson, Dr Ray 138
Watt, Jim 76, 109, 134
WBA *see* World Boxing Association
WBO *see* World Boxing Organisation
Weekes, Wayne 80
Weiss, Jimmy 245
Wellington pub 1
Wembley Arena (*formerly* Empire Pool)
    64, 129
    Astaire and 'cartel' 75, 78, 79, 98–9,
        105, 110
West Ham Baths 58
West Ham Boxing Club 60, 61
West Ham gymnasium 68
White City stadium 64
White Hart Lane stadium 64, 244

Whiteson, Dr Adrian 146–7, 157–8, 223
Whiting, Harry 175, 195
Wicks, Jim 25
Wiggins, Det-Insp Peter 205–6
Williams, Jeff 182, 262
Williams, Mike 117, 153
Williams, Rex 170, 172, 183
Williams, Sanderline 181
Windsor, Blazers Club 121
Winners Worldwide 250, 251
Winston, Howard 256
Witherspoon, Tim ('Terrible Tim') 86, 129, 156
Wonderland 9

Woodcock, Bruce 64
World Boxing Association (WBA) 43, 50
World Boxing Corporation 246
World Boxing Council 49–50
World Boxing Organisation (WBO) 50, 233, 246, 251, 255, 266, 267
World Sports Corporation (WSC) 123, 223, 251, 263, 256, 259, 260, 267
World Sports Federation 156
WSC see World Sports Corporation

Yates, Paula 161
York Hall, Bethnal Green 47, 106, 156, 174